World War II
Almanac

World War II
Almanac VOLUME 2

George Feldman
Edited by Christine Slovey

AN IMPRINT OF THE GALE GROUP

DETROIT · SAN FRANCISCO · LONDON
BOSTON · WOODBRIDGE, CT

World War II: Almanac

George Feldman

Staff

Christine Slovey, *U•X•L Editor*
Carol DeKane Nagel, *U•X•L Managing Editor*
Tom Romig, *U•X•L Publisher*

Rita Wimberley, *Senior Buyer*
Dorothy Maki, *Manufacturing Manager*
Evi Seoud, *Assistant Production Manager*
Mary Beth Trimper, *Production Director*

Margaret A. Chamberlain, *Permissions Specialist*

Eric Johnson and Martha Schiebold, *Cover Art Directors*
Pamela A. E. Galbreath, *Page Art Director*
Cynthia Baldwin, *Product Design Manager*
Barbara J. Yarrow, *Graphic Services Supervisor*

Linda Mahoney, LM Design, *Typesetting*

Laura Exner, XNR Productions, Inc., *Cartographer*

Front cover photographs reproduced by permission of the National Archives and Records Administration.

Library of Congress Cataloging-in-Publication Data

World War II: Almanac / George Feldman

    cm.

    Includes bibliographical references and index.

    ISBN 0-7876-3830-7 (set), — ISBN 0-7876-3831-5 (v. 1). — ISBN 0-7876-3832-3 (v. 2)

    1. World War, 1939-1945 Juvenile literature.   I. Feldman, George II. Title: World War two. III. Title: World War 2.

D743. 7.W673 1999

940.53—dc21

99-36179
CIP

Contents

Advisory Board vii

Reader's Guide ix

Timeline. xi

Words to Know. xxi

Research and Activity Ideas. xxxi

Three children sit in front of their bombed house in London. *(Reproduced by permission of the National Archives and Records Administration)*

Volume 1

Chapter 1: Background to War. 1

Chapter 2: The Beginning of the War in Europe 35

Chapter 3: The War Expands 61

Chapter 4: Japan Attacks and America Goes to War . . . 83

Chapter 5: The Home Front. 105

Chapter 6: Europe Under Occupation 131

U.S. Army tank in Aachen, Germany. *(Reproduced by permission of AP/Wide World Photos)*

Chapter 7: The Holocaust 157

Chapter 8: The Impact of Total War 181

Volume 2

Chapter 9: The Allies and the Axis 205

Chapter 10: Turning Points:
    The Allies Begin to Win the War 227

Chapter 11: The Great Invasion:
    Operation Overlord 251

Chapter 12: The Defeat of Germany 277

Chapter 13: The War Against Japan 305

Chapter 14: The Defeat of Japan 323

Chapter 15: Spies and Scientists 345

Chapter 16: Art, Entertainment,
    and Propaganda 369

Chapter 17: The World After the War 391

Where to Learn More xxxvii

Index xlv

Advisory Board

Special thanks are due to U•X•L's World War II Reference Library advisors for their invaluable comments and suggestions:

- Sidney Bolkosky, Professor of History, University of Michigan-Dearborn, Dearborn, Michigan

- Sara Brooke, Director of Libraries, The Ellis School, Pittsburgh, Pennsylvania

- Jacquelyn Divers, Librarian, Roanoke County Schools, Roanoke, Virginia

- Elaine Ezell, Library Media Specialist, Bowling Green Junior High School, Bowling Green, Ohio

- Melvin Small, Department of History, Wayne State University, Detroit, Michigan

.

Reader's Guide

etween 1939 and 1945 a war was fought among all the major powers of the world. By the end of it, more than fifty countries were involved. It was a war in which more people died than had died in any previous war and it changed the political, social, and economic face of the entire world. *World War II: Almanac* provides a comprehensive range of historical information and current commentary on World War II. The set explores how events after World War I (1914–18) led to World War II; the impact of the rise of dictatorial governments in Europe and of militarism in Japan; how world leaders attempted to avoid war; the relationships among the Allied countries and among the Axis countries; major battles and turning points; life on the home fronts and the nature of German occupations in Europe; scientific developments; art and entertainment during the war; and finally, how the world was changed by the war.

Other Features

World War II: Almanac is divided into seventeen subject chapters, each focusing on a particular topic, such as The Beginning of the War in Europe, Europe Under Occupation,

The War Against Japan, and Spies and Scientists. The chapters contain numerous sidebar boxes, some focusing on people associated with the war, others taking a closer look at pivotal events. More than 150 black-and-white photos and maps illustrate the text. Each volume begins with a timeline of events, a "Words to Know" section, and a "Research and Activity Ideas" section. The volumes conclude with a list of sources students can go to for more information and a subject index so students can easily find the people, places, and events discussed throughout *World War II: Almanac*.

Comments and Suggestions

We welcome your comments on *World War II: Almanac* and suggestions for other topics in history to consider. Please write: Editors, *World War II: Almanac,* U•X•L, 27500 Drake Rd., Farmington Hills, Michigan 48331-3535; call toll-free: 1-800-877-4253; fax to (248)414-5043; or send e-mail via http://www.galegroup.com.

Timeline

1917: The czar (emperor) is overthrown in Russia and a Communist government comes to power. The Russian empire is eventually renamed the Union of Soviet Socialist Republics (USSR), known as the Soviet Union.

1919: Germany signs the Treaty of Versailles, officially ending World War I. Extreme nationalist groups in Germany blame socialists, communists, and Jews for Germany's defeat.

1919: Communist revolutions in various parts of Germany are put down with great bloodshed.

1919: Adolf Hitler joins the tiny German Workers' Party in Munich. The party soon changes its name to the National Socialist German Workers' Party (NSDAP), called the Nazi Party for short.

1908
The Model T Ford is introduced

1914
World War I begins

1918
World War I ends

1920
The League of Nations is formed

1905   1910   1915   1920

Unemployed workers turn to a German soup kitchen for a free meal. *(Reproduced by permission of Bildarchiv Preussischer Kulturbesitz)*

1922: Benito Mussolini and his Fascist Party march on Rome, Mussolini is named premier of Italy.

1923: Hyperinflation hits Germany; its currency becomes worthless, causing severe economic distress.

1923: In November, Adolf Hitler leads a failed attempt to take over the German government. Police end the rebellion, called the Munich Beer Hall Putsch, and arrest Hitler and other leaders of the party.

1924: At his trial for treason and armed rebellion, Adolf Hitler gains the attention of extreme nationalists. While serving only eight months of a five year prison sentence, Hitler dictates *Mein Kampf* (*My Struggle*).

1924: Benito Mussolini becomes dictator of Italy.

1926: Hirohito becomes emperor of Japan, giving his reign the name Showa ("enlightened peace").

1927: Chiang Kai-Shek establishes the Kuomintang or Nationalist government in Nanking, China.

1930: A worldwide economic depression hits Germany especially hard. Thirty-three percent of the workforce is unemployed.

1931: The Japanese army seizes Manchuria in a short war with China, establishing Manchuria as the independent country of Manchukuo, which is actually controlled by the Japanese.

1932: In German parliamentary elections held in July, the Nazis become the largest party in Germany, with about 37 percent of the vote. Nazi stormtrooper violence increases.

1932: Franklin D. Roosevelt begins the first of four terms as president of the United States.

1933: Adolf Hitler becomes chancellor (head of the government) of Germany on January 30. Within a few

1922
Harlem Renaissance begins

1924
Vladimir Lenin dies

1926
Germany joins the League of Nations

1929
Great Depression begins; it ends in 1939

1922   1924   1926   1928

months he and his National Socialist German Workers' Party take control of the German government.

1933: The Reichstag building is set afire. Nazis blame the Communists and Hitler receives emergency powers from President Paul von Hindenburg. Free speech and press are restricted. Nazi stormtroopers receive police powers.

1933: Dachau, the first permanent concentration camp, is opened in a suburb of Munich in March. Ten thousand opponents of Nazis, especially communists, are arrested and sent to the newly established concentration camps.

1933: In April, Nazis organize a national boycott of Jewish-owned businesses. The first anti-Jewish laws are passed, removing almost all Jews from government jobs including teaching.

1934: Upon the death of German president Paul von Hindenburg, the office of chancellor is combined with president. Adolf Hitler is now the Führer (leader) of the Third Reich (empire) with absolute powers. All officers and soldiers of the army swear allegiance to Hitler.

1935: March 16, Germany announces the reintroduction of the military draft and a major expansion of its army, violating the Treaty of Versailles.

1935: Germany passes the Nuremberg laws, which define Jews in racial terms, strip them of German citizenship, and ban marriages between Jews and non-Jews.

1935: Italy invades Ethiopia on October 3. By May 1936, Ethiopia is conquered.

1936: Germany and Italy enter into agreements that establish a political and military alliance between the two countries called the "Rome-Berlin Axis."

1936: Germany and Japan sign the Anti-Comintern (anti-communist) Treaty.

German soldiers examining the remains of the burned Reichstag. *(Reproduced by permission of Bildarchiv Preussischer Kulturbesitz)*

1930
The planet Pluto is discovered

1931
The *Star Spangled Banner* is made the national anthem of the United States

1933
Francis Perkins is appointed Secretary of Labor, becoming the first woman to hold a U.S. cabinet post.

1936
The Spanish Civil War begins

1930 | 1932 | 1934 | 1936 ▶

Adolf Hitler in Austria.
(Reproduced by permission of AP/Wide World Photos)

1937: In the first example of aerial bombing against a civilian population, the German air force bombs Guernica, Spain, on April 26, aiding Francisco Franco's fascist troops during the Spanish Civil War.

1937: Japan invades China, captures Peking (Beijing), Shanghai, Canton, and other major cities. In Nanking, invading Japanese troops rape, torture, and murder tens of thousands of Chinese civilians.

1938: Austrians vote in favor of the *Anschloss,* an agreement that makes their country part of Nazi Germany. Crowds cheer the German dictator Adolf Hitler as he enters the Austrian capital Vienna.

1938: Soviet and Japanese troops engage in bloody battles on the border of China and Soviet east Asia.

1938: Europe is at the brink of war as Adolf Hitler makes territorial demands on Czechoslovakia. At a conference in Munich in September, leaders of France and Britain agree to grant Germany a section of Czechoslovakia with a large German-speaking population.

1938: November 9, the Nazis stage *Kristallnacht* (Crystal Night or "night of broken glass"), in which homes, businesses, and synagogues of German Jews are destroyed.

1939: Adolf Hitler violates the Munich agreement by taking over the remainder of Czechoslovakia by March 1939.

1939: August 23, Germany and the Soviet Union sign the Nazi-Soviet Pact. The two countries promise not to attack each other and secretly agree to divide Poland after Germany conquers it.

1939: World War II officially begins. Germany invades Poland on September 1; Britain and France declare war on Germany two days later. Poland surrenders on September 27.

1936
The Olympic Games are held in Berlin, Germany

1937
Joseph Stalin conducts purges of the Soviet military and the Communist Party

1938
The first nuclear fission of uranium is produced

1937   1938

1939: Britain begins evacuating children from London to rural towns to protect them from German air raids.

1939: Jews in German-occupied Poland are ordered to wear a yellow star at all times.

1940: April 10, Germany invades Norway and Denmark. Denmark soon surrenders, but fighting continues in Norway, aided by British and French forces. The Norwegian government flees to Britain.

1940: Winston Churchill becomes prime minister of Great Britain.

1940: Germany invades the Netherlands, Belgium, Luxembourg, and France on May 10. The Netherlands surrenders on May 14 and Belgium on May 28.

1940: Italy declares war on France and Britain and invades France on June 10.

1940: French troops evacuate Paris on June 13 and German forces enter the city the next day. France signs an armistice with Germany on June 22. German troops occupy northern France, while a government friendly to Germany (Vichy France) has some independence in the south.

1940: The Germans begin bombing England in a long air campaign called the Battle of Britain. The Germans are defeated by the fighter pilots of Britain's Royal Air Force (RAF) and Hitler abandons plans to invade Britain.

1940: Germany, Japan, and Italy sign a military alliance called the Tripartite Pact. Within six months, Hungary, Romania, Slovakia, and Bulgaria will also join the alliance.

1941: President Franklin D. Roosevelt signs the Lend-Lease Act.

1941: April 13, Japan and the Soviet Union sign a treaty promising that neither will attack the other.

The Polish Cavalry was no match against Germany's tanks.
(Reproduced by permission of AP/Wide World Photos)

1938
The Volkswagen ("people's car") makes its first appearance

March 1939
The Spanish Civil War ends

April 1939
Television broadcasting is introduced at the World's Fair in New York

1939

1940

The Japanese raid on Pearl Harbor. *(Reproduced by permission of the National Archives and Records Administration)*

1941: June 22, Germany invades the Soviet Union in an offensive called Operation Barbarossa and quickly takes control of much of the country.

1941: Winston Churchill and Franklin D. Roosevelt meet aboard a warship off the coast of Newfoundland and issue the Atlantic Charter, in which they agree to promote peace and democracy around the world.

1941: Kiev, the capital of Ukraine, falls to the German army on September 19. On September 29 and 30, thirty-three thousand Jews are killed at Babi Yar outside Kiev.

1941: Japan bombs the U.S. naval base at Pearl Harbor in Hawaii on December 7. The United States and Britain declare war on Japan. Japan's allies, Germany and Italy, declare war on the United States on December 10.

1942: In January, the U.S. Ration board announces rationing of rubber. In May, sugar is rationed. By the end of the year, gasoline is also being rationed.

1942: Manila, capital of the Philippines, surrenders to the Japanese on January 2.

1942: Executive Order 9066 directs all Japanese Americans living on the West Coast to internment camps.

1942: May 6, American and Filipino troops on the island of Corregidor in Manila Bay surrender to the Japanese.

1942: May 7, the U.S. Navy defeats the Japanese fleet in the Battle of the Coral Sea in the Pacific.

1942: In May, 1,000 British bombers destroy Cologne, Germany's third largest city.

1942: The Americans defeat the Japanese fleet at the Battle of Midway, June 4 to 7, in one of the most decisive naval battles in history.

1942: In July, British bombers attack Germany's second largest city, Hamburg, on four straight nights, causing a firestorm that kills 30,000 civilians.

1940
The Olympic Games Committee cancels the games

1941
Hideki Tojo becomes prime minister of Japan

1942
Oxfam is founded to fight world famine

1941   1942

1942: August 7, American troops land on Guadalcanal in the Solomon Islands in the mid-Pacific, the first American offensive operation of the war.

1942: In the Battle of El Alamein in Egypt, the British Eighth Army wins a strategic victory against Italian forces and the German Afrika Korps.

1942: November 8, the Allies launch Operation Torch, an invasion of German-occupied North Africa that ends with the Germans being chased from the region.

1943: January 31, the Germans surrender to the Russian troops at Stalingrad, marking a major turning point of the war.

1943: Small groups of Jews in the Warsaw ghetto begin attacking German troops on April 19. They continue fighting for almost one month until the Germans have killed almost all of the Jewish resisters and completely destroyed the ghetto.

1943: July 10, American, British, and Canadian troops land on Sicily, a large island south of the Italian mainland, and defeat German forces there.

1943: Italian dictator Benito Mussolini is removed from office by the Fascist Grand Council on July 25 and tries to establish a separate government in northern Italy.

1943: The Allies invade the Italian mainland on September 3; the new Italian government surrenders to the Allies on September 8.

1944: June 6, Allied forces land in Normandy in the largest sea invasion in history, called Operation Overlord.

1944: On the third anniversary of the German invasion of the Soviet Union, June 22, the Soviets launch a massive offensive called Operation Bagration, inflicting immense losses on the German army and driving them back almost 400 miles in a month.

American and Filipino troops surrender at Corregidor. (Reproduced by permission of the Corbis Corporation [Bellevue])

1942
Physicist Enrico Fermi achieves the first sustained nuclear chain reaction

1943
Prohibition of Chinese immigration into the United States is repealed

October 1943
Chicago's first subway is dedicated

1943

1944

Survivors of the Warsaw Ghetto uprising are rounded up at gunpoint. *(Reproduced by permission of AP/Wide World Photos)*

1944: July 20, a group of German army officers attempt to kill German leader Adolf Hitler and make peace with the Allies. Many of the conspirators, along with their families, are tortured and executed in retaliation.

1944: August 25, Paris is liberated by Free French and American forces.

1944: The largest naval battle in history, the Battle of Leyte Gulf in the Philippines, October 23 to 26, ends in the almost total destruction of the Japanese fleet.

1944: December 16, the Germans launch a major counter-offensive against the Americans in the Ardennes Forest, known as the Battle of the Bulge.

1945: January 12, the Soviets begin an offensive along the entire Polish front, entering Warsaw on January 17, and Lodz two days later. By February 1, they are within 100 miles of the German capital of Berlin.

1945: January 18, the Nazis begin evacuating the Auschwitz death camp. Almost 60,000 surviving prisoners are forced on a death march out of the camp.

1945: February 14, Allied raids on Dresden result in firestorms while the city is crammed with German refugees from the fighting farther east.

1945: February 19, American Marines land on Iwo Jima in the Pacific.

1945: March 7, American troops cross the Rhine River in Germany, the last natural obstacle between the Allied forces and Berlin.

1945: American troops land on Okinawa on April 1, beginning the largest land battle of the Pacific war. The Japanese forces are defeated by June.

1945: April 12, U.S. president Franklin D. Roosevelt dies; Harry S. Truman becomes president of the United States.

1946
Cold War begins

1947
India gains independence from Great Britain

1948
Israel is declared an independent state

1945 — 1946 — 1947 — 1948

1945: April 28, former Italian dictator Benito Mussolini is captured by resistance fighters and executed.

1945: With Soviet troops in the city limits, Adolf Hitler commits suicide in his fortified bunker beneath Berlin on April 30. The new German government surrenders unconditionally on May 8.

1945: July 16, the first atomic bomb is tested in the desert near Alamogordo, New Mexico.

1945: August 6, the United States drops an atomic bomb on Hiroshima, Japan. A second bomb is dropped on Nagasaki, Japan, on August 9.

1945: August 8, the Soviet Union declares war on Japan; a large Soviet force invades Manchuria the following day.

1945: August 15, the Allies accept the unconditional surrender of Japan. Formal surrender papers are signed aboard the USS *Missouri* in Tokyo Bay on September 2.

1945: War crimes trials begin in Nuremberg, Germany, in November.

1948: The Soviets block all overland traffic between Berlin and the Allied-controlled zones of Germany. Allies airlift food and fuel to West Berlin for eleven months.

1949: The Soviets establish East Germany as a Communist state called the German Democratic Republic; France, England, and the United States join their power zones into a democratic state called the Federal Republic of Germany (West Germany).

1949: Communists led by Mao Zedong take control of China; Chiang Kai-shek and the Nationalists are forced into exile on Taiwan.

1952: General Dwight D. Eisenhower becomes president of the United States.

1961: Communists build the Berlin Wall around East Berlin

1949
The North Atlantic Treaty Organization (NATO) is created

1950
The Korean War begins; it ends in 1953

1951
J. D. Salinger's *Catcher in the Rye* is published

1949   1950   1951   1952

in order to stop East Germans seeking a higher standard of living from fleeing to West Germany through West Berlin.

1988: The U.S. Congress formally apologizes to Japanese Americans for interning them in concentration camps during World War II. Living persons who spent time in the camps are offered a one-time payment of $20,000.

1989: The Berlin Wall is destroyed.

1990: East Germany and West Germany are reunited.

1998: Volkswagen agrees to pay reparations to slave laborers who worked in their factories during the war.

1999: Dinko Sakic, the last known living commander of a World War II concentration camp, is tried for war crimes.

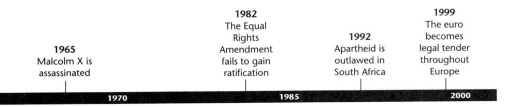

1965
Malcolm X is assassinated

1982
The Equal Rights Amendment fails to gain ratification

1992
Apartheid is outlawed in South Africa

1999
The euro becomes legal tender throughout Europe

1955   1970   1985   2000

Words to Know

A

Afrika Korps: The experienced, effective German troops who fought under German field marshal Erwin Rommel in the North African desert.

Allies: The countries who fought against Germany, Italy, and Japan during World War II. The makeup of the Allied powers changed over the course of the war. The first major Allied countries were Great Britain and France. Germany defeated France in 1940 but some Free French forces continued to fight with the Allies until the end of the war. The Soviet Union and the United States joined the Allies in 1941.

Annex: To add territory to an existing country.

Anschloss: The 1938 agreement that made Austria a part of Nazi Germany.

Anti-Comintern Treaty: Comintern refers to the Communist International organization, a group of world Communist parties that was run by the Soviet Union. Germany, Japan, and Italy called their military alliance

Anti-Comintern to make it sound like a defensive agreement against communism.

Anti-Semitism: The hatred of Jews, who are sometimes called Semites.

Appeasement: Making compromises in order to stay on neutral terms with another party or country.

Armistice: A temporary halt to a war, until a peace treaty ends it permanently.

Armored division: A division of the army that uses tanks.

Atlantic Charter: An agreement signed in 1941 by President Franklin D. Roosevelt and British prime minister Winston Churchill in which the United States and Great Britain stated their commitment to worldwide peace and democracy.

Atom bomb: A weapon of mass destruction in which a radioactive element such as uranium is bombarded with neutrons to create a chain reaction called nuclear fission, releasing a huge amount of energy.

Axis: During World War II, Germany, Italy, and Japan formed a coalition called the Axis powers. Eventually, they were joined by Hungary, Romania, Slovakia, Finland, and Bulgaria.

B

Black market: Where rationed goods are bought and sold illegally, in violation of government restrictions.

Blitzkrieg: Meaning "lightning war" in German, this is the name given the German's military strategy of sending troops in land vehicles to make quick, surprise attacks while airplanes provide support from above. This strategy was especially effective against Poland and France.

C

Calvary: Originally referred to horse-mounted troops. In modern times calvary refers to troops using armored vehicles such as tanks.

Chancellor: In some European countries, including Germany, the chief minister of the government.

Collaborate: To work together toward a common goal; during wartime this term refers to working with the enemy force that has occupied one's country.

Communism: An economic system that promotes the ownership of most property and means of production by the community as a whole. By 1939, the Soviet Union was a harsh dictatorship run by the Communist Party and its all-powerful leader, Josef Stalin.

Concentration camps: Places where the Germans confined people they considered enemies of the state. These included Jews, Roma (commonly called Gypsies), homosexuals, and political opponents.

Convoys: Large groups traveling together, sometimes with military protection, for safety.

D

D-Day: Usually refers to June 6, 1944, the day the Normandy Invasion began with a massive landing of Allied troops on the beaches of northern France, which was occupied by Germany; also called Operation Overlord. D-Day is also a military term designating the date and time of an attack.

Death camps: Concentration camps built by the Nazis for the single purpose of killing Jews.

Depression: An economic downturn with falling industrial production, lower prices, and increasing unemployment. The United States experienced the worst depression in its history from 1929 to 1939, which is referred to as the Great Depression.

Dictator: A ruler who holds absolute power.

Division: A large unit of an army, usually about 15,000 men.

Draft: The system by which able young men are required by law to perform a term of military service for their country.

E

Einsatzgruppen: Meaning "special-action groups" in German, these were specially trained strike forces in the military wing of the Nazi Party that were responsible for murdering approximately 2 million Jews, Communists, and other people in the Soviet Union.

Embargo: A government ban on trade.

Executive Order 9066: President Franklin D. Roosevelt's order directing all Japanese Americans living on the American West Coast to be sent to internment camps.

Exile: Living away from one's native country, either by choice or by force.

Extermination camps: Concentration camps built by the Nazis with the single purpose of killing Jews.

F

Fascism: A political system in which power rests not with citizens but with the central government, which is often run by the military and/or a dictator.

Final Solution: The code name given to the Nazi plan to eliminate all the Jews of Europe.

Free French Movement: The movement led by Charles de Gaulle, who, from a position outside France, tried to organize and encourage the French people to resist the German occupation.

Führer: The German word meaning "leader"; the title Adolf Hitler took as dictator of Germany.

G

G.I.: Standing for government issue, a nickname for enlisted soldiers or former members of the U.S. armed forces.

Genocide: The deliberate, systematic destruction of a racial, national, or cultural group.

Gestapo: An abbreviation for Germany's *Geheime Staats Politzei* or Secret State Police.

Gliders: Planes without motors that are towed by ropes behind regular planes and then cut loose and allowed to float down to land.

Guerillas: People who fight behind enemy lines, usually employing hit-and-run tactics against a more powerful enemy.

H

Hitler Youth: An organization that trained German boys to idolize and obey German leader Adolf Hitler and to become Nazi soldiers.

Holocaust: The period between 1933 and 1945 when Nazi Germany systematically persecuted and murdered millions of Jews, Roma (commonly called Gypsies), homosexuals, and other innocent people.

I

Internment camps: A guarded facility usually used to hold citizens of an enemy country during wartime. The United States had ten camps located throughout the western part of the country to which about 120,000 Americans of Japanese ancestry were forced to move due to the ungrounded suspicion that they were not loyal to the United States.

Isolationism: A country's policy of keeping out of other countries' affairs. Isolationism was a strong force in American politics after World War I (1914–18) and continued to be an important factor until Japan attacked the United States in December 1941.

L

Lebensraum: A German term meaning "room to live." The Nazis told the German people that they needed expanded living space to survive and used this idea as justification for invading and occupying other countries.

Lend-Lease Program: A program that allowed the United States to send countries fighting the Germans (such as

Great Britain and the Soviet Union) supplies needed for the war effort in exchange for payment to be made after the war.

Luftwaffe: The German air force.

M

Manhattan Project: The project funded by the U.S. government that gathered scientists together at facilities in Chicago, Illinois, Los Alamos, New Mexico, and other places to work on the development of an atom bomb.

Martial law: Temporary rule of the government by the military, often imposed during war or other emergencies. Under martial law, many normal legal rights are suspended.

***Mein Kampf* (*My Struggle*):** The 1924 autobiography of Adolf Hitler, in which he explains his racial and political philosophies, including his hatred of Jews.

Merchant ships: Commercial or trading ships.

Militarists: Extremists in the military and their supporters who believe the government should be controlled by the army and society should be organized on military principles.

Mobilized: Called to active duty in the armed services.

Morale: The state of a person's or group's spirit and willingness to work toward an established goal.

N

Nationalism: Strong loyalty to one's nation, combined with a belief that one's country will benefit from acting independently and in its own best interest rather than in cooperation with other countries. Nationalism often leads to dislike of other countries.

Nazi: The abbreviated name for the National Socialist German Workers' Party, the political party led by Adolf Hitler, who became dictator of Germany. Hitler's Nazi Party controlled Germany from 1933 to 1945. The

Nazis promoted racist and anti-Semitic (anti-Jewish) ideas and enforced complete obedience to Hitler and the party.

Noncombatant: A job in the military that is not directly involved with combat or fighting.

O

Occupation: Control of a country by a foreign military power.

Operation Overlord: The code name for the Normandy Invasion, a massive Allied attack on German-occupied France; also called D-Day.

P

Partisans: Groups fighting behind enemy lines or in occupied territory, usually employing hit-and-run tactics.

Pearl Harbor: Inlet on the southern coast of the island of Oahu, Hawaii, and the site of a Japanese attack on a U.S. naval base on December 7, 1941. The attack prompted the United States to enter World War II.

Prime minister: Chief executive of the government or of parliament.

Propaganda: Material such as literature, images, or speeches that is designed to influence public opinion toward a certain doctrine. The content of the material may be true or false and is often political.

Purge: To remove (often by killing) all those who are seen as enemies.

R

Ration: To make something available in fixed amounts; limiting access to scarce goods; the allotted amount of something.

Red Army: Another name for the Soviet Union's army.

Refugee: A person escaping from danger or persecution.

Reich: The German word meaning "empire"; Adolf Hitler's term as Germany's leader was called the Third Reich.

Reichstag: Germany's parliament or lawmaking body.

Reparations: Compensation required from a defeated nation for damage or injury during war.

Resistance: Working against an occupying army.

S

SA: An abbreviation for *Sturmabteilungen,* or stormtroopers. They were members of a special armed and uniformed branch of the Nazi Party.

Sabotage: Intentional destruction of military or industrial facilities.

Segregation: The forced separation of black and white people, not only in public places and schools but also in the U.S. military. The opposite of segregation is integration.

Socialism: A political system in which the means of producing and distributing goods are shared or owned by the government.

Soviet Union: Short for the Union of Soviet Socialist Republics or USSR, the country that the Communists had set up after overthrowing the Russian Empire.

SS: An abbreviation for *Schutzstaffel,* or Security Squad, the unit that provided German leader Adolf Hitler's personal bodyguards as well as guards for the various concentration camps.

Stormtroopers: Another name for members of the *Sturmabteilungen,* a special armed and uniformed branch of the Nazi Party.

Swastika: The Nazi symbol of a black, bent-armed cross that always appeared within a white circle set on a red background.

Synagogue: A Jewish house of worship.

T

Theater: An area of operations during a war. The main areas of operation during World War II were the European theater and the Pacific theater.

Tripartite Pact: An agreement signed in September 1940 that established an alliance among Germany, Italy, and Japan. The countries promised to aid each other should any one of them face an attack.

U

U-boat: Nickname given to German submarines because the German word for submarine is *unterseeboots*.

Underground: Engaged in secret or illegal activity.

V

Versailles Treaty: The agreement signed by the countries who had fought in World War I that required Germany to claim responsibility for the war and pay money to other countries for damage from the war.

Veteran: A person who has served in the armed forces.

Vichy Government: The government set up in France after the Germans invaded the country; headed by Henri Petain, it was really under German control.

W

WACs: The Women's Army Corps, an organization that allowed American women to serve in a variety of non-combat roles.

Waffen-SS: Also known as the "armed SS," military units of the SS that fought as part of the regular army.

War crimes: Violations of the laws or customs of war.

Research and Activity Ideas

The following research and activity ideas are intended to offer suggestions for complementing social studies and history curricula, to trigger additional ideas for enhancing learning, and to suggest cross-disciplinary projects for library and classroom use.

Ration Recipes: Look in cookbooks published during the 1940s or in women's magazines published during World War II and note how the recipes account for rationing. Make one of the recipes and invite others to rate the flavor, or adapt a recipe from a modern cookbook to account for rationing.

Personal History: Interview a veteran of World War II or someone who lived during the war. Create a list of questions before the interview. You might find out where your subject was during the war, how the war changed his or her life, his or her impression of the importance of the war both at the time and in the world after the war.

Atom bomb debate: Study the decision to drop atom bombs on Hiroshima and Nagasaki. Taking into consideration only what was known at the time about the bombs, form two teams, one in favor of dropping the bomb and the other against it, and debate the issues. Then, repeat the debate taking into consideration what we know now about the effects of atomic bombs. Discuss how the debate changed.

Turning Points: On a large map of the world use pushpins to mark the sites of battles that were important turning points during the war. For each site create a notecard that explains who fought in the battle, who the was the victor, and why the battle there was important.

Modern opinions from historical figures: Form a group of four to six people. Choose a current event in world politics (such as NATO's actions in Kosovo); prepare for a panel discussion on the topic by reading magazine and newspaper articles and Internet news stories on the subject. Choose one person to serve as a discussion moderator. Everyone else in the group should choose a prominent individual involved in World War II whom he or she will represent in a panel discussion. Each person should research the individual he or she has selected and have a clear understanding of the historical figure's role in the war. The group will then have a panel discussion on the selected current event with students presenting the positions they think their historical figure would take on the subject.

War-inspired artwork: Choose a creative work related to World War II. This can be anything from one of the many War memorials, like the memorial to the USS *Arizona* in Pearl Harbor, Hawaii, to a poem, song, or painting inspired by the war, such as Randall Jarrell's poem "The Death of a Ball Turret Gunner." Explain the work's relationship to the war: is it about a battle, or an individual's experience of the war? What emotions does the piece evoke: bravery, fear, loneliness, anger?

War journal: Imagine that you are a child living during the war. You can choose to have lived in any of the countries involved in the war. Write a journal of your activities over the course of one week.

Propaganda: Rent a video of a film created during the war and one that has a war theme. Some examples of films that are available on videocassette include: Frank Capra's *Why We Fight* series of documentaries, *Casablanca, Mrs. Miniver,* and *Der Führer's Face.* Write an essay discussing whether the film has a particular political message and discuss what that message is.

Battlefield tour: Pretend that you are a travel agent and create a World War II battlefield tour. You could choose to focus the tour on sites in the Pacific, sites throughout Europe or North Africa, or focus on a specific country. List the sites you'll be visiting on the tour, giving the name of the battle, if there was a codename for the operation, key events of the battle and the commanders involved, who won the battle, and why it was important.

D-Day Newspaper article: Imagine you are a war correspondent for either a U.S. paper or a German paper covering the June 6, 1944, invasion of France. Write an article about the events you see.

World War II
Almanac

The Allies and the Axis

9

Two sets of countries fought World War II. The alliance of Nazi Germany, Italy, and Japan was known as the Axis. Several other countries were members of the Axis or cooperated with it at different times. The countries fighting them were called the Allies. Originally, the major Allies were Great Britain and France, but France surrendered to Germany in June 1940. In June 1941, Germany invaded the Soviet Union, which then allied with Britain. In December 1941, Japan bombed Pearl Harbor in Hawaii and attacked British and American possessions in the Pacific. The United States declared war on Japan. A few days later, Germany and Italy declared war on the United States. The United States, Britain, and the Soviet Union were now fighting Germany. The United States and Britain were at war with Japan.

The lineup of countries fighting the war was complicated, as were their relationships with one another. Britain, the Soviet Union, and the United States were not allies before they went to war, as Britain and France were. Each went to war against Germany at different times and for different reasons. Each had different goals. And although all

American master spy Allen Dulles. Dulles's secret contacts with German officials raised Soviet fears that the United States might make a separate peace with Germany.
(Reproduced by permission of AP/Wide World Photos)

three wanted to win the war, each had different ideas about the best way to do this. These ideas were strongly influenced by each country's goals for the war and by their hopes for the kind of world they wanted to see afterward.

Western Allies and the Soviet Union

The most serious differences were between the Soviet Union and the Western Allies (Britain and the United States). These differences arose out of basic mistrust. The Soviet Union was a communist country. (Communism is a political and economic system based on government ownership of factories, banks, and most other businesses.) The British and Americans were always afraid that the Soviets were planning to impose communism wherever their army conquered. The Soviets feared that the Western Allies still wanted to strangle their communist system, which they had in fact tried to do before World War II.

In addition, both sides were always worried that the other would seek to make peace with Germany without their consent. Each thought it had good reasons to fear this. The Soviets had signed a treaty with German leader Adolf Hitler in August 1939 that allowed Germany to fight Britain and France without fear of Soviet intervention. (See Chapter 2.) The Soviets believed that Britain and France had given in to Hitler for years, seeing him as an insurance policy against communism and hoping to encourage him to attack Soviet Russia. (See Chapter 1.)

These disputes were significant, but they should not be exaggerated. Germany always hoped and predicted that suspicions would destroy the Alliance, but that was never a real possibility. Even in the most serious arguments, both sides recognized how important it was to stay together until Germany was defeated. Afterward, the Alliance fell apart quickly. (See

Chapter 17.) But as long as the danger of Hitler's Germany existed, the three members of the Grand Alliance stayed together.

The United States and Britain

The closest relationship, and the one with the fewest disputes, developed between the United States and Britain. But even this association was marked by strong differences on some issues.

Cooperation between the British and Americans began very early in the war. In September 1940, the United States gave the British old but much-needed warships in return for the use of naval bases on British islands in the Caribbean. In March 1941, Congress passed the Lend-Lease law, which, in effect, allowed Britain to purchase huge quantities of arms and supplies on credit. Then, even though the United States was still neutral, the American navy played an increasing role in protecting the ships that carried these supplies from America to England. (Early U.S.-British cooperation is described in Chapter 3.)

In November 1940, more than a year before Pearl Harbor, high-ranking military officers from the two countries met secretly to discuss a common military strategy if the United States entered the war. They decided that in case of war with both Japan and Germany, both countries would concentrate on defeating Germany first.

The Atlantic Charter

In August 1941, American president Franklin D. Roosevelt and British prime minister (head of the government) Winston Churchill met aboard a warship off the coast of Newfoundland (now part of Canada) in the North Atlantic, the first in a series of personal meetings that continued until Roosevelt's death almost four years later. Privately, Roosevelt reaffirmed the Germany first strategy to Churchill.

Publicly, the Newfoundland meeting resulted in a joint British-American declaration called the Atlantic Charter. The

Cooperation between the British and Americans began very early in the war.

Atlantic Charter committed Britain and the United States to oppose territorial changes unless they were the "freely expressed" desire of the people involved. This statement was a promise to restore the borders of the European countries Nazi Germany had taken over. But it also seemed to support independence for the Asian and African colonies of European powers such as Britain, France, and the Netherlands if the native people of those countries wanted it.

The issue of colonies reflected one of the basic disagreements between the United States and Britain. Roosevelt was very hostile to colonies, an attitude shared by most Americans. Some historians have said this attitude comes from the fact that the United States itself was once a group of thirteen British colonies that fought a revolution to win their freedom.

Critics of American policy have often argued that the United States opposed colonies because it could influence and even dominate other countries through its economic power, without having to use its army or run a country directly. They point to U.S. influence in Latin America as an example. Whether or not this is true, Roosevelt's attitude and American public opinion encouraged colonized people to seek independence. At that time, there was a strong independence movement in India, the largest and most important British colony. And of all British political leaders, Churchill was the most strongly opposed to Indian independence.

The Arcadia Conference

Immediately after Pearl Harbor, Churchill and top British military leaders flew to Washington, D.C., for a series of meetings code-named Arcadia, that lasted from December 22, 1941, to January 14, 1942. The fact that the head of the British government, together with his most important military officers, spent that much time away from his country in wartime shows how vital these meetings were.

The Arcadia Conference made several decisions that directed the entire war effort. The Germany first policy became official. The two countries agreed that they would make decisions on how to use all economic and military resources together. This was an extremely unusual arrangement, even for close allies. The two countries also created a Combined Chiefs of Staff made up of the commanders of the army, navy, and air force of each country. Since this committee met in Washington, the British commanders each named a permanent substitute to represent them when they were not present.

This system worked for the rest of the war. The British representatives, who were in constant contact with Britain, met to decide their positions, and the Americans did the same. Then the Combined Chiefs of Staff met—200 times during the war—to agree on all British-American war operations. They often disagreed on details, but they usually worked them out. Roosevelt and Churchill settled the major disagreements.

Roosevelt and Churchill

In addition to their personal meetings, Roosevelt and Churchill constantly exchanged opinions, information, and arguments by coded radio messages. According to Churchill, he sent 950 messages to Roosevelt during the war and got 800 messages in return.

Through these messages and their face-to-face meetings, Roosevelt and Churchill developed a genuine respect and affection for each other. Although some writers have probably exaggerated the importance of this personal relationship, historians generally agree that it played a significant part in making British-American cooperation work so well.

Roosevelt loved sailing, ships, and the navy, and as president he was commander in chief of all U.S. armed forces. But he was not really interested in military strategy and did not pretend to be an expert. Instead, he listened to and trusted his advisers on the purely military aspects of the war. The most important American military leader was General George C. Marshall, the army chief of staff. But the final decision on how America would fight the war, such as defeating Germany first, Roosevelt made himself.

Churchill had been an army officer as a young man and had been in charge of the British navy during World War I. He not only expressed opinions about military matters but also tried hard to convince Roosevelt—and everyone else— about strategy, tactics, and personnel. As one British naval

Roosevelt and Churchill developed a genuine respect and affection for each other.

writer put it after the war, there was not a single British admiral from 1939 to 1943 whom Churchill did not try to fire. He did the same with plenty of generals as well. (In fact, Hitler told his own generals that they were lucky that, compared with Churchill, he generally left them alone.)

Military strategy and the second front

The most important disagreement between the British and Americans also involved the Soviet Union. This was the question of the timing and location of a second front in Europe. A front is a combat zone, the area where two opposing armies are in contact. After France surrendered in June 1940, no major Allied army fought the Germans for a year. Then in June 1941, Germany invaded the Soviet Union, and the two armies fought, with immense losses on both sides, until the end of the war.

After the invasion, the Soviets immediately pressed the British to open a second front in western Europe. They wanted British troops fighting the Germans as close to Germany as possible to take pressure off the Soviet armies. But in 1941, the British did not have the troops, landing ships, tanks, artillery, or planes to mount a successful invasion. When the United States entered the war, the Soviets pushed the Americans as well as the British for a second front.

The United States, Britain, and the Soviet Union all agreed on the Germany first strategy. But to the American military leaders and the Soviets, Germany first meant a major invasion of western Europe—probably in France—as soon as possible. After crossing France, the British and Americans could attack Germany from the west, while the Soviets closed in from the east. They thought this was the fastest—and probably only—way to defeat Germany.

The British, however, resisted an invasion of western Europe. They feared that an invasion before they were fully prepared would end in disaster. They remembered the way the German army had defeated them in France in 1940 (see Chapter 2) and the terrible bloodshed of World War I, when armies attacked built-up defensive positions. The Americans had never been defeated by the Germans and were far more optimistic.

Fighting around the edges

Instead, Churchill and his military chiefs preferred fighting around the edges of German-controlled Europe. One example was the campaign in Egypt and Libya, mostly against the Italians. Another was Churchill's ongoing interest in sending British troops to fight the Germans in Greece. (See Chapter 3 for details on both operations.)

The British-American invasion of North Africa in November 1942 (Operation Torch) was part of this strategy to fight around the edges. (Operation Torch is described in more detail in Chapter 10.) The British convinced the Americans that while it was impossible to invade France in 1942, Torch would be a good way to get American troops fighting the Germans, something Roosevelt, Marshall, and the American people all strongly favored. It took until May 1943 to clear Axis forces out of North Africa. At that point, Churchill and the British argued for an invasion of Sicily (a large Italian island at the toe of the boot-shaped Italian peninsula), which began in July 1943, and then of Italy itself, beginning in September. These operations were designed to knock Italy out of the war, which they did. (See Chapter 10.) But the United States agreed to them only on condition that they would not delay the main second front against Germany. However, it became clear that an invasion of France would not be possible in 1943—partly because of the military personnel and equipment tied up in the Italian campaign.

General Marshall and other American leaders always saw the North African and Italian campaigns as sideshows that did not really advance the war against Germany. Worse, they came to believe these operations actually hurt this goal by diverting scarce resources. At the beginning of 1944, with the invasion of France scheduled for spring, Churchill was still trying to postpone it in favor of other strategies. He wanted to send the Allied armies from Italy into Yugoslavia and toward Vienna, the capital of Austria. But Churchill's plan could take years: the Allied armies were still bogged down in southern Italy.

Roosevelt and his advisers always suspected that Churchill's arguments were aimed at keeping British economic and political influence in Greece, southeastern Europe, and the Mediterranean. Many historians also believe Churchill was

Churchill and his military chiefs preferred fighting around the edges of German-controlled Europe.

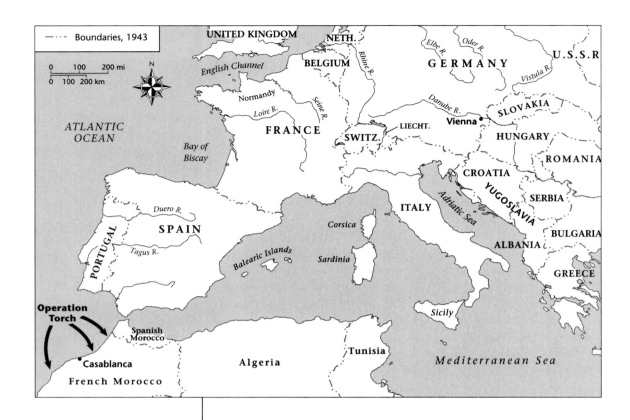

Europe and the Mediterranean, showing the movement of Operation Torch, 1943.

afraid that otherwise the Soviets would control these areas after the war.

Western military historians generally agree with the British that an invasion of western Europe in 1942 would have resulted in disaster. Most also believe that the British were right not to invade in 1943 either. Soviet historians, while admitting that an earlier invasion probably would have cost the lives of many more British and American soldiers, point out that, in the meantime, *their* soldiers were dying instead.

This view reflects the attitude of the Soviet leaders during the war. They always suspected that their allies wanted the Soviet Union to come out of the war in a very weak condition. At the very least, the British seemed to be saying that they would invade western Europe only after the Soviets spent years fighting and severely weakening the German army. Since the Soviets lost far more soldiers and civilians than any other country (an incredible 7 million soldiers and at least 13 million civilians), it is easy to understand the Soviet leaders' resentment. (In comparison, about 250,000 British troops and 60,000 civilians died; the United States lost about 300,000 soldiers and almost no civilians.)

The Free French

Another disagreement between Churchill and Roosevelt involved their attitudes toward General Charles de Gaulle and his Free French movement. De Gaulle had been a little-known French one-star general who had refused to surrender to the Germans in 1940 and had instead retreated to England. (The defeat of France in 1940 is described in Chapter 2.) From there, he had used the British radio to call on the French to keep fighting alongside the British. He had organized the Free French (later called Fighting France) troops, which were part of the Allied armies.

DeGaulle leads the Free French

After much maneuvering over several years, the many different resistance organizations within German-occupied France had accepted de Gaulle as their overall leader and his organization as the rightful government of their country. But the Allies had not. Churchill was the most favorable to de Gaulle, partly because he was grateful that de Gaulle had urged France to continue fighting alongside Britain at a time when it looked as if Britain would lose the war. But Churchill had concluded that because of its superior economic strength, the United States would play the key role in the war. That meant that on issues that were important to the Americans, Churchill would always side with them.

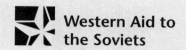

Western Aid to the Soviets

Although there is no question that the Soviet Union suffered far more in the war against Germany than the Western Allies, it is also true that the West provided important aid to the Soviet effort. For many years, convoys of Allied ships sailed across the North Atlantic and through icy Arctic waters to the Soviet port of Murmansk, carrying huge amounts of supplies. German submarines attacked these convoys at every opportunity, causing heavy losses. In one convoy, only eleven out of thirty-six ships reached Murmansk safely. Sometimes the submarine attacks were so heavy the convoys had to be canceled.

Although the Soviet leaders constantly complained about the amount of supplies getting through, the total value of American aid to the Soviet Union was $11 billion, an enormous sum at that time. In November 1943, Soviet dictator Joseph Stalin told President Franklin D. Roosevelt that without the American supplies received in the first two years of the German invasion, the Soviet Union would have lost the war.

Henri Giraud, Franklin D. Roosevelt, Charles de Gaulle, and Winston Churchill at the Casablanca conference, January 1943.
(Reproduced by permission of AP/Wide World Photos)

United States supports General Giruad

And the Americans did not support de Gaulle. Part of the reason was Roosevelt's personal dislike of de Gaulle, who, everyone agrees, was a difficult person to get along with. The more help de Gaulle got, the less grateful he seemed. But Roosevelt also felt that de Gaulle was an old-fashioned military man who did not believe in democracy. He did not want the Allies to impose de Gaulle and his movement on the French people.

Instead, the Americans seemed to be searching for some other military man to replace de Gaulle. They came up with General Henri Giraud, who had commanded an army in 1940, been captured by the Germans, and escaped. But there were several problems with Giraud. He was not nearly as skillful a politician as de Gaulle. He was distrusted by the French resistance. And, whatever Roosevelt thought of de Gaulle, Giraud really *was* antidemocratic.

De Gaulle and Giraud at Casablanca

In January 1943, Roosevelt and Churchill held a series of talks near Casablanca in Morocco. Both de Gaulle and Giraud were invited to attend, and Roosevelt and Churchill forced the generals to accept a compromise by which they shared power. Before long, however, Giraud began to fade out of the picture, and de Gaulle's movement was eventually accepted by the Soviet Union, Britain, and the United States as the provisional (temporary) government of France.

The Soviet Union, the Western Allies, and Poland

The second front was one of the major sources of disagreements between the Soviet Union and the Western Allies. Another set of disputes concerned Poland, and it went back to the earliest days of the war.

Just before it invaded Poland on September 1, 1939, and started World War II, Germany signed a treaty with the Soviet Union, usually called the Nazi-Soviet Pact. (The treaty is described in Chapter 2.) The pact assured Germany that it could fight Britain and France, which had promised to protect Poland, without having to fight the Soviet Union at the same time. Secret parts of the treaty provided that the Soviets would take over the eastern part of Poland.

So, on September 17, while the desperately retreating Polish army tried to escape the Germans and make a stand in the eastern part of their country, the Soviet army entered Poland from the east. The Soviets then annexed (made part of their country) the eastern half of Poland, where one-third of the population lived.

Soviets claim eastern Poland

To many people, it seemed that the Soviets had joined with Germany to grab their neighbor's land. But the Soviets did not see it this way. They pointed out that these areas had been taken by Poland from the new Soviet government in a war in 1920. The Soviets pointed out that in 1919, before the Polish-Soviet war, the British Foreign Minister, Lord Curzon,

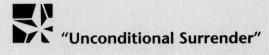

"Unconditional Surrender"

At the Casablanca Conference, U.S. president Franklin D. Roosevelt publicly announced that the "aims of the war" could be reduced to "a very simple formula: the unconditional surrender of Germany, Italy, and Japan." Roosevelt emphasized that the Allies did not want to destroy the people of the Axis countries or the countries themselves. The Axis powers were controlled by "a philosophy based on the conquest and subjugation of other peoples," however, which Roosevelt did find necessary to destroy.

The demand for unconditional surrender is quite unusual in war. More commonly, countries fight for limited goals, such as control of a particular region. One purpose of Roosevelt's declaration was to reassure the Soviet Union that the Western Allies would not make peace with Germany without including the Soviets. The declaration was also intended to influence American and British public opinion and reassure the people in German-occupied European countries. It promised that the Allies would not make deals with the Nazis. The demand for unconditional surrender also showed that the war was being fought between two ways of life that could not coexist. Some historians think that Roosevelt was influenced by the example of President Abraham Lincoln in dealing with the slave-holding Confederacy during the American Civil War.

Roosevelt's declaration has been strongly criticized ever since, on the grounds that it encouraged Germany and Japan to continue fighting and prolonged the war. The British military writer B. H. Liddell Hart called it the "biggest blunder of the war." Other historians disagree, arguing that Germany and Japan would never have negotiated any terms that the Allies could have accepted.

had tried to define the border between Poland and the Soviet state. The boundary that he drew, known as the Curzon Line, put most of this territory that the Soviets now annexed on the Soviet side of the line.

Less than two years later, in June 1941, the Germans had invaded the Soviet Union and conquered eastern Poland in the process. Poland was now under German control. By the end of 1943, however, the Red Army (the Soviet army) had pushed the Germans far back toward the west. As the Soviet military approached eastern Poland, the Soviet leaders made it

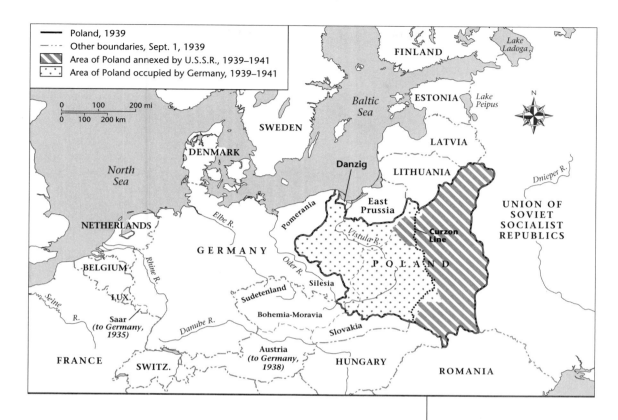

Legend:
— Poland, 1939
‒ ‒ ‒ Other boundaries, Sept. 1, 1939
▨ Area of Poland annexed by U.S.S.R., 1939–1941
▨ Area of Poland occupied by Germany, 1939–1941

Poland with 1939 and 1941 borders.

clear to the British and Americans that they considered this area part of the Soviet Union and that they would not restore Poland's 1939 borders.

Although the Soviets had not consulted the people who lived there, violating the principles of the Atlantic Charter, the British and Americans realized there was not much they could do. The Red Army would physically control the area, and only a serious threat to break up the alliance against Germany might have changed the Soviet leaders' minds. Dissolving the alliance was too high a price to pay. At the first meeting among Roosevelt, Churchill, and Stalin, held in Teheran, Iran, in November 1943, the two western leaders agreed generally to the Soviet demand regarding Poland's eastern border.

Plans to move Poland west

However, the British and Americans also suggested that to make up for the loss of territory on its east, Poland

General Wladyslaw Sikorski, head of the Polish government-in-exile in London, who later died in a plane crash. His death removed the most respected and capable leader of the London Poles, who might have been able to reach a compromise with the Soviet Union.
(Reproduced by permission of AP/Wide World Photos)

should be given land on its west, taken from Germany after its defeat. In essence, Poland would be moved westward. The Soviets agreed with this suggestion, partly because it might weaken Germany permanently and partly because it would mean that Poland would never side with Germany against the Soviets.

In 1939, the Polish government had escaped the Germans and was now in London. Britain and the United States considered this government-in-exile the legal representative of the Polish people. The London Poles, as the government-in-exile was often called, absolutely refused to give up the eastern half of Poland to the Soviets.

The Katyn massacre

The territorial dispute was made much worse by a stunning accusation from the Germans. In the spring of 1943, the Germans announced they had discovered a mass grave in the Katyn forest region of eastern Poland. They initially said that the grave contained 1,700 bodies, a number that eventually reached 4,000. The dead were officers of the Polish army, each with a bullet in his head. The Germans blamed the Soviets, who had controlled the area between September 1939 and June 1941.

The Soviets strongly denied the German accusation, claiming the Germans themselves had committed the murders. At first, most people in the west believed the Soviets. This was natural, since some of the terrible massacres committed by the Germans in Poland and Russia were becoming known. An accusation of mass murder, coming from the Nazis, was not to be trusted.

The Polish government-in-exile, however, refused to accept the Soviet explanation. It demanded an investigation by the International Red Cross. The Soviets considered this an insult and maintained that the London Poles were siding with the Nazis against them. The Soviet government soon broke off all relations with the London Poles.

Today it is known that the Soviet secret police murdered the Polish officers in the spring of 1940. The reason may have been to eliminate Poles who might have been leaders in regaining their country's independence. Some historians believe the killings may have been caused by a misunderstanding of orders sent by Soviet leaders.

The future of eastern Europe

The argument over borders became closely connected to the question of what kind of government Poland would have after the war. The Western Allies were afraid the Soviets would impose communist governments in the areas they liberated. These fears increased in July 1944 when the Soviets created a Polish Committee of National Liberation, dominated by Polish communists, which the Soviets soon recognized as the legitimate Polish government instead of the government-in-exile of the London Poles.

At almost the same time, the underground Home Army, which was loyal to the London Poles, led a major uprising against the Germans in Warsaw, the Polish capital. The Red Army, which was very close to Warsaw, did not help the uprising and did not enter the capital until months later, after the Germans had crushed the Home Army. The Soviets said that the Red Army had been unable to advance for military reasons, but most Poles believed that the Soviets had purposely allowed the Germans to destroy the Home Army. In either case, relations between the Soviet Union and the London Poles worsened. (The Warsaw uprising is described in Chapter 12.)

By the last year of the war, it was becoming obvious that the Soviet Union was determined to install a communist government in Poland. Historians have strongly disputed the Soviet motivation for this. Some believe that the Soviets always wanted to install communist governments throughout eastern Europe, either because they believed in spreading communism or because they wanted to control those countries.

Other historians think the Soviets acted defensively, in response to British and American actions elsewhere—such as in

The Western Allies were afraid the Soviets would impose communist governments in the areas they liberated.

Italy. In the summer of 1943, Stalin asked that the Soviet Union be allowed to take part in governing newly liberated territory in southern Italy. In October, the Allies created an Advisory Council for Italy, which included the Soviet Union and France. But this council had no power, and Italy was really governed by the Anglo-American Control Commission. ("Anglo" is a prefix referring to England that is often used to mean "British.")

According to some historians, the Soviets responded to being shut out of governing Italy by deciding to run Poland themselves, without allowing the British and Americans to participate. In this view, the Soviets felt that only communist governments would be friendly to the Soviet Union and would prevent countries such as Romania and Hungary from ever again attacking the Soviet Union. The argument about who was to blame for these actions became very bitter in the years after World War II, when the disputes between the Western Allies and the Soviet Union became a worldwide struggle called the Cold War. (See Chapter 17.)

The Soviet Union and Japan

Another important series of disagreements between the Western Allies and the Soviet Union concerned the war against Japan. Japan and the Soviet Union had signed a treaty in April 1941 in which each country promised that it would remain neutral if the other went to war. When Germany, Japan's ally, invaded the Soviet Union two months later, Japan stood by its agreement and did not join in. Japan was planning to go to war with the United States and Britain and did not want to fight the Soviet Union at the same time.

In December 1941, when Japan attacked the United States, Germany quickly declared war on America in support of Japan, but Japan still did not enter the war against the Soviet Union. Hitler believed that Germany could defeat the Soviets alone and, at least at first, did not want Japan's help. So for most of the war, the United States, Britain, and the Soviet Union were at war with Germany, but only the United States and Britain were at war with Japan.

In the first years after Germany invaded, the Soviet Union could not have helped very much in the war against

Japan, and the Western Allies understood this. Even then, the United States wanted to use air bases in the far eastern Soviet Union to send American bombers against Japan. But the Soviets, afraid this action would cause Japan to attack Soviet territory, would not allow the Americans to use their bases. Both Japan and the Soviet Union were afraid of going to war with each other, even if each country's allies wanted it to.

United States presses Soviets to invade Manchuria

By 1944, however, it became clear that the Allies would soon defeat Germany and that Japan would keep fighting. American military leaders believed that the United States would have to invade Japan and that tens of thousands of American soldiers would be killed. The United States pressed the Soviets to agree to join the war against Japan after Germany surrendered. They wanted the Soviet army to invade Manchuria, in northern China, and engage the large Japanese army stationed there.

Winston Churchill, Franklin D. Roosevelt, and Joseph Stalin at Yalta on the Crimean Peninsula, February 1945. At this final meeting of the "Big Three," Roosevelt pressed the Soviet Union for a commitment to join the war against Japan. Roosevelt's health was quickly deteriorating; he died two months after this picture was taken. *(Reproduced by permission of the Library of Congress)*

That way, the Japanese could not use those troops to defend Japan itself. Destroying the Japanese army in China might also make the Japanese leaders see that continuing the war was hopeless. Then an American invasion might not be necessary.

Getting the Soviet Union to declare war on Japan was so important to the United States that the American government was willing to agree to many Soviet demands. The Americans promised that the Soviets could have special economic privileges in Manchuria (a promise they made without asking the Chinese government) and that it could take over some islands belonging to Japan. The United States was also willing to agree to some Soviet demands about the war in Europe. This give-and-take influenced many of the discussions among the Allies about Europe.

Generalissimo Chiang Kai-Shek, leader of the Republic of China. Although his government had been supported by American military aid for many years, President Franklin D. Roosevelt finally determined that Chiang would never seriously fight Japan.
(Reproduced by permission of AP/Wide World Photos)

Soviets invade Manchuria

The Soviets eventually promised to join the war against Japan as soon as possible after Germany's final defeat, usually saying it would take about three months. Following Germany's surrender, the Soviets shifted some of their most experienced troops, with their best equipment, from Europe to the Far East. On August 8, 1945, exactly three months after Germany's surrender, the Soviet Union declared war on Japan, and a huge Soviet army invaded Manchuria the next day. Despite a hard fight put up by the Japanese, the Soviets soon broke through the Japanese defenses, taking many prisoners. In less than two weeks, the Soviets drove what was left of the Japanese army back into northern Korea.

A-Bomb changes everything

By then, however, the Americans were no longer sure they wanted the Soviets in the war against Japan. On July 16,

◢◣ Secrets and Spying Among Allies

The atomic bomb project illustrates some of the suspicions between the Western Allies and the Soviet Union. The atomic bomb was developed in secret in the United States by scientists working for the U.S. Army. (The project is described in Chapter 15.) Scientists and engineers from many countries were involved, but no Russian (Soviet) scientists were asked to participate.

Although there were some disputes, the United States generally kept the British government informed about the development, construction, and testing of the new weapon. Officially, British prime minister Winston Churchill's agreement was required before the United States could use the bomb, though the decision was really made by Harry S. Truman, who became president after Franklin D. Roosevelt's death in April 1945.

At the same time, the Western Allies kept the existence of the project secret from the Soviets. It was only after they had successfully tested the bomb, in July 1945, that Truman told Soviet leader Joseph Stalin of its existence. Even then, he spoke in very general terms, saying only that the United States had a new, very powerful weapon. He gave no details, and Stalin did not ask for any.

In fact, it is now known that spies kept the Soviet government informed of the progress of the atom bomb project, although it is not clear whether the Soviet leaders appreciated its immense power. In any case, the atom bomb project shows how neither side fully trusted the other: the Americans tried to keep the most vital military secret of the war from one of their most important allies, while the Soviets used every possible method to spy on the United States.

1945, the United States had successfully tested the first atomic bomb in the desert of New Mexico. (The development of the atomic bomb is described in Chapter 15.) American leaders now believed atomic weapons could force Japan to surrender without an American invasion and without help from the Soviet Union. If so, then a Soviet invasion of Manchuria would increase Soviet influence in China without any benefit for the United States. But it was too late to change the plan for a Soviet invasion, and no one knew for sure if the atomic bomb would defeat Japan.

On August 6, 1945, two days before the Soviet declaration of war, an American plane dropped an atomic bomb on

Compared with the complicated relationships among the three major Allied powers, the connection between Germany and Japan, the two most important Axis powers, was much simpler.

the Japanese city of Hiroshima, completely destroying it. On August 9, a second atomic bomb was dropped on Nagasaki. On August 15, the emperor of Japan told the Japanese people in a radio broadcast that the war was lost. Although the threat of further atomic bombs was probably the most important reason for his admission of defeat, many historians believe that the Soviet invasion of Manchuria was also a key factor. (The use of the atomic bomb and the defeat of Japan are discussed in Chapter 14.)

The Axis powers

Compared with the complicated relationships among the three major Allied powers, the connection between Germany and Japan, the two most important Axis powers, was much simpler. Basically, Germany and Japan shared some information but never planned any military operations together. Their top military and naval officers never met, never discussed strategy, never timed campaigns to take advantage of what the other was doing. In effect, Germany and Japan were fighting parallel wars. Each was fighting Britain and the United States, and each hoped that the other would succeed. Allied propaganda during the war implied that Germany and Japan had a plan to divide up the world between them. This plan really amounted to vague ideas about the Japanese conquering India and moving west while the German army moved south from the Caucasus region of the Soviet Union with the two armies meeting somewhere around Iran. Neither side actually planned any operations to put this offensive into action. The two armies never got within 3,000 miles of each other.

The third major member of the Axis was Italy. In many ways, German leader Adolf Hitler had originally followed the example of the Italian dictator Benito Mussolini. When the Nazis took over Germany, Hitler and Mussolini began to work together. For example, Italy sent troops to help General Francisco Franco's rebels in the Spanish Civil War that began in 1936, while Germany sent airmen and planes. Soon, however, it became clear that Germany, with its much greater economic and military power, was the senior partner.

Germany's dominance became even more true once Italy entered World War II in June 1940. Both in the North

African desert and in Greece, the Germans had to help save Italian armies from defeat. (See Chapter 3.) The German generals had a very low opinion of the Italian army, which they did not attempt to hide. The alliance with Germany was never popular among the Italian people, who increasingly wanted Italy to get out of the war. By the time the Allies invaded Italy in the summer of 1943 and Mussolini was overthrown (see Chapter 10), Germany was treating Italy more like a conquered country than an ally.

Germany treated Italy more like a conquered country than an ally.

Other members of the Axis

The military alliance signed by Germany, Italy, and Japan in September 1940 was called the Tripartite Pact, which means three-party treaty. In November 1940, Romania and Hungary also signed the pact. Both countries bordered on the Soviet Union, and Germany wanted them to join its planned invasion. Though both countries had antidemocratic governments that were sympathetic to Nazi Germany, this alliance was always complicated.

Romania and Hungary Romania and Hungary were strongly influenced by Germany, but they were still independent countries. And although they were allied with Germany, they were each other's traditional enemies. In August 1940, under German pressure, Romania gave up large sections of its country to Hungary, which satisfied neither side. Both suffered tremendous losses in the Soviet Union, and by the summer of 1943 both were secretly (and separately) trying to contact the Western Allies to make peace. The British and Americans, in effect, told them they would have to deal with the Soviet Union directly.

Afraid that Hungary was secretly planning to get out of the war, the Germans took over the country in March 1944. An extreme pro-Nazi government was put into power, and soon Germany controlled every aspect of Hungarian life. Romania was luckier. As the Red Army crossed into the country in August 1944, the Romanians surrendered, declared war on Germany, and joined the Soviets in attacking Hungary.

Reluctant allies There were three other allies of Germany, although two of them did not really act like allies. Bulgaria signed the Tripartite Pact and joined in the German invasion of Yugoslavia in 1941, but it refused to declare war on the Soviet Union—though it did declare war on the United States and Britain. Soon after the Soviet Union declared war on Bulgaria in September 1944, Bulgaria declared war on Germany and sent 150,000 troops to fight its former allies.

Finland fought with Germany against the Soviet Union because it wanted to regain territory it had lost to the Soviets in the winter of 1939–40. It never declared war on Britain or the United States, and Germany had very little influence on how Finland acted. (See the box in Chapter 12 on p. 279.)

On the other hand, Slovakia, which the Germans had recently set up as an independent country, was really a puppet of Germany and did whatever Hitler wanted. It signed the Tripartite Pact in November 1940 and provided troops to invade the Soviet Union.

Turning Points: The Allies Begin to Win the War

10

B etween the fall of 1942 and the summer of 1943, the Allies (the countries fighting Germany) won a series of military victories that changed the course of World War II. One of these victories was in the Atlantic Ocean, which finally forced the German submarines, in May 1943, to abandon their attempt to prevent North American supply ships from reaching Britain. (The Battle of the Atlantic is described in Chapter 3.) The other victories occurred on the shores of the Mediterranean Sea and at the eastern end of Europe, in Russia. At the beginning of this period, the possibility of a German victory was still very real. By the end, however, most people knew that Germany, although far from being defeated, could not win the war.

Africa

The British Eighth Army had been fighting in the desert of Egypt and Libya in North Africa since September 1940. The Axis forces (the name used for Germany and its allies) it opposed were mostly Italian, but they were reinforced by the Afrika Korps, German armored and mechanized troops.

This time, Montgomery wanted to destroy the Axis forces.

The Axis commander was a German general, Erwin Rommel, known as "the Desert Fox." Rommel was a daring leader who had embarrassed the British with his lightning attacks and had become a national hero in Germany. (These events are described in Chapter 3.)

In August 1942, the British appointed a new commander of the Eighth Army, General Bernard Montgomery. Within two weeks, Rommel attacked the British, but this time the Eighth Army held its position, and Rommel broke off the attack.

The Battle of El Alamein

Montgomery prepared the Eighth Army's next move carefully. The British now had far more troops and planes than the Axis. They had six times as many tanks and most of them, including the recently arrived American-built Sherman tanks, were better than Rommel's. The Axis troops were dangerously short of fuel and shells. On October 23, 1942, Montgomery attacked, beginning the Battle of El Alamein. He was not aiming to chase the Axis army from Egypt into Libya. That had already happened twice in the war, and each time the British had eventually been chased back. This time, Montgomery wanted to destroy the Axis forces.

Rommel had been home in Germany, recovering from an illness, and rushed back to Africa by plane. But he could not change the outcome of the Battle of El Alamein. The fighting continued for ten days. After suffering heavy losses, Rommel began a long retreat westward along the single coast road. By the end of the year, he had retreated 1,000 miles, deep into Libya. The retreat had cost him 40,000 prisoners; he had only 60,000 troops and fewer than 100 tanks left.

Operation Torch: The invasion of North Africa

Meanwhile, a new battlefront had opened in Africa, behind Rommel. On November 8, 1942, while Rommel was retreating, American and British forces landed in three locations much farther west. Under the overall command of American General Dwight D. Eisenhower, Operation Torch began with one landing near Casablanca, on the Atlantic coast of Morocco, and two on the Mediterranean Sea, near Algiers and Oran, the two largest cities of Algeria.

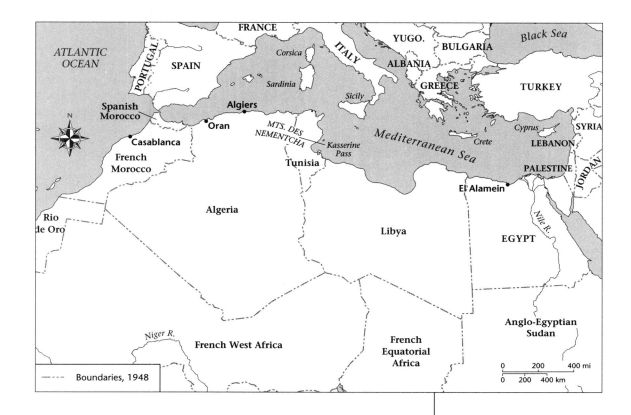

Boundaries, 1948

North Africa, 1948.

Morocco and Algeria, as well as neighboring Tunisia, were French colonies. After France surrendered to Germany in June 1940, the Germans allowed a French government to remain in power in the southern part of the country. This government, known as Vichy (the town where the government was based), still controlled most French colonies overseas. The Vichy government was officially neutral in the war, although it was influenced by and cooperated with Germany, since the German army controlled most of France.

In November 1942, about 100,000 French troops were stationed in North Africa. The Allies hoped that these troops would not oppose their landings. In fact, they wanted the French to join them. American representatives had secretly contacted some Vichy military and civilian officials, as well as opponents of the Vichy government, both in France and in North Africa. (See box on p. 230.) Many Vichy supporters were beginning to believe that Germany would lose the war, and they wanted to get on the right side.

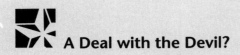

A Deal with the Devil?

It was by pure chance that Vichy admiral Jean François Darlan was in Algiers, visiting his critically ill son, when the Allies landed in November 1942. The Allies considered it very lucky because French troops throughout Morocco and Algeria quickly obeyed Darlan's order to stop fighting the Allies. In return, the Allies put Darlan in charge of North Africa.

But this deal created a major political controversy. Darlan had cooperated closely with the Germans for the past two years. The French resistance, the network of secret organizations inside France that opposed the Germans, hated him, as did the Free French movement, the London-based organization led by General Charles de Gaulle that had refused to accept France's surrender and had continued fighting on the Allied side from the very beginning. (The French resistance is discussed in Chapter 6; the Free French and de Gaulle are discussed in Chapter 9.)

Putting Darlan in charge of North Africa also caused outrage in Britain and the United States that the Allies had not expected. Many people in the two countries believed it was wrong to put a man who had worked closely with the Nazis into power, that it betrayed all the things the Allies said they were fighting for. They worried that there would be more deals with pro-Nazi officials in other countries who wanted to switch sides, and maybe even with Nazis in Germany who wanted to stay in power if Germany lost the war.

On Christmas Eve 1942, Darlan was assassinated. Although the Allies had nothing to do with it, Darlan's death was a relief to them. As Winston Churchill, the British prime minister (head of the government), wrote after the war, the Allies had already gotten the benefit of the deal with Darlan, and his death ended their embarrassment at having to work with him.

There was a great deal of confusion among French officials when the Allies landed. Some pro-Allied French officers arrested those who wanted to resist the Allies—but then they were arrested themselves. In Casablanca and Oran, the landings were resisted. In Algiers, there was little fighting, partly because pro-Allied residents had taken over the city before the landings. The French troops stopped fighting when the Allies made a deal with Admiral Jean François Darlan, the second-highest official of the Vichy government and the commander in chief of all its military forces, who happened to be in Algiers at the time.

The end of the Axis in Africa

Although they no longer faced any resistance, the Allied troops moved slowly. They were heading for Tunisia, between Algeria and Libya, where they planned to trap Rommel's forces between them and Montgomery's Eighth Army, which was advancing westward. But their hesitation gave Gemany and Italy time to rush troops into Tunisia, first by air and then by ship. The French authorities in Tunisia followed Vichy's orders, rather than Admiral Darlan's, and allowed the Axis troops to enter the country unopposed.

It looked at the time as if the Allies' delay was a major mistake because they could have taken Tunisia before the new Axis troops arrived. As it turned out, Germany and Italy made the mistake by sending those troops. Although there was hard fighting, eventually all the Axis forces in North Africa—including Rommel's army and the new troops in Tunisia—would be destroyed or captured.

The flag-draped coffin of Admiral Jean François Darlan after his assassination in December 1942. *(Reproduced by permission of AP/ Wide World Photos)*

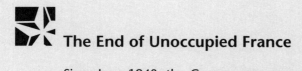

The End of Unoccupied France

Since June 1940, the German army had held direct control of the northern half of France and the entire Atlantic coast. This area was known as occupied France. (A military occupation is when a victorious country stations troops in a defeated country to control it.) Italy occupied the southeast corner of the country. The rest of France, known as the unoccupied zone, was under the authority of the Vichy government. When the Allies landed in French-controlled North Africa in November 1942, the German army immediately poured troops into most of the unoccupied zone while the Italians took over the rest. There was no more unoccupied France. Although the Vichy government still existed, it was even more strongly dominated by Germany.

The Germans also wanted to gain control of the French fleet, anchored in the port of Toulon on the Mediterranean coast of southern France. The Allies urged its commander to sail his warships to North Africa and join them, but the commander hesitated. When the Germans attacked the Toulon naval base, it was too late for the ships to sail away. Determined not to hand over their warships to the Germans, the French naval officers and sailors blew them up instead.

When they reached Tunisia, the Allied forces faced determined German resistance in the mountainous countryside. Rommel's forces had retreated into Tunisia and established defensive positions against Montgomery's troops coming from the east. At the same time, Rommel launched several counterattacks against the Allied forces to his west, some quite successful. At the Kasserine Pass, a narrow pass through the mountains, Rommel took an American force by surprise, inflicting serious casualties on them, capturing some American prisoners, and forcing them to abandon a great deal of equipment. Like almost all American troops, these soldiers had never been in serious combat before. Their generals were also inexperienced, and Rommel took advantage of both of these facts.

But the Axis forces did not have the men or equipment to turn these small victories into bigger successes. Their supplies, coming across the Mediterranean by ship and plane, were not reaching them in sufficient quantities. As the fighting continued through the winter months, the Allied forces, which now included French troops, grew stronger. The Americans, now led by General George S. Patton, became more experienced in fighting the Germans. Believing the situation was hopeless, German leader Adolf Hitler ordered Rommel to return to Germany on March 6, leaving his army behind.

In late March 1943, Montgomery's troops broke through the Axis defensive positions and attacked from the rear. The Germans and Italians retreated and continued to fight defensive battles for more than a month. Early in May, the Axis troops, low on supplies and ammunition, began to surrender in large numbers. The last holdouts gave up on May 13. Although estimates of the exact number vary, the Axis probably lost more than 200,000 men. The war in Africa was over.

Map of Italy showing the Gustav Line and Gothic Line, 1943.

Italy: The invasion of Sicily

On July 9, 1943, less than two months after the end of the fighting in Africa, the Allies invaded Sicily, the large island at the toe of the boot-shaped Italian peninsula. Ten divisions (about 150,000 men), including two parachute divisions, were involved. Twelve Axis divisions were defending the island, but only two were German. Some of the Italian troops treated the Allies as liberators rather than invaders—in some cases helping them unload their landing boats. Large numbers of Italian troops surrendered as soon as the Allied troops reached them.

The American forces, commanded by General Patton, raced up the western side of the island, while the British, led by General Montgomery, went up the east side. The British met strong resistance from first-rate German units, including two more German divisions sent as reinforcements. Even so, the Italians began evacuating their troops to the Italian mainland on

American soldiers landing on a beach in Sicily.
(Reproduced by permission of AP/Wide World Photos)

August 3, and the Germans began to do the same a week later. Most of the Germans successfully evaded capture. By the middle of August, however, the Allied troops controlled all of Sicily.

The fall of Mussolini

The series of Axis defeats in Africa had hurt Germany, but they had been a disaster for Italy. It had lost the empire that the Italian dictator, Benito Mussolini, had dreamed would bring back the glory of ancient Rome. Now Sicily, part of Italy itself, had been invaded. More than 300,000 Italian soldiers were prisoners of war in Africa. Another Italian army, with more than 200,000 men, had been wiped out in Russia. In both Russia and Africa, the Allies had captured vast quantities of arms and equipment. This was a much greater loss for Italy than for the other major powers, whose economies were far stronger. Most Italians were much poorer than they had been before the war, and there were increasing shortages of almost everything. Allied planes constantly bombed Italian cities, and the Italian and German air forces seemed unable to protect them.

Few Italians had ever been enthusiastic about the war, especially after Italy declared war on the United States. Many Italians had relatives in America, and most admired the country. The alliance with Hitler's Germany had never been popular with the Italian people, and it became even more unpopular because many Italians believed Germany did not treat Italy as an equal. As dissatisfaction grew, many of the country's most powerful people, including King Victor Emmanuel III and top military officers, decided that Italy had to get out of the war. The king and the army had supported Mussolini for more than twenty years, but now they plotted to get rid of him.

On July 25, 1943, while the fighting in Sicily was still going on, the king and his men removed Mussolini from his position as prime minister and placed him under arrest. The new leader of the government was Marshal Pietro Badoglio, the senior general of the Italian army, while the king took over direct command of the armed forces. The new government promised the Germans that Italy would continue to fight alongside them. In fact, it immediately entered secret negotiations with the Allies for Italy to surrender.

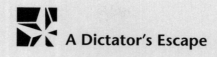

A Dictator's Escape

After his arrest in July 1943, Italian dictator Benito Mussolini was held in a series of locations, and finally in a mountaintop house. On September 16, a small force of German commandos led by Otto Skorzeny landed in gliders and rescued him. Soon, the Germans set him up in northern Italy, where he declared himself head of the Italian Socialist Republic. This new government helped the Germans in fighting the Italian anti-Nazi resistance movement in German-held areas. Near the end of the war, the resistance captured and executed Mussolini.

Surrender and invasion

The Italians signed the surrender on September 3, 1943, but kept it secret. On the same day, a British force commanded by General Montgomery crossed the narrow strait from Sicily and landed at the toe of Italy. This was not the main invasion; it was only a diversion to draw German troops into the area. It failed, mainly because the region—like much of Italy—is very mountainous, and the only way Montgomery's troops could move forward was on a few roads along the coastline. These could be defended by relatively few German troops.

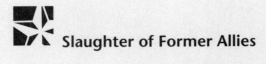

Slaughter of Former Allies

In addition to occupying Italy after the Italians surrendered to the Allies in September 1943, the Germans also took over areas outside Italy that had been controlled by Italian forces. In southeastern France and Croatia (the western part of Yugoslavia), as in Italy itself, the Italian troops usually did not resist. But on several Greek islands, there was heavy fighting between the Italians and the Germans. In revenge, the Germans executed every Italian officer they captured there.

On September 8, 1943, British radio announced the Italian surrender, and the next morning the main Allied invasion force landed near Salerno, south of Naples, the largest city of southern Italy. The Allies had hoped that the announcement would mean that they could land without facing any serious opposition. But Hitler had expected Italy's surrender and had made plans to deal with it. German troops moved quickly to take over all important cities, roads, and bridges. They disarmed the Italian soldiers, who usually did not resist. Some became prisoners and were sent to Germany to work in arms factories. Others were allowed to go home. The fact that the new Italian government soon declared war on Germany had little practical effect.

The Germans rushed their own troops to Salerno and nearly forced the American and British invasion force to return to its ships. But the Allied planes, artillery, and especially the big guns of their nearby warships prevented this evacuation. By September 18, the Germans began to withdraw from the invasion area. But this retreat was planned. The Germans were preparing a defensive position that stretched all the way across Italy, called the Gustav Line. Most of the Gustav Line was in rugged terrain in the mountains. It would be almost impossible to attack the dug-in Germans directly. The Allies would have to advance along the two narrow plains between the mountains and each coast. And these plains were crossed by a series of rapidly flowing—and easy to defend—rivers that came down from the mountains to the sea.

Anzio and Cassino

British troops entered Naples on October 1, 1943. The advance up the Italian peninsula would prove to be very slow. The Gustav Line soon became known as the Winter Line, as the Allied armies attacked it throughout the winter of 1943–44. Unable to get past it, the Allies finally decided to go

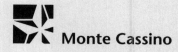

Monte Cassino

Allied troops from all over the world carried out the attacks on the great abbey of Monte Cassino in Italy. The first attack, in early February 1944, was by Americans. The second and third were by soldiers from New Zealand, India, and Britain. In the last battle, French troops, including Moroccans, broke through near Cassino, and Polish troops finally reached the ruins of the great monastery. So, in the end, the German army was forced back from the Gustav Line by soldiers from France and Poland, two countries that it had conquered in the first few months of the war.

The Monte Cassino monastery had great historic importance. Founded by Saint Benedict in the sixth century, it had survived fourteen centuries of war and turmoil. The German troops around Cassino apparently did not actually take defensive position inside the historic buildings, though they may have stored ammunition in them. It is not clear whether the Allies knew this. In any case, on February 15, 1944, massive Allied bombing destroyed the monastery buildings. After that, the Germans did set up positions in the ruins and the piles of wreckage created even more obstacles for the attacking Allied troops. Military historians agree that the bombing of Cassino only helped the Germans.

around it. In January 1944, a large Allied force landed on the beaches around the town of Anzio, north of the Gustav Line and only 30 miles south of Rome, Italy's capital. Again, the Germans rushed reinforcements to the area, and they kept the invasion force from moving away from the beaches. In mid-February, the Germans counterattacked at Anzio and nearly succeeded in pushing the Allies back into the sea. After heavy fighting with many deaths on both sides, the Allies stopped the Germans, but they were still penned in near the beaches. The Anzio landings had not freed Rome, and they had not forced the Germans to abandon the Gustav Line.

On its western end, the Gustav Line was dominated by the mountaintop abbey (church) of Monte Cassino. As it became clear that the Allied troops at Anzio could not reach the Gustav Line from the rear, the Allies tried repeatedly to attack Cassino. Three major assaults were defeated, with heavy casu-

alties. The fourth attempt, in May, finally succeeded. As British and American armored divisions could now move past the Gustav Line, the Germans at last abandoned it and retreated north.

At the same time, the Allies finally broke through the German encirclement at Anzio. The Americans entered Rome on June 4, 1944. But the Germans retreated to another position in the mountains farther north, the Gothic Line. The Allies did not reach the great cities of the north, where most of Italy's industries are located, until the spring of 1945. By that time, the British and American troops that had invaded France were fighting deep in Germany, and the Soviet army was at the gates of Berlin, the German capital, itself.

The war in Soviet Russia

While the fighting was going on in Africa, much larger battles were being waged in the Soviet Union. That was where

the main part of the German army, including most of its best troops, its tanks, and its air force, was fighting. The German invasion in June 1941 had driven the Soviet army back hundreds of miles, killed 1 million Soviet soldiers, and taken 3 million prisoners. But the Soviets had stopped the German advance in the fall, and Soviet counteroffensives in the winter of 1941–42 had pushed the Germans back from Moscow, the Soviet capital. Although for a while it looked as if a large part of the German army might be overwhelmed by the Soviet attack and the terrible winter conditions, it pulled back and established defensive positions. (These events are described in Chapter 3.)

The ruins of the Abbey of Monte Cassino after the Allied bombing. *(Reproduced by permission of AP/Wide World Photos)*

A weakened German army

When the winter of 1941–42 ended, the Germans prepared to attack again. But the battlefront stretched 2,100 miles from north to south, and the Germans were not strong enough

Adolf Hitler (center right with mustache), Benito Mussolini (center left), and German generals study battle maps. *(Reproduced by permission of AP/Wide World Photos)*

to attack everywhere, as they had the previous year. They had lost too many men, tanks, and horses—a quarter million—which were needed to pull their cannons and supply wagons.

The German air force, the Luftwaffe, was weaker than it had been the previous summer, and the Soviet air force was stronger. (One of the reasons was that the Luftwaffe needed more planes to defend German cities from British bombing raids, which are described in Chapter 8.) The Soviets were producing more tanks than the Germans, and supplies from the United States, especially trucks, were beginning to arrive in large quantities. The Red Army, as the Soviet forces were called, was being reinforced to make up for the huge losses of the past year. It had many new generals, often younger men who had succeeded in the earlier fighting. They had learned the strategy and tactics of modern war and were beginning to equal the German generals in skill.

The German generals also had to deal with increasing interference from Hitler. The Nazi dictator had always made

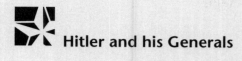

Hitler and his Generals

German leader Adolf Hitler's increasing interference in running the army was partly a result of his distrust of his generals. Top German officers usually came from old, noble families that often looked down on Hitler as half-educated and ill-mannered. Although they went along with the Nazis, many officers considered them street thugs. In return, the Nazis hated the old-line officers, believing they just wanted to return to the good old days instead of the entirely new Germany that the Nazis wanted.

Hitler believed that most of his generals were too cautious and did not understand the finer points of politics. Hitler appreciated the fact that military policy and political issues are closely connected. For example, the military men tried to talk him out of sending troops into the Rhineland area of Germany in 1936 because they knew they could not fight France, which opposed this move. But Hitler believed, correctly, that France would not use force to stop the Germans.

Especially in the early years, Hitler was often right—and the generals wrong—about these kinds of issues. Hitler came to believe he was a military genius. He also had a very good memory and understood military details, such as specific types of weapons and where each army division was located. But sometimes he became so involved in these details that he lost sight of larger issues.

Hitler's distrust of his generals also led him to divide authority among them, without clear lines of command. This meant that disputes between generals had to be settled by Hitler himself. In fact, the whole Nazi government ran this way. For the army, however, this practice meant that commanders in the field often did not have the authority to make immediate decisions, even though delay could mean defeat.

Hitler's belief that only he understood the big picture led to disastrous mistakes. He was very reluctant to ever order a retreat, even when it was the only way to save his army. The worst example was the battle of Stalingrad (discussed later in this chapter), but there were many others.

As military events began to go against Germany, Hitler blamed his generals and constantly replaced them. By the end of the war, Hitler was increasingly unrealistic. He would not believe reports that he did not like; he gave orders that were impossible to carry out (such as vast increases in building tanks), and he put more and more faith in the introduction of new weapons that he believed would change the course of the war even when it was clear to his generals that the war was lost.

the big decisions, such as the Soviet invasion, but now he was insisting on much more direct control of army operations. In the spring of 1942, Hitler decided that the German armies should capture the Caucasus, the part of the Soviet Union between the Black Sea and the Caspian Sea, north of Iran. The Caucasus was a major producer of petroleum, and Germany was beginning to experience serious oil shortages.

The attack on the Caucasus

Early in May 1942, the Germans began an offensive to clear Soviet troops out of the Crimean Peninsula. The Germans were afraid that the Soviets could use Crimea, which jutted into the Black Sea, as a base to attack the Germans in their offensive on the Caucasus. In a week, the Germans had taken another 170,000 prisoners and controlled the entire peninsula except for the fortress city of Sevastopol. The city, which had been surrounded by the Germans since the previous October, did not surrender until July 2.

Around the same time, the Soviet army launched its own offensive, around the city of Kharkov, north of Crimea. Although this attack at first threatened to disrupt German plans, it ultimately played into their hands. German forces north and south of the city moved forward and encircled the Soviet troops. The Russians lost another 250,000 prisoners and more than 1,000 tanks.

On June 28, the main German attack began. Four German armies, with strong tank forces, swept south from the Kharkov area, down the grassy plain that stretched between the Donets and Don Rivers. They drove down into the Caucasus, forcing the Soviet troops back. But the Germans were taking far fewer prisoners than in previous advances. The Soviets were retreating rather than allowing themselves to be encircled by the attacking German tanks. Soviet resistance, intense summer heat, and the ever-greater distance that German supplies had to travel to reach the troops began to slow the German advance. As the flat terrain began to change to the foothills of the Caucasus mountains, the Germans ground to a halt.

The Eastern front in 1941 and 1942.

The battle for Stalingrad was the most significant battle of World War II.

Stalingrad: The turning point of the war

As they moved south into the Caucasus, the Germans also sent a strong force eastward across the river Don toward the city of Stalingrad, on the great river Volga. Their purpose was to block the route to the Caucasus for Soviet reinforcements and supplies. Stalingrad itself, a city of 600,000 people, was originally not an important military target. But it became important, and partly because of that, it was the most significant battle of World War II.

In mid-August, the German Sixth Army reached the outskirts of Stalingrad from the west. The Fourth Panzer (tank) Army was coming from the southwest. The Soviets rushed reinforcements to the city, dug defensive ditches, and ordered troops not to retreat. The attack on the city turned into a battle for every street and every building. The entire city was destroyed as the German troops slowly pushed the Russians back toward the banks of the mile-wide Volga. One German officer described fighting for more than two weeks to capture one house. Stalingrad, he said, "is an enormous cloud of burning, blinding smoke; it is a vast furnace lit by the reflection of the flames." General Vasili Chuikov, the Russian commander, said that it was impossible to hear separate shots or explosions: everything was one single, continuous roar.

By the middle of October, the Russians controlled only a few pockets of the city. Although German radio announced that they had captured Stalingrad, the fighting inside the city continued. The Germans were exhausted by two months of the worst fighting of the entire war. Neither side made any progress.

On November 19, 1942, the Soviet armies finally sprang their trap. They had carefully prepared two Soviet forces with vast quantities of artillery and tanks. One was many miles west of Stalingrad, on the river Don. It struck southward, through an area defended by troops from Germany's allies Hungary, Italy, and Romania. They were there because Germany did not have enough troops of its own. None were as well-equipped as the Germans, and the Soviets smashed through them, as well as any German units they met.

The next day, the second Soviet force attacked from southeast of Stalingrad, heading west. When the two armies

Trapped by a Name?

Part of the reason that Stalingrad became so significant was something that happens in many wars. It is natural for military commanders to try to win a battle once it begins rather than retreat. The attackers think that one more effort will meet success. The defenders think that if they stop one more attack, the enemy will give up.

But there was another factor at work in Stalingrad. The city was named for Joseph Stalin, the Soviet dictator. Its loss would represent a major symbolic defeat for Stalin, so he wanted it defended at all costs. Further, Stalin and his military leaders had planned to use Stalingrad as a trap for the Germans.

Hitler, on the other hand, became obsessed with capturing the city, even if it did not make military sense. For months he obsessed about it. He refused to listen to any military advice that contradicted this goal. Because of this fixation, he sent a German army into the Soviet trap and ordered it to stay, even when it became clear that his troops would be destroyed. No one knows for sure, but it is possible that the destruction of the battle for Stalingrad would never have happened if the city had a different name.

met on November 23, they had the German Sixth Army trapped in Stalingrad. There was still time for the Germans to retreat westward and possibly break through the trap, but Hitler personally ordered that there would be no retreat. Instead, Hitler wanted the troops supplied by air while German tank forces attempted to break through the Soviet ring and get into Stalingrad.

But the winter weather and the Soviet air force and antiaircraft guns prevented the Luftwaffe from supplying anywhere near enough food and ammunition. The Sixth Army—freezing, starving, and short of ammunition—stayed in Stalingrad as the Russians began to retake the city.

The German force sent to break through the trap was far too small and did not have enough tanks. It had to travel 60 miles; it went 30 and then was driven back. On Hitler's orders, the Germans in Stalingrad did not try to break out to meet the advancing column and retreat with it.

Soldiers of the German Sixth Army after their surrender at Stalingrad. Few of them survived the war. *(Reproduced by permission of the Corbis Corporation [Bellevue])*

Meanwhile, on December 16, 1942, the Soviets attacked again, even farther west. In a blinding snowstorm, they destroyed the Italian Eighth Army and retook much of the area between the Don and Donets Rivers. This meant that the German troops in the Caucasus were nearly trapped too. Even Hitler agreed that there was no choice but to retreat. In January, the German troops managed to escape from the Caucasus before the Soviet army could block the way.

But there was no retreat from Stalingrad, where the temperature was twenty below zero. On January 10, 1943, as the Russians began their final attack to retake Stalingrad, 7,000 cannons blasted the Germans, the largest artillery bombardment in history. The German-held area was split in two and then into smaller pockets. On January 30, the Russians captured the German headquarters, and the German commander finally surrendered. In the battle's last three weeks, 100,000 German soldiers died. Another 100,000 were prisoners, including 24 German generals. The entire Sixth Army, with 22 divisions, was destroyed. In Germany, all regular radio programming was stopped for three days. Only somber music was played.

The Red Army advances

The main battle lines were already far west of Stalingrad. In the next weeks, the Soviet army pushed the exhausted Germans back. But the Germans regrouped and counter-attacked. The city of Kharkov, already captured and recaptured, changed hands twice more in bitter fighting. By March 1943, the spring thaw again flooded the dirt roads and turned the countryside into marshes that tanks could not cross. Both sides paused to try to replace the men and equipment that had been lost in these battles.

Many of the top German generals wanted to withdraw their forces much farther west and prepare a defensive line that was shorter and closer to its sources of supply. In effect, this meant the German military no longer believed that they could destroy the Soviet armies. Now their plan was a defensive war against Russia, in which they would try to hold on to some of the vast territory they had conquered in the summer of 1941.

But Hitler still believed in the possibility of a total German victory. Instead of a general withdrawal, he ordered the German army to attack again. Its goal this time was to encircle and destroy large Soviet forces—as it had done in 1941.

The winter battles had left the two armies facing each other for hundreds of miles. But the line between them was not straight. In some places, German positions jutted out toward the east. In others, Soviet forces were positioned farther west. These bulges, or salients, were classic military targets. The idea was to attack the two sides of the bulge at its base, cutting off the main enemy forces inside the bulge from supplies and reinforcements. The attack would disrupt the ability of each unit's headquarters to communicate with its troops and control their movements.

The Kursk salient

The largest Soviet bulge centered on the city of Kursk. Known as the Kursk salient, the bulge extended 150 miles west on its northern side and 50 miles west on its southern

The German army would never again be able to launch a major offensive in the Soviet Union.

side. It was almost 100 miles wide. Inside the salient were 60 Soviet divisions.

On July 5, 1943, the Germans attacked both sides of the salient. Their force included 2,700 tanks, almost all the Germans hadstationed in the entire Soviet Union. Despite this powerful force, they made relatively slow progress. The Soviet military leaders had expected the attack and had issued large numbers of antitank weapons to the troops there. They had laid 5,000 explosive mines on every mile of the front line. The troops and civilians in the area had built a series of strongly fortified positions so that even if the Germans did overrun one, the Soviet troops could withdraw to the next and escape capture. Soviet tanks fought it out with the advancing Germans. The two German forces could not reach each other to cut off the salient.

On July 12, the Red Army began its counterattack. In one engagement, each side sent 900 tanks against the other in a battle that raged all day. The Germans lost 300 tanks that day, the Russians even more—but they stopped the Germans. In other battles throughout the area, the result was the same. The Soviets pushed the Germans back, with both armies suffering heavy losses. On July 13, Hitler ordered an end to the German offensive.

For the next two months, the Soviets followed up their victory at Kursk by pushing the Germans eastward. By September, they were in Ukraine and White Russia (Belarus) and had driven the Germans from all of southern Russia. On November 3, the Red Army entered Kiev, the capital of Ukraine, which the Germans had captured more than two years earlier.

Although both sides had suffered heavily at Kursk and the battles that followed, the Soviets could replace their lost troops and equipment. The Germans could not. Russia had more people and therefore more soldiers. The Red Army also had more tanks than the Germans, and every month Soviet factories turned out more. The same was true for planes, cannons, and bullets. When aid from the United States was added in, the same was true for every other category of military supplies. In addition, the Germans were fighting the British and Americans in Italy and would soon be fighting them in France.

The losses at Kursk meant that the German army would never again be able to launch a major offensive in the Soviet Union. From then until the end of the war almost two years later, the Germans would retreat. Almost always, they fought hard, inflicting heavy losses on the Soviets. Sometimes they would stop the Red Army for a while, especially while the Soviets were being resupplied. Sometimes they would even launch counteroffensives, but these were never major threats. The battles that came later were among the bloodiest of the war. But whatever the cost, the Soviets were prepared to pay it. No amount of blood, German or Soviet, could stop the Red Army now.

The Great Invasion: Operation Overlord

11

By the end of 1943, the Allies (the United States, Great Britain, and the Soviet Union) had won a series of victories that had changed the course of World War II. Yet the final defeat of Germany still seemed far away.

In the Soviet Union (Russia), the Red Army had fought and won a great tank battle around Kursk in July and continued to drive the Germans westward. But powerful German armies remained on Soviet territory. Millions of Soviet soldiers had already died in battle, and the Germans had captured millions more in the early part of the war. (See Chapter 3.) No one could be certain that the Russians could continue to bear the major part of the fighting against Germany.

The Americans and British had successfully invaded French North Africa in November 1942 and Sicily in July 1943, but this had not taken much pressure off the Soviet armies. The invasion of Italy, which began soon afterward, was going much more slowly than expected. Italy had changed its government, ended its alliance with Germany, and even declared war on its former ally. But the American and British armies were bogged down by strong German defensive positions

By the end of 1943, the Allies agreed that the great invasion could not be delayed any longer and set it for the spring of 1944.

along the mountainous Italian peninsula. (The events in Russia, North Africa, and Italy are described in Chapter 10.)

Pressure and delay

The Russians had constantly pressed Britain and the United States to open a second front in western Europe. (A front is a combat zone, the area where two opposing armies are in contact.) American military leaders had favored an invasion of France almost from the time America had entered the war. After crossing France, the British and Americans could attack Germany from the west while the Russians closed in from the east. (See Chapter 9.)

The planning for the invasion had been going on for years, but it had always been delayed. The British feared that an early invasion, before they were fully prepared, would result in many deaths and would end in disaster. They remembered the way the German army had defeated them in France in 1940 (see Chapter 2), and they remembered the terrible bloodshed of World War I, when armies tried to attack built-up defensive positions.

Political factors also played a part. Winston Churchill, the British prime minister (head of the government), wanted to maintain British influence in the Mediterranean and southeastern Europe. That was one of the reasons the Allies had invaded Italy. Churchill wanted to send the Allied armies from Italy into Yugoslavia and toward Vienna, the capital of Austria. Many historians believe he was afraid that otherwise the Russians would control these areas after the war. But Churchill's plan might take years: the Allied armies were still in the southern half of Italy. (The political disputes among the Allies are discussed in Chapter 9.)

By the end of 1943, the Allies agreed that the great invasion could not be delayed any longer and set it for the spring of 1944. A supreme commander was named—Dwight D. Eisenhower, the American general who had commanded the invasions of North Africa and Italy. He was in charge of all land, sea, and air forces for the invasion. The commander of the ground troops was a British general, Bernard Montgomery, who had defeated the German Afrika Korps at the Battle of El Alamein in

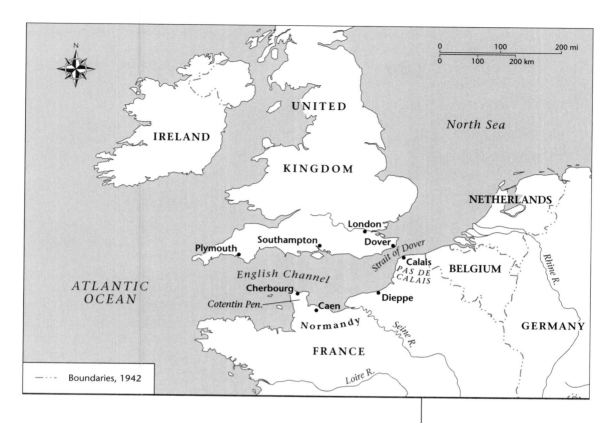

Egypt and led the British troops in Sicily (see Chapter 10). The invasion was code-named Operation Overlord. The day of the invasion would come to be known as D-Day.

Choosing a location

The Allied planners had to decide the location of the invasion. It had to be within easy range of the fighter planes that would take off from airfields in England. The planners believed that the invasion would fail unless Allied planes covered the troops in their first hours onshore. (So important was protecting the troops sufficiently, the American and British air forces would assign more than 5,000 fighter planes to the operation, while the German air force [the Luftwaffe] had only 169 fighters to cover a much larger area.) The closer the invasion was to the airfields, the longer the fighter planes could stay in action before they had to return to their bases to

The landings would have to be on the French coast facing the English Channel, somewhere between Belgium and the tip of the Cotentin Peninsula in Normandy.

refuel. In addition, the shorter the distance, the easier it would be to transport the troops and the enormous amount of equipment and supplies they would need.

This meant that the landings would have to be on the French coast facing the English Channel, somewhere between Belgium and the tip of the Cotentin Peninsula in Normandy. The English Channel, separating the island of Great Britain from France, is quite narrow, only 30 miles wide in some places. Although there were strong currents and storms sometimes blew up suddenly, causing high waves, it was still an easy crossing when the weather was good. Since the troops would land from fairly small boats, not large troopships, rough seas would endanger their safety and their ability to come ashore.

An invasion farther east would have the advantage of putting the Allied armies closer to Germany itself. But it would be too far for the fighter planes and would require a much more difficult journey in the North Sea. Anyplace farther west or south would mean sending the landing boats across a section of the open Atlantic, again without fighter support.

The Atlantic Wall

Of course, the Germans understood these factors too. Two German armies guarded the English Channel coast of France. The Germans had lined the coast with high-quality artillery (cannon) units, including coastal artillery that could fire on invading ships, and antiaircraft and antitank guns. Often concrete blockhouses protected the artillery. Other fortifications (built-up strong points) protected the troops. Networks of barbed wire would make it difficult to attack the German machine gunners firing on the invading Allies. In some places, concrete tunnels connected the machine gun and artillery positions.

The Germans had dug ditches and placed large metal obstacles in the open fields behind the coast, making it difficult for planes or gliders carrying troops to land and for tanks to cross. (Gliders are engineless planes that are towed behind a regular plane by ropes and then allowed to float down to land.) They purposely flooded some of the fields so that para-

chute troops who landed there might drown. They placed other obstacles underwater near the beaches to tear out the bottoms of landing boats as they approached the shore. A quarter of a million of these obstacles were in place by the time of the invasion. The water obstacles often had mines (explosive devices) attached, so that a boat that bumped into them would blow up. Other mines were placed in the water and on the beaches. By May 1944, there were 4 million mines along the French coast.

This system of fortifications, obstacles, and mines was called the Atlantic Wall. The Germans tried frantically to strengthen it, and by the time of the invasion, it had become a very powerful defensive position. But it was never really a wall. There were many gaps along the coast, manned by second-rate troops.

The Germans could not guard every place on the coast equally well. Most of their best troops were fighting in

Germany had a system of fortifications, obstacles, and mines called the Atlantic Wall protecting the coast of France.
(Reproduced by permission of AP/Wide World Photos)

Russia. Others were needed to block the Allied armies that were moving up through Italy. The Germans did not have enough material or manpower to fortify every section of the hundreds of miles of coast where the invasion might take place. They had to guess where the Allies would land—and they guessed wrong.

Capturing a port or landing on the beaches?

Ideally, the Allies would have liked to capture a major port in the invasion. Then they could bring supplies across the English Channel—or even directly from America—on large ships, which could be unloaded at the docks. Having a port would also make it much easier, in the days after the first troops landed, to bring in tanks, trucks, and artillery and vast quantities of gasoline to keep them going; ammunition and food for the troops; and more and more troops. The Germans expected that the invasion would center on one of the large ports on the Channel.

Problems attacking a port

But the raid on Dieppe in 1942 (see box) had convinced the Allied planners that it would be impossible to land the troops at a major port. The German defenses at these ports were too powerful. That was where the Germans positioned the most cannons and built the best fortifications against Allied air attack. The Dieppe raid had shown that a small number of well-fortified defenders could destroy a much larger attacking force. Even if an invading force succeeded in getting past the beach into a port city, every house would become a German strongpoint, hiding machine guns and riflemen. The Allied troops would have to fight their way through the town street by street and house by house.

While the Allies fought to take the city, the Germans would have time to bring in reinforcements from other parts of France. This would happen quickly, since the ports were always on roads and railway lines. If the Germans could bring in enough soldiers and tanks before the Allies could reinforce their troops, the invasion would fail.

Dieppe

In August 1942, almost two years before the Normandy invasion, the Allies attempted to capture the French port of Dieppe. At that time, the war was going very badly for the Allies. They needed a victory to help keep up the spirits of their people and their soldiers. Dieppe would not be a real military victory because the Allies knew they could not hold the port for long. They just wanted to capture it briefly and then evacuate the troops back to England. This would also show the people of Europe, suffering under German rule, that the Allies were planning to return to Europe—that Germany's power would not last forever.

Unlike the small raids launched by special British troops called commandos, the invasion of Dieppe was not aimed at destroying a specific target, such as a German submarine base, and it involved many more troops. It was really a rehearsal for the great invasion that would come someday. The Allies wanted to know how difficult it would be to capture a port. The rehearsal made them believe it was impossible.

The Canadian troops who attacked Dieppe outnumbered the German defenders by about twelve to one. The German troops guarding the port were not special elite units: they were the same kind of troops the Allies would meet wherever they landed. But the Germans had not even needed reinforcements. They were dug in and protected from the Canadians' firing. The Germans had carefully placed machine guns and artillery to cover the area an attacker would have to cross.

The raid was a disaster: many of the Canadians were killed before they could leave their landing craft. The rest were trapped on the beach. In one section, three waves of Canadian soldiers landed. Within three hours, every man was either dead or a prisoner.

Almost 5,000 Canadian soldiers landed at Dieppe. Only 2,110 returned to England, 378 of them wounded. More than 1,000 were killed and another 1,800 were captured, including 500 who were wounded. Almost 40 percent of the troops were killed or wounded in action, in only a few hours of fighting. Every one of the 29 tanks the Allies sent were destroyed, most by the German artillery.

Largely because of the fear of civilian casualties, the Allies chose not to bombard Dieppe from the air. That left the Canadian soldiers helpless before the dug-in German defenders. The Allied generals were determined that they would not make the same mistake for the big invasion.

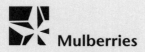

Mulberries

To make up for not capturing a port in the invasion, the Allies decided to build two artificial harbors near the invasion beaches. They were called Mulberries. Two million tons of steel and concrete were used to build more than 600 separate sections of the harbors. Tugboats towed the sections across the Channel in the days immediately following the Normandy landings.

The harbors included more than 200 concrete structures that were 60 feet tall. The Allies sank them in thirty feet of water to create a seawall that protected the Allied supply ships from the wind and waves of the Channel. They also sank old freighters as part of the plan. Then they built a floating pier inside the protected water and built roadways from this pier to the beaches. Large ships would unload at the floating piers, and trucks, jeeps, and tanks could be driven from their ships right onto the shore.

The Mulberries were a gigantic job of engineering and construction: one of them could hold 500 vessels at a time. Despite the size, the job was accomplished with amazing speed. The first ship unloaded at one of the Mulberries only ten days after the first troops landed.

Just three days later, however, one of the worst June storms in decades hit the English Channel. For three days, heavy winds and high waves tore at the piers, smashing them into each other. The Mulberry used by the Americans was completely destroyed, and the British Mulberry was severely damaged. Within a few days, the British, using parts from the wrecked American harbor, were again unloading ships. The Americans could not rebuild their Mulberry, but they were able to land enough supplies on the beaches without it.

Finally, attacking a port would greatly increase the number of French civilians who were killed or wounded. The Allies had learned this lesson from Dieppe as well. They would blast the area picked for the invasion with the giant guns of the warships and the bombs of the planes before the troops landed. This would kill many German soldiers and destroy some of their tanks, artillery, and fortifications. The Allied planners hoped it would also make it harder for the surviving German soldiers to fight when the Allied troops landed, their being stunned and confused by the naval and aerial bombardment. Some would have been deafened by the noise. They would be afraid. They might run away or surrender when the Allied soldiers came onshore.

Allies choose a beach landing

For all these reasons, the Allies decided that the invasion force would land on beaches. The troops would then capture a port as soon as possible after they had landed. In the meantime, although it would be more difficult, the Allies would land supplies and reinforcements on the beaches that they had captured at the beginning of the invasion.

The British Mulberry helped make up for the fact that the Allies could not capture a port on the coast of France. Supplies were unloaded from the prefabricated harbors. *(Reproduced by permission of the Corbis Corporation [Bellevue])*

The beaches of Normandy

The location of the invasion came down to two choices. The planners had ruled out the places where the beaches were not wide enough or were faced by high cliffs that the troops would have to climb while the Germans shot down at them. They also rejected targets that were too far from good ports.

The eastern end of the English Channel coast was one of the remaining options. This was the area of France called the Pas de Calais (pronounced pah de kal-LAY), on the narrowest part of the Channel, a short hop from the English port of Dover. Besides being close to England, this area was also relatively close to Germany, especially to the industrial areas whose factories built the weapons that the German army needed. A successful invasion at the Pas de Calais would put the Allied armies in a good position to drive into Germany and end the war quickly. But, because it seemed the most logical

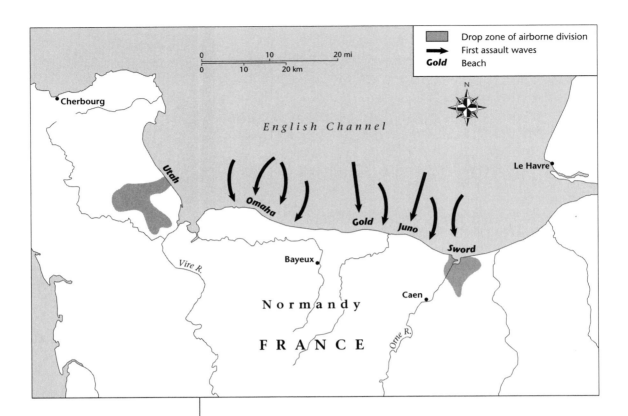

The Normandy invasion area, including the five beaches and the drop zones of the three airborne divisions.

place to attack, the Germans were concentrating on defending this area.

The Allies decided that the invasion force would land on the beaches of Normandy, just west of the town of Caen. The landing would be on five separate beaches, stretching along 50 miles of coast. Each beach had a code name and was assigned to a different part of the Allied armies. The code names have become famous. From east to west, the beaches were called Sword, Juno, Gold, Omaha, and Utah. The British would attack Sword and Gold, the Canadians would land at Juno, and American troops would take Omaha and Utah. Five infantry divisions would land from the sea, one at each beach. (A division is a large unit of an army, usually around 15,000 soldiers.) In addition, a British airborne division, including parachute troops and glider-carried soldiers, would land east of the five beaches to prevent the Germans from attacking the invasion from the side. Two American parachute divisions would land on the west side of the invasion area, inland from Utah beach, to protect that area.

The plan was that the soldiers would win control of the beaches and push inland several miles. Meanwhile, reinforcements would be landing constantly. The five separate forces, plus the airborne troops, would then link up so that the Allies would control an area 50 miles wide and several miles deep. Then part of the invasion force would turn north to capture the port of Cherbourg, on the Cotentin Peninsula.

Weather: The uncontrollable factor

The invasion was scheduled for June 5, 1944. On that day and the next two, there would be the right combination of tides and moonlight. Moonlight was needed so that the parachute troops could see when they dropped into France the night before the invasion. The tides had to be just right so that the obstacles and mines that the Germans had placed on the beaches would not be hidden underwater when the landing craft reached the beaches at dawn. If the invasion did not happen on one of these three days, it would be two more weeks before the conditions were right again.

On the evening of June 4, the weather in England was terrible. Heavy winds blew the rain almost parallel to the ground. It would be difficult for the bombers to see their targets and for glider pilots to find their landing zones. Pilots would have trouble delivering the parachute troops over the correct drop zone, and the wind would scatter the soldiers and make it almost impossible for them to land in large groups. The small landing craft were not designed for rough seas. Many might sink, drowning the soldiers before they could even get to the beaches. And bad weather and heavy clouds immediately after the invasion meant that German tanks and troop-carrying trucks could travel toward Normandy without being seen—and attacked—by Allied planes.

The German commanders knew that the invasion would need good weather. They were sure the Allies would not land in the storm, and many of them took the opportunity to relax. General Erwin Rommel, the commander of German forces on the coast, went home to Germany for a few days to celebrate his wife's birthday.

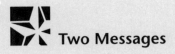

Two Messages

Around noon on June 6, 1944, official British radio broadcast a simple message to the people of England and the world: "Under the command of General Eisenhower, Allied naval forces supported by strong air forces began landing armies this morning on the coast of France."

But in Eisenhower's wallet was a slip of paper on which he had written a different message—one that never needed to be broadcast. "Our landings in the Cherbourg-Havre area have failed to gain a satisfactory foothold and I have withdrawn the troops," he wrote. "My decision to attack at this time and place [was] based on the best information available. The troops, the air and Navy did all that bravery and devotion to duty could do. If any blame or fault attaches

But the Allied weather forecasters predicted that the winds would die down just long enough to launch the invasion. It was probably the most important weather forecast ever made, but no one could be sure that it was right. And once the invasion was set in motion, it would be difficult to stop. The soldiers were packed tightly on the ships that would later transfer them to the landing boats. Many of the soldiers—who would soon have to fight a major battle—were becoming seasick. They could not be left waiting on the ships much longer. To maintain secrecy, they had not been allowed to communicate with anyone. If they were unloaded and returned to their bases, it would be impossible to prevent the Germans from learning which ports were being used—and that would tell them that the invasion was heading for Normandy, not the Pas de Calais. In addition, the bases the invasion troops had left in England were filling with new soldiers. Sending them back would create a transportation nightmare.

For days, the Allies had been bombing the railroads and roads in northern France so that they could not be used to bring German reinforcements to Normandy. If the invasion were delayed, the Germans could repair some of the damage. In addition, the bombing had not yet focused on Normandy itself, to keep the location secret. Just before the invasion, the bombers would concentrate entirely on Normandy. If that happened and the invasion were delayed, it would probably reveal the location, and the Germans would be waiting when the Allies did land.

Sometime after midnight on the morning of June 5, while the wind and rain continued over England, the Channel, and Normandy, General Eisenhower made his final decision. The landings would begin at dawn on June 6, 1944. The parachute landings would begin several hours before. The invasion was on.

The airborne attack

The three airborne divisions began landing east and west of the invasion beaches during the night. At the eastern edge of the area, the British troops, many landing by glider, captured several important bridges over rivers and canals that German reinforcements would have to cross. The lightly armed airborne troops were to hold these positions until the main invasion force, with its more powerful weapons and its tanks, fought its way to them from the beaches.

At the western end, the wind and poor light made it impossible for the American paratroopers of the 101st and 82nd Airborne Divisions to land in large groups, as intended. Many fell miles away from their drop zones. They were scattered all over the countryside, many drowning in the flooded fields, others shot by the Germans while they hung helpless above the ground, their parachutes tangled in trees.

Combat units that had been trained to fight as a team found themselves separated from the other soldiers in their

General Dwight D. Eisenhower visits paratroopers of the American 101st Airborne Division, just before they head for Normandy.
(Reproduced by permission of the National Archives and Records Administration)

The ships, including seven battleships, twenty-three cruisers, and more than one hundred destroyers, fired shells —some as heavy as automobiles—into the German fortifications.

squads. Each unit had been assigned specific targets to attack. In most cases, this was now impossible. For hours—and in some cases, for days—small groups of paratroopers from different units searched for others, formed a bigger group, and attacked a crossroad or a bridge or an artillery position. Little by little, the groups became larger and better organized and began to go after their assigned targets.

Although the confusion cost many paratroopers their lives, some military historians believe it may have actually helped make the invasion successful. The Germans were not sure what was happening; they had no idea how many paratroops had landed or what their targets were. For a long time, they remained uncertain about whether this was just another commando raid or part of an invasion.

The bombardment

More than a thousand bombers of the British Royal Air Force began their attack on the defenses at the beaches code named Sword, Juno, and Gold at three in the morning. The bombing continued for two hours, and in that time they dropped more than 10 million pounds of bombs. The American bombers did the same at Utah and Omaha beaches.

Then at five in the morning, the bombing stopped, and the big guns of the navy warships opened fire from off the coast. The ships, including seven battleships, twenty-three cruisers, and more than one hundred destroyers, fired shells— some as heavy as automobiles—into the German fortifications. Many of the soldiers waiting on their landing ships claimed they could actually see the shells flying over their heads toward the beaches. Every witness, Allied and German, who later described the bombardment mentioned the incredible noise. No one had ever heard anything as loud. No one had ever seen so much firepower aimed at so small a place. Some American soldiers waiting to land later remembered thinking that not a single German could still be alive.

The landings

Behind the smoke of the bombardment, more than 6,000 ships, including 4,000 landing craft, were waiting. It was the largest fleet ever assembled. Between 6:00 and 7:30 in the morning (depending on the tides at each of the five beaches), the troops began to land. The sea was rough, and many of the small landing boats began to fill with water. In many cases, the soldiers had to use their helmets to bail the water out. Others were not so lucky: their boats sank, and the soldiers, wearing combat boots and carrying heavy backpacks and other equipment, often drowned.

Other boats hit mines and blew up. Sometimes they hit sandbars and had to let the soldiers out too far from shore. Then the troops charged out into water that was over their heads, trying desperately to run toward the beach. All the time, the Germans fired on them.

Despite these setbacks, at four of the five beaches the landings went very well. At Sword, Juno, and Gold, the boats landed tanks right onto the beaches, where they could protect the troops immediately. The three attacking divisions of British and Canadian troops overwhelmed the single, poor-quality German division that opposed them. By 10:00 A.M., the invaders had landed 30,000 men, 3,000 cannons, and 700 armored vehicles, including tanks. Soon, the British troops who landed on Sword beach, the farthest east of the landing areas, linked up with the paratroopers and glider-borne soldiers of the British airborne division. German resistance was somewhat stronger at Gold beach, but by the end of the day, the British had pushed several miles inland.

At Utah beach, the American 4th Infantry Division completely surprised the Germans. The German troops, another poor-quality division, were stunned by the bombardment. They felt surrounded by the landings in front of them and the American paratroopers behind them. After relatively little resistance, most of the Germans surrendered. Twenty-three thousand American troops landed on Utah Beach on D-Day. Only a dozen Americans were killed and less than two hundred wounded.

At Utah beach, everything went right. Even the mistakes—which happen in every large military operation—helped the Americans. Strong currents had carried many of the boats away from their intended landing areas. Although at first confused and unsure of where to go, the troops accidentally landed in an area that was almost undefended.

At Utah beach, everything went right.

Omaha beach: The American agony

But at Omaha beach, everything went wrong. Much of the beach led to steep banks, some of them 200 feet high. The German defenders could fire down on the Americans from these banks. In addition, at each end of Omaha there were high cliffs, with German cannons on top of them. The huge air and sea bombardment had not destroyed these guns, probably because of the cloud cover. (Elite American units called Rangers, which were like the British commandos, attacked the cliffs on D-Day, using ropes to climb the cliffs in the face of German fire.)

This was the kind of beach that the planners of Operation Overlord had wanted to avoid, but Omaha was in the center of the invasion area. It was the link between Utah beach and the American paratroopers on the west and the British and Canadians on the east.

There was more bad news at Omaha. It was defended by the best German troops in the area, tough combat veterans who had recently been sent to Normandy for more training. The landing boats were blasted by German fire long before they reached the beaches. Many of the soldiers died in the boats or in the water before they could reach shore. The specially designed swimming tanks launched from their boats too far from shore, and most of them sank, often drowning their crews. (These tanks had canvas covers that were filled with air. When the tank reached land, the covers were removed.) Many of the combat engineers, whose job was to clear the beach of obstacles, also died, and their special equipment was lost in the water.

The first wave of soldiers at Omaha beach had no tanks to protect them and no way to clear the beach of obstacles. They were pinned down by German artillery, machine gun, and rifle fire. Some clung to the half-submerged obstacles, trying to get any cover they could from the devastating enemy fire. The bodies of their dead friends floated beside them. The wounded lay screaming around them. Moving forward seemed impossible. Staying where they were, at the edge of the water, was just as bad. Finally, little by little, one or two soldiers at a time, then in small groups, they began to advance toward the Germans. One of their officers (no one is certain which) summed up their situation in words that became

World War II: Almanac

famous: "Two kinds of people are staying on this beach," he shouted. "The dead, and those about to die. Now let's get the hell out of here."

By the end of D-Day, more than 3,000 Americans had been killed or wounded at Omaha beach. But the Germans could not drive them back into the sea. As night fell on June 6, 1944, the Allied armies had five footholds on the coast of France.

Supplies and reinforcements move inland from Omaha Beach some days after the invasion, while more ships wait their turn. *(Reproduced by permission of AP/Wide World Photos)*

The Battle of Normandy

The Germans were slow to send reinforcements to the battle. They were still afraid that another invasion would attack the Pas de Calais. Allied bombing and sabotage (destruction of military targets) by the French resistance made it difficult to move their armored (tank) divisions to the battlefield. The armored troops were the best in the German army, and only the tanks could now defeat the Allies. But the German divisions arrived one at a time, and too late.

By June 12, the Allies had connected their troops into a continuous front. By June 18, they had landed more than 600,000 soldiers in Normandy. Also on that day, American troops who had cut across the neck of the Cotentin Peninsula reached the Atlantic coast. They captured the port of Cherbourg on June 26, but the Germans had heavily damaged the harbor and the Allies could not use it for several weeks. It took months before the port became an important unloading point. Even so, Allied reinforcements kept pouring into the battle area, until the Americans and British had more troops, tanks, artillery, and—as throughout the fighting—air power than the Germans.

The German army was under increasing pressure. They could not bring reinforcements from Russia. As the Soviets had promised the British and Americans, the Soviet army began a massive offensive on June 22. Within a week, almost 200,000 German troops had been killed, wounded, or captured, and the entire German army in the Soviet Union was in danger. (See Chapter 12.)

Heavy fighting continued in Normandy for more than two months. The British failed several times to capture the town of Caen, which they had almost reached on D-Day. The fighting was made especially difficult by the way the Normandy countryside was divided. Each farm was surrounded by tall mounds of earth covered with thick plant growths. These hedgerows, as they are called, made it impossible for the Allied tanks to cross the fields. Instead, they had to creep along the narrow roads, between the hedgerows, where they made easy targets for the Germans. The Allied foot soldiers had to take each field under fire from the Germans, who used the hedgerows for cover.

On July 25, the Americans at the west end of the Normandy front attacked the German defenders near the town of

Saint-Lô. The Germans had fought with tremendous determination since D-Day, but now they were exhausted. The units in this area began to retreat and then to fall apart, as many of the soldiers surrendered. The American armored divisions of General George S. Patton's Third Army broke through the gap in the German lines toward the south and then swung east. The British and Canadian troops attacked from the north. Much of the German army in Normandy was between these two forces near the town of Falaise.

The Germans, on German dictator Adolf Hitler's direct orders, tried to counterattack on August 7, attempting to cut off Patton's Third Army from its supplies. But the counterattack was defeated. The Germans had committed their last tank forces to this attack. Now they too were trapped, under constant bombardment from the Allied air forces, with the Allied ground troops closing the circle around them. There was only a narrow gap separating the advancing Allied troops. The Ger-

After the landing at Normandy, the Allied armies moved east and south through France. General George S. Patton's Third Army advanced south and east and British and Canadian troops drove east from the Caen area.

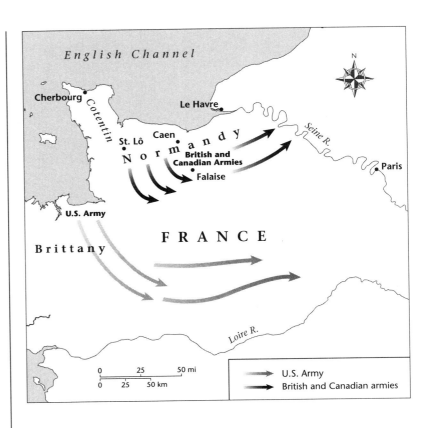

mans got about 300,000 soldiers and 25,000 vehicles through this gap before it closed on August 20. They retreated east, trying to establish a new defensive line closer to the German border. But 50,000 German soldiers were dead, and 200,000 had surrendered. Two German armies, with their tanks and artillery, had been destroyed.

The Allies race across France

The Battle of Normandy was over. The German defenses had crumbled. Patton's tanks, almost unopposed, raced east across France. The British chased the retreating Germans through the northern part of the country. At one point, they advanced more than 100 miles in two days. Within two weeks they had entered Belgium, freeing its capital, Brussels, on September 4, 1944.

Meanwhile, on August 15, the American Seventh Army landed eight divisions that had been fighting in Italy, five of them French, on the Mediterranean coast of France, between Nice and the great port of Marseilles. The second invasion, code-named Operation Anvil, had finally come—at the other end of the country from the Pas de Calais, where the Germans had expected it. The Allied forces overwhelmed the German troops, capturing Marseilles and racing north from the Mediterranean deep into France. The German army retreating from Normandy was now in danger of being cut off and surrounded if it tried to make a stand too far west (see map on p. 272). This was one of the reasons that the Germans moved so far east so quickly.

U.S. Army medical corpsmen try to comfort a young French girl who was wounded during the Battle of Normandy. *(Reproduced by permission of AP/Wide World Photos)*

Paris

On August 17, 1944, Patton's troops had reached the river Seine, northwest and southeast of Paris. But the Allies were not planning to capture Paris immediately. They did not

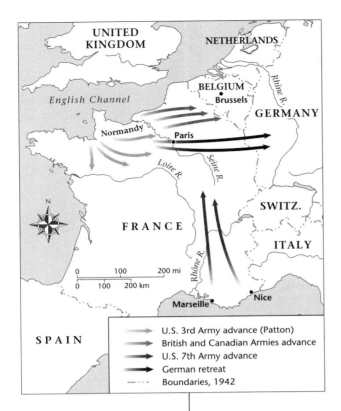

As the Allies moved through France, the German forces were in danger of being trapped between the two Allied invasion forces unless they retreated far enough east. The Allied code name for the second invasion was Operation Anvil, because the German army would be smashed down on it by the "hammer" of the Allied troops coming from Normandy.

want a battle that might destroy the famous monuments, historic buildings, and artistic treasures of the city. They did not want to risk the lives of the people of Paris. And, perhaps most of all, they did not want to have to supply the city with food and fuel. All their trucks were being used to supply the armored divisions that were trying to destroy the retreating German army.

But Paris was not just a great city; it was the symbol of France. Liberating Paris from the Germans had political as well as military importance. General Eisenhower had long since promised that the first Allied troops to enter Paris would be French.

Although the different resistance organizations and movements were supposed to be united under the authority of General Charles de Gaulle, the leader of the Free French (see Chapter 9), there were many conflicts among them. One of the most important resistance organizations was dominated by the French Communist Party. They did not trust de Gaulle's plans for postwar France, and he did not trust theirs. The Communists wanted the people of Paris to rise up and liberate themselves from the Germans, not wait for the American army to free them. De Gaulle's supporters were afraid this would lead to a bloodbath if it failed, and they were also afraid that it would lead to Communist control of the city if it succeeded. On the other hand, de Gaulle's supporters also wanted to fight the Germans and regain the honor that France had lost in the surrender of 1940.

As tensions mounted in Paris and the Allied armies began to break out of Normandy, the Germans ordered the French police in Paris to be disarmed, fearing their weapons would be used by the resistance. The police went on strike instead. Other workers were also on strike, defying the Germans.

On August 17, 1944, the police took over the main police headquarters in central Paris, barricaded themselves, and raised the French flag above the building—the first time it had flown in Paris since June 1940.

Soon other barricades appeared on the streets of the city. Young men and women, armed with rifles, pistols, and homemade gasoline bombs called Molotov cocktails, attacked German patrols. Resistance groups began taking over official buildings. Some of the buildings were now empty; in others, there was heavy fighting against the Germans. Similar small actions occurred throughout the city. By the standards of the great battles in Russia and Normandy, these did not amount to a major military action. Even so, about 1,500 French resistance fighters died in the next few days, and another 3,000 were wounded—more than the number of American soldiers who had been killed or wounded on Omaha beach on D-Day.

A German general's honor

For the next several days, the fighting in Paris spread. After a short truce, arranged by the representative of neutral Sweden, the fighting broke out again. On August 22, Hitler ordered the Germans to destroy Paris rather than surrender. He told the German military commander Dietrich von Choltitz that only a "field of ruins" should be left. Von Choltitz did not want to be remembered as the man who had blown up Paris, no matter what Hitler ordered. Destroying bridges, to prevent the Allies from crossing the Seine, was one thing. But dynamiting famous landmarks like the Eiffel Tower or the Louvre Museum made no military sense. It went against his idea of military honor.

But von Choltitz's sense of honor also would not allow him to surrender without putting up a fight. And he felt he could not surrender to a bunch of armed civilians, only to officers of a regular army. In addition, on July 20 there had been an attempt by some German officers to kill Hitler. (See Chapter 12.) Von Choltitz knew that any sign of disobeying Hitler's orders would put him under suspicion of being part of the anti-Hitler plot and would endanger his family back home in Germany.

On Augutst 17, 1944, the police raised the French flag above the building— the first time it had flown in Paris since June 1940.

The people of Paris and the French army had freed Paris together.

The Second Armored Division

As news of the uprising reached the Allied commanders, the French Second Armored Division, which had been among the best Allied forces in the recent battle around Falaise, received new orders. It was to move immediately to Paris, 120 miles away. The next day, August 23, the division sped along the roads toward Paris, avoiding the Germans as much as possible. On August 24, as they reached the suburbs, they were held up several times by German antitank defenses.

Their advance was also slowed by the crowds and celebrations that broke out along their route. One American general accused them of "dancing to Paris." Afraid that American troops would be ordered to take the city, the French commander, General Philippe Leclerc, decided to send a small force into Paris that night.

One platoon of soldiers (about thirty men) and three tanks headed into the city, turning down side streets and going around any defended position. At 9:30 that night, they reached the Paris City Hall, near the center of town. Even though it was only three tanks, church bells began to ring all over Paris, as the fighting between the resistance and the Germans continued.

At seven the next morning, Leclerc's main force entered the city from the south. Huge crowds—sometimes twenty deep—cheered them. At first, the Parisians thought that American troops had arrived, since the tanks and jeeps and even the uniforms were American. The celebrations were even more joyful when it became clear that the soldiers were French.

The crowds passed them food and drink and flowers. They opened bottles of champagne that had been hidden away for more than four years, waiting for this day. Women hugged and kissed the liberating troops.

Many of the French soldiers were from Paris. They passed notes to people in the crowd, asking them to phone their families with the news they had come home. Some of these soldiers died before they could see their families, however. In the rush of happiness, the crowds had forgotten that the Germans were still fighting in Paris.

As Leclerc's men approached the center of Paris, many German positions held out fiercely. At about 2:30 in the afternoon of August 25, 1944, some of the French troops reached German headquarters, fought their way in, and captured General von Choltitz. The French drove him to police headquarters, where Leclerc was waiting. The two generals signed the terms of the German surrender of Paris. A little while later, one of the leaders of the resistance added his name. The people of Paris and the French army had freed Paris together.

The Defeat of Germany

12

The two-front war

In the last year of the war in Europe, two powerful forces closed in on Germany from the east and west. One was the Red Army, the army of the Soviet Union (present-day Russia, one of the eastern Allies). The other was the combined army of the western Allies, the United States and Britain. (The Allies were the countries fighting against Germany, the leading Axis power.) Germany had to defend first one and then the other of these fronts.

For a while, Germany could shift troops and resources from one front (or combat zone, the area where two opposing armies are in contact) to the other, depending on where the greatest danger lay. But the Allied bombing of the railroad system in Germany and German-controlled Europe made maneuvering like this difficult. More significantly, too many German soldiers died or were captured, and too many tanks, planes, and cannons were destroyed: Germany couldn't replace all of them. In the long run, Germany was not strong enough to defend itself against all its enemies, and eventually it was crushed between them.

The western front

On June 6, 1944, American and British troops landed in Normandy, on the northwest coast of France. The Allies had been eager to begin this invasion ever since the United States entered the war in 1941, but they waited until the armies were fully prepared and they had enough supplies to be fairly sure it would be successful. In two weeks, the Allied force in Normandy had grown to 600,000 troops. The German army fought desperately to keep the Allies from breaking out of Normandy and moving east across France and Belgium toward Germany. (The D-Day invasion and the Battle of Normandy are described in Chapter 11.)

The eastern front

At the same time, on the other side of Europe, the Germans faced the Red Army along a front that stretched 2,000 miles from north to south. For three years, ever since the German invasion of the Soviet Union in June 1941, the Red Army had fought massive battles against the Germans. In the largest and bloodiest campaigns of World War II, the Soviets succeeded in driving the invaders back toward the western border of their country. (The German invasion of the Soviet Union is described in Chapter 3 and the Red Army's first major victories are described in Chapter 9.)

The Soviet leaders had promised the British and Americans that the Red Army would begin a major offensive immediately after the invasion of western Europe. That would prevent the Germans from shifting troops, tanks, and planes to Normandy from Russia. Just two weeks after D-Day, the Soviets kept their promise.

Operation Bagration: The liberation of White Russia

The Soviets chose the central part of the eastern front for this new offensive, where large Soviet and German armies faced each other on the western edge of Soviet territory in White Russia or Belorussia (today the independent country of Belarus). This region belonged to Poland before 1939 but became Russian territory early in the war. The German army in

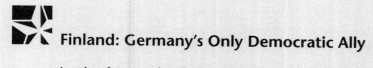

Finland: Germany's Only Democratic Ally

In the far north of the eastern front, the Red Army also faced the army of Finland. The Soviet Union had attacked Finland in the winter of 1939–40, fighting a short, bitter war. The much smaller Finnish army had won admiration all over the world for how strongly it resisted the attack. But Finland had been forced to ask for peace and give up some of its territory to the Soviet Union.

When Germany invaded the Soviet Union in June 1941, Finnish troops fought alongside the Germans, trying to get back their land. However, despite German pressure, the Finns refused to cross the old border—they would fight only on land that they considered part of Finland.

Although it had agreed to be Germany's ally along the eastern front, Finland refused to cooperate with Germany in other ways. It did not declare war on Britain or the United States. It chose to remain a democracy, unlike any other country fighting on the German side. Unlike Germany's other allies, the Finnish people were never attracted to Nazi ideas. The Finnish government successfully resisted Nazi pressure to arrest Finnish Jews and deport (forcibly remove) them to other parts of German-occupied Europe, where they would have been murdered.

On June 9, 1944, just before their great offensive in White Russia, the Soviets began an offensive against the Finnish army. By the end of July, Finland was negotiating with the Soviets to get out of the war. The Germans no longer had enough power to prevent this, and Finland agreed to the Soviet Union's terms early in September.

White Russia was organized as Army Group Center and had 37 divisions. (A full-strength division is usually around 15,000 men, although Soviet divisions were usually smaller and many German divisions were below full strength because of losses in previous battles.) Unknown to the Germans, there was a massive buildup of Red Army forces in White Russia. They had 166 divisions with 2,700 tanks, far outnumbering the Germans. Forty-five hundred planes waited close by. For several days before the attack, Soviet partisans blew up railroad tracks and other targets in German-controlled territory. (Partisans or guerrillas are troops operating behind enemy lines, usually employing hit-and-run tactics. The role of partisans in World War II is described in Chapter 6.)

The Red Army had now won back almost all the territory that had been part of the Soviet Union when the Germans invaded.

On June 22, 1944, the third anniversary of the German invasion, the Red Army began its attack along an 800-mile section of the front. The operation was code-named Bagration, after a Russian general killed fighting French emperor Napoleon Bonaparte's invasion of Russia in 1812. Within days they surrounded and destroyed the German Ninth Army. The rest of the German forces retreated rapidly. In the first week of the Soviet attack, 200,000 Germans were killed, wounded, or captured. Nine hundred German tanks were destroyed.

On July 3, the Red Army pushed the Germans west and entered Minsk, the capital of White Russia. A few days later, about 60,000 men of the German Fourth Army were taken prisoner, after tens of thousands of its soldiers had been killed. Northwest of Minsk, on July 10, Soviet forces freed Vilna, which had been part of Poland at the start of World War II. After Poland was defeated by the Germans in 1939, Vilna became the capital of Lithuania. Farther south, they reached the Polish city of Lublin on July 23 and captured Lvov, another formerly Polish city, on July 27.

The Red Army had now won back almost all the territory that had been part of the Soviet Union when the Germans invaded. In one area, the Soviet forces were on the border of East Prussia, part of Germany. In the center of the front, leading units of the Red Army reached the river Vistula in two widely separated areas. On the other side of the Vistula, between these units, was Warsaw, the capital of Poland.

The Red Army stops

Now, at the beginning of August, the great Soviet offensive came to a halt. The Soviets had pushed the Germans 300 miles west in six weeks—in some places they had moved more than 400 miles. Army Group Center and 30 German divisions had been destroyed. More than 300,000 German soldiers had been killed, wounded, or captured in White Russia alone.

Part of the reason for the end of the Soviet advance was that German resistance became tougher. By retreating, the Germans had a chance to catch their breath, regroup, and defend positions, such as river crossings, that gave them an

Western Soviet territory, showing 1920 to 1938 and 1941 Polish-Soviet borders.

Map legend:

- - - - Boundaries, 1920–1938
▬ ▬ ▬ Western frontier of U.S.S.R., June 1941
- - - - Eastern Front (at the end of 1941)

advantage. In addition, German reinforcements, including three armored (tank) divisions, arrived to help hold these positions.

Another possible reason for the Soviet slow down was that their forces had moved forward so quickly that it had become difficult to supply them. A modern army depends on huge quantities of fuel, ammunition, and food. Now supplies had to be brought a longer distance, over roads and railroads

The reason the Soviet army stopped on the Vistula is one of the most debated topics in World War II military history.

that had been badly damaged or destroyed. It was a common pattern in World War II for a powerful offensive—whether German or Allied—to slow down and then stop because it had been so successful that it had outrun its supply lines.

Many military historians think this is exactly what happened in Operation Bagration. However, the reason the Soviet army stopped on the Vistula is one of the most debated topics in World War II military history. Many people believed at the time, and still believe, that the offensive was not stalled because of a lack of supplies. Instead, they think the Soviet government purposely stopped the offensive because of political disputes it had with Poland. For as the Red Army waited on the Vistula, the people of Warsaw rose up in armed rebellion against the Germans.

Poland and the Soviet Union

Warsaw, which the Germans had bombed into surrender in September 1939, suffered under German occupation longer than any other capital city of Europe. (An occupation is when foreign military forces are stationed in a country to control it.) The Germans had treated the Polish people much more harshly than it treated people of western Europe. Poland lost a higher percentage of its people in the war than any other country. A very large underground movement (a network of secret organizations opposed to the Germans) had grown up in Poland. One part of this underground movement was the Home Army, also called the AK, which stands for *Armai Krajowa*. The Home Army was the armed military branch of the Polish underground. It was loyal to the Polish government that had escaped from Warsaw to London in 1939. Britain and the United States considered this government-in-exile the legal representative of the Polish people. (See Chapter 9.)

The London Poles, as members of the government-in-exile were often called, were very suspicious of the Soviet Union. The most important issue between the Soviet and Polish governments concerned Poland's borders. The Soviets wanted the eastern parts of prewar Poland—the White Russian region just freed from the Germans in Operation Bagration—to remain part of the Soviet Union. Most of the people in this region were not Polish. The Soviet Union had taken this area from Poland in September 1939 as part of a deal with Nazi Germany. In effect, the Soviet Union had helped Nazi dictator Adolf Hitler eliminate Poland as an independent country. That deal, known as the Nazi-Soviet Pact, added to the Polish distrust and anger toward the Soviets. (The Nazi-Soviet Pact and the events of September 1939 are described in Chapter 2.)

Another major difference concerned the kind of government Poland would have after the war. The London Poles were strongly opposed to communism, while the Soviet Union was officially a communist country. (Communism is a political and economic system based on government control of the production and distribution of goods and the abolition of private ownership of factories, banks, and most other businesses.) The London Poles were afraid the Soviets would use the Red Army to impose a communist government on Poland. These fears increased at the end of July 1944, when a Polish Committee of National Liberation, dominated by Polish communists, was created in the newly freed city of Lublin. With Soviet support, this committee soon claimed that it, and not the London Poles, ought to be the legitimate Polish government. (The political controversies between Poland and the Soviet Union are described further in Chapter 9.)

Late in July, the Lublin radio called on the Polish underground to rise up against the Germans, promising that the Red Army would soon arrive. In fact, those in Warsaw could clearly hear the Soviet artillery across the Vistula. The London Poles came to agree that the Home Army should begin a general uprising. One reason for this decision was fear that if the Home Army did nothing, the Soviets and the Lublin committee would accuse them of being a phony resistance movement, or even—as the Soviet leaders sometimes already claimed—that the Home Army was really pro-German.

General Wladyslaw Sikorski, head of the London Poles, was killed in plane crash; he had the most stature among the London Poles and was the least fanatically anti-Soviet.
(Reproduced by permission of AP/Wide World Photos)

A group of Polish soldiers about to leave for the front is addressed by Wanda Wasilewska, chair of the Union of Polish Patriots (ZPP). *(Reproduced by permission of AP/Wide World Photos)*

The London Poles also hoped to obtain great advantages from a successful uprising. Many of the men and women of the Home Army were pleading for a chance to fight the hated Germans. If Polish forces played a major role in driving the Germans from their country, it would restore the pride of the Poles who had been severely defeated by the Germans. Most important, it would also leave the Home Army a powerful military force, in control of Warsaw and independent of the

Red Army. The Home Army could then guard Poland's political and territorial interests against the Soviets.

The Warsaw uprising

The commander of the Home Army ordered the uprising to begin on August 1, 1944. About 20,000 fighters, armed with rifles and submachine guns, took control of half of Warsaw. They carried enough ammunition for about one week of fighting. It turned out they had to fight for two months.

At first the Germans used security troops rather than front-line combat soldiers to fight the Poles, but soon they brought in regular army units with tanks and artillery. In slow, bloody, house-to-house fighting, the Germans recaptured large areas of the city and forced the Home Army into a few pockets.

The Home Army's fighters desperately needed more arms and ammunition. Before long, they and the rest of the population would also need food, as the Germans cut off all supplies into the city. British planes based in England and American bombers from Italy tried to drop supplies by parachute, but many of the supplies fell into German-controlled areas. The planes could not carry heavy loads because of the large amount of fuel needed to fly such long distances. The distance was made twice as long because they had to make a round trip without landing. Despite repeated British and American requests, the Soviet government, in all but one case, refused permission for these planes to land on Soviet territory to refuel.

The official Soviet attitude toward the uprising was very hostile. Joseph Stalin, the Soviet dictator, called it a reckless and even criminal adventure—in other words, a stunt that endangered many lives without good reason. These charges are one of the reasons that many people believe the Soviets purposely allowed the Germans to crush the Poles.

On the other hand, at the end of August, the Soviet forces did make serious attempts to break through to Warsaw. Polish units fighting in the Red Army led these attacks and were driven back with heavy casualties. In the middle of September, the Soviets began dropping food and ammunition

The Polish Home Army carried enough ammunition for about one week of fighting. It turned out they had to fight for two months.

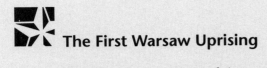

The First Warsaw Uprising

The Warsaw uprising of August 1944 was a different event from the uprising of the Warsaw ghetto, which began in April 1943. The Warsaw ghetto was a walled-off section of the city in which the Germans forced all the city's Jews to live. Beginning in July 1942, the Germans began deporting the Jews of Warsaw to a secret destination. In fact, they were sending them to special death camps to be murdered. (The creation of the ghettos, the deportations, and the death camps are described in Chapter 7.)

Small groups of Jews, especially young people, were determined to resist the Nazis. Although they had almost no weapons and little military training and were cut off from the rest of Warsaw, they fought fiercely against the German troops for more than a month. In the end, almost all the Jewish fighters were killed, and the Germans totally destroyed the ghetto.

In both these respects, the ghetto uprising was like a smaller version of the later uprising of the Home Army. In other ways, however, the situation of the Warsaw Jews was very different from that of the non-Jewish Poles. The young leaders of the ghetto uprising did not expect to defeat the Germans or to be rescued by the arrival of a friendly army. Rather, their goal was to save the honor of the Jewish people, since they could not save their lives. They had urged their fellow Jews not to allow the Nazis to slaughter them "like sheep" but instead "to die as human beings."

into Warsaw by plane, sending at least fifty tons. Perhaps, as the French historian Henri Michel has argued in *The Second World War*, that the Soviets were now willing to help because the Home Army was no longer strong enough to present a challenge to the Soviets but was still large enough to be useful against the Germans.

With the Poles driven into small sections of the city by the Germans, even supply by air became impossible. On October 2, the Home Army surrendered. Ten thousand of its 20,000 fighters had been killed and another 7,000 wounded. But this was only a small part of the cost. More than 200,000 citizens of Warsaw died, many in savage German revenge actions. Ninety percent of the city was destroyed.

The plot to kill Hitler

Crushing the Warsaw uprising could not hide the fact that Germany had suffered a series of immense defeats in the middle of 1944. From the beginning of June to mid-September, at least 1 million German soldiers had been killed or captured throughout Europe. These were months of disaster for the German army.

In the middle of this period, on July 20, a group of anti-Hitler Germans, most of them army officers, tried to kill Hitler, take over the government, and end the war. The leaders of the plot, which included some high-ranking generals, believed that killing Hitler was absolutely essential for taking over the government. They were certain that until he was dead, most of the army would follow Hitler's orders.

Hitler and the army officers

It is not surprising that army officers were at the center of the plot. Although they had achieved high rank and great honors under the Nazi government, Germany was a police state, with spies everywhere, and anyone found opposing the government was arrested and sent to a concentration camp (the brutal prison camps run by the SS, the black-uniformed security units of the Nazi Party). Individually, army officers were among the few Germans who still had some freedom to act as they wanted. Most important, as a group they had the power within the military to resist the Nazis if they wanted to.

Some of the officers involved in the plot had secretly opposed Hitler and the Nazis for a long time. Some of them had been horrified by the crimes committed by the German armed forces, such as the mass shootings of civilians. They blamed Hitler and the Nazis for bringing shame on Germany and its army. Some blamed Hitler for starting the war. Others blamed him only for losing it.

Critics have pointed out that these plotters took action only when it was clear that Germany would lose the war. Many of them, whatever their private beliefs, continued to act with loyalty to Hitler, despite the Nazis' terrible crimes, as long as he was winning. Many of them wanted Germany to make peace without surrendering. They understood that the Allies would

Some of the officers involved in the plot to kill Hitler blamed Hitler for starting the war. Others blamed him only for losing it.

The fairly small number of officers at the center of the plot, however, had come to believe that Hitler and the Nazis, not the Allies, were Germany's real enemies.

never agree to this while Hitler and the Nazis were in power. But they hoped that a new government, headed by military men, could negotiate an end to the war. Some of them even hoped to make peace with the United States and Britain and continue the war against the Soviet Union.

The plotters had to be very careful in approaching other officers to support the plan. One word to the Gestapo (the secret police), and their lives, and perhaps the lives of their families, would be in danger. Some of the people they spoke to, including important generals, refused to promise their support. But they did not inform the Gestapo either. These generals seemed to take a wait-and-see approach. If Hitler were killed and it looked like the plot to end the war might succeed, they would support it. If it failed, they would not have been involved.

German officers were taught that duty and honor were very important. Every one of them had sworn an oath of obedience to Hitler personally. (This oath is described in a box on p. 18 in Chapter 1.) For many of them, betraying this promise meant losing their honor—or, at least, many claimed this was their reason for not supporting the scheme. In addition, some of them thought that trying to overthrow the government while their country was at war amounted to treason. The fairly small number of officers at the center of the plot, however, had come to believe that Hitler and the Nazis, not the Allies, were Germany's real enemies.

Stauffenberg

One of the leaders of the group was Count Claus von Stauffenberg, a colonel who had been badly wounded in North Africa, losing a hand, several fingers of his other hand, and an eye. He was now on the staff of the Replacement Army in Berlin, the German capital. The Replacement Army (*Ersatzheer* in German) was the organization that drafted and trained new soldiers to replace combat losses. Stauffenberg prepared a plan for the Replacement Army to take over emergency powers in major German cities. His excuse was that they would use this plan if there were an uprising by the millions of foreign laborers who had been forced to work in Germany. In fact, he intended to use the plan to take over the government after Hitler had been killed.

Stauffenberg also had regular personal access to Hitler, who was very concerned with finding replacements for the army's losses. On July 20, 1944, Stauffenberg was at Hitler's headquarters in East Prussia for a meeting. (Hitler had several headquarters outside Berlin during the war.) Stauffenberg entered the wooden building, almost a hut, where Hitler and two dozen others were gathered around an oak table, looking at maps. Stauffenberg placed his briefcase under the table and then left, explaining that he needed to phone Berlin.

Within minutes, a tremendous blast shook the area, as the time bomb that Stauffenberg had placed in his briefcase exploded. The walls and roof of the building were destroyed, and fire and smoke were pouring out. In the confusion, Stauffenberg got to the airstrip for the three-hour flight to Berlin. He thought the next part of the plan would have already begun.

The commander of regular army troops in Berlin, the Berlin chief of police, and some top leaders of the Replacement Army were all part of the plot. They should have taken over the radio station and the Gestapo headquarters, disarmed SS units in the city, and arrested top Nazi leaders. The same should have been done throughout Germany and in the rest of German-occupied Europe. But except in Paris, where the German military governor of France had arrested all SS and security police forces in the city, none of these thing had been done.

Hitler's revenge

The reason for the failure was simple. Hitler was not dead. He had survived Stauffenberg's bomb with only minor injuries. It's possible that the briefcase was moved farther from Hitler or that the heavy oak table over which he was leaning had protected most of his body from the blast.

Although a member of the plot cut off communications from Hitler's headquarters for a while, they were soon restored. Orders from the plotters in Berlin were canceled by loyal officers, but for a while army units in Berlin and other cities did not know whom to obey. But Hitler's voice on the radio convinced them to remain true to the Nazi government. Some of the leaders of the plot, including Stauffenberg, were quickly arrested and shot. Like many other officers, the general

Field Marshall Erwin Rommel—one of those who knew about the plot but probably did not participate—killed himself. The Nazis told the German people that Rommel died of a heart attack. He was given a hero's funeral and praised as a loyal supporter of Hitler.

who had them shot had known about the plot and had taken a wait-and-see attitude. Now he wanted to cover his tracks by shooting the plotters before the Gestapo could question them. Despite this, he too was later arrested by the Gestapo and shot.

The Gestapo began its work immediately and continued almost until the war was over. Using torture to obtain information, they hunted down officers and civilians who had participated or known about the plot. About 5,000 people were executed and several thousand more were sent to concentration camps. A few, such as Field Marshal Erwin Rommel, Germany's most popular war hero, were given a choice between committing suicide or facing arrest and trial. To protect his family, Rommel—one of those who knew about the plot but probably did not participate—killed himself. The Nazis told the German people that Rommel died of a heart attack. He was given a hero's funeral and praised as a loyal supporter of Hitler.

Others were not treated so gently. After torture by the Gestapo, those leaders of the plot who had not been shot were immediately tried before a special Nazi People's Court. Then they were hanged with piano wire from meat hooks to make their deaths more painful. On Hitler's orders, these trials and hangings were filmed. He'd watch the film that night.

After the failure of the July plot, as it is usually called, the Nazis kept closer control over the army and its officers. To prove their loyalty, some officers participated in military Courts of Honor that expelled the plotters from the army. Then they could be turned over to the People's Court to be tried—and hanged—as civilians. The stiff-armed Nazi salute, with its barked "Heil Hitler" ("hail Hitler"), replaced the normal military salute.

The results of July 20, 1944, also had an impact on military events. German generals were more afraid to retreat, fearing that Hitler would see it as proof of disloyalty. And Hitler, even more than before, distrusted the military advice of his generals. All these developments made it more likely that the German army would continue to fight even though there was no chance of victory and the only result was to increase the destruction of Germany and the suffering of the German people.

The last months of 1944

Even while the Germans were crushing the people of Warsaw, the Allies were making tremendous gains in western Europe. Breaking out of Normandy and destroying huge German forces, the Allied tanks raced across France, freeing Paris late in August; reaching Brussels, the capital of Belgium, on September 3; and reaching the Belgian port of Antwerp, the largest in Europe, on September 4. From Switzerland almost to the North Sea, the Allied armies were approaching the borders of Germany. (The Allied breakout from Normandy and the liberation of Paris are described in Chapter 11.)

The Allies now faced two major obstacles. One was a line of defensive positions built before the war and recently strengthened, which the Germans called the West wall. The Allies called it the Siegfried line. Although not a wall, this series of protected cannons, machine-gun emplacements, and tank barriers would severely slow the Allied advance. The second obstacle was the Rhine River, which separated the Allied armies from the heart of Germany.

Supply difficulties played an even greater role in slowing down the Allies. Much of their gasoline and other needs had to be brought all the way from Normandy by truck because the Allied air forces had done such a good job of destroying the French railroad system (to cripple Germany's defense of the Atlantic shore). The problem became worse as the armies advanced farther from Normandy. The port of Antwerp, in Belgium, was much closer to the fighting, but the Allies could not use it because the Germans still controlled the mouth of the river that separates Antwerp from the sea.

The United States Army organized a system of high-speed, one-way highways to bring supplies to the front from Normandy. The most famous was called the Red Ball Express. Although this system worked better than anyone had expected, it still could not meet the Allied armies' needs.

The supply problem led to arguments and rivalries between General Bernard Montgomery, whose British and Canadian troops were on the northern end of the front, and General George S. Patton, whose American Third Army was farther south. Each believed that his forces could break through into Germany and end the war quickly if they had enough fuel

The supply problem led to arguments and rivalries between General Bernard Montgomery, whose British and Canadian troops were on the northern end of the front, and General George S. Patton, whose American Third Army was farther south.

and other supplies. But that would mean sending most of the supplies to one army and leaving the rest of the Allied forces without enough resources to resist the Germans.

Dwight D. Eisenhower, the American general who was supreme commander of the Allied forces in western Europe, refused to give either Montgomery or Patton all the supplies at the expense of the other. Instead, he decided that the Allies would enter Germany all along a broad front and would not concentrate all their strength in one area. Many military historians have criticized Eisenhower for this decision, saying it was based on political considerations of keeping both the British and Americans happy. Others have defended Eisenhower, pointing out that the Germans could have attacked whichever Allied force was deprived of supplies.

Germany's successful offensive in the Ardennes Forest created a bulge in the Allies' front line, giving this famous battle its name, the Battle of the Bulge.

The last German attack: The Battle of the Bulge

The Germans soon proved that they could still mount one more large offensive. Near the center of the front was the Ardennes Forest of Belgium and Luxembourg. It was thinly defended by four American divisions because the Allies were sure the Germans would not attack in this area. The Ardennes was heavily forested, with steep hills and narrow roads, and the Americans did not think it was suitable for tanks. This belief is remarkable because it is exactly what the French thought in 1940. But the German tanks had smashed into France through the Ardennes and destroyed the French and British armies. (The German victory in 1940 is described in Chapter 2.) Four-and-a-half years later, the Americans would make the same mistake.

The Ardennes offensive (soon called the Battle of the Bulge by the Americans because the German attack created a large bulge in the American lines) was Hitler's idea, not that of the German generals. He sent Germany's last available tank divisions to the area. The German generals worried that these divisions would be needed if the Soviets attacked in the east. Further, they could see some of the plan's weaknesses from the beginning. For example, they could not stockpile enough gasoline to ensure that their tanks would have fuel for more than a few days. Instead, they had to rely on capturing the large quantities of fuel that the Americans had collected nearby.

At first Hitler's plan was a success. The narrow roads and thick forests prevented Allied airplanes from seeing the German tanks being brought forward for the attack. In addition, the Germans purposely planned the offensive to take place in poor weather so that Allied planes, which had complete control of the skies, could not fly.

When the Germans attacked through the fog on December 16, 1944, they completely surprised the outnumbered Americans and made rapid progress, taking a substantial number of prisoners. But very soon the resistance of the GIs (ordinary American soldiers, nicknamed GI by the initials stamped on all their equipment and clothing, which stood for "government issue") began to slow the German attack. The town of Bastogne, even though it was surrounded by the Germans, refused to surrender.

After some confusion on the part of the American commanders, the Allies rushed several divisions to reinforce the Ardennes area. As the weather cleared, the Allied air forces began to pound the German tanks. The German advance slowed and then stopped. Strong Allied forces attacked the bulge from both north and south, wearing down the Germans until they retreated to their original positions. The Allies could afford to lose men and equipment; the Germans could not.

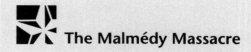

The Malmédy Massacre

A few miles north of Bastogne, at Malmédy, a group of Americans surrendered to troops of the First SS Panzer (tank) Division. Like many of the German troops in the Ardennes offensive, this division was part of the *Waffen-SS* ("armed SS"). These were military units of the SS that fought as part of the regular army. They were Hitler's favorite units, and they were the best equipped and supplied because they were more "Nazified" than the regular army and Hitler trusted their officers. The SS troops took at least seventy American prisoners into a field and machine-gunned them all. The same unit also murdered Belgian civilians in the area. Soldiers from this unit were tried after the war and a dozen were executed for these crimes.

Dead soldiers near Malmédy, Belgium.
(Reproduced by permission of AP/Wide World Photos)

The Ardennes offensive has often been described as Hitler's last gamble. He knew that if he lost, as he did, he would use up almost all of Germany's remaining offensive ability. Its best additional armored divisions would not be available against the Soviets, even for defensive purposes, as well.

But even a German victory in the Ardennes would not have changed the course of the war. Hitler hoped to recapture the port of Antwerp to disrupt Allied supplies and perhaps even drive the British army back to the sea. Something like this had happened after the Ardennes breakthrough in 1940. But this plan was completely unrealistic. Now, at the end of 1944, the Germans no longer had the resources to turn a victory in the Ardennes into a victory in western Europe. The Battle of the Bulge may have temporarily slowed the progress of the western Allies, but it helped ensure that when the next big Allied offensive finally came, there would be nothing to stop it.

From Warsaw to Germany

For many months, the great majority of new German divisions had gone to the western front. The German army in Poland received few new tanks or planes. This area had been comparatively quiet since the end of the great Soviet offensive in August 1944. In their positions east of the Vistula River, however, the Soviets had prepared for their next major attack. Almost 2 million tons of supplies were gathered, along with more than 6,000 tanks and 32,000 pieces of artillery (cannons).

African American Soldiers of the 3201st Quartermaster Service Company, assigned to dig up the bodies of American soldiers massacred at Malmédy. *(Reproduced by permission of the Corbis Corporation [Bellevue])*

Many Germans believed that the Red Army would slaughter them in revenge for what Germany had done in Russia. The Germans' fears turned out to be accurate.

The attack began on January 12, 1945, along a 30-mile-section of the front. Over the next few days, Soviet forces on either side of this sector joined in. Soon, 180 Soviet divisions were attacking along a battlefront 200 miles long. They had twice as many troops as the Germans, four times as many tanks, seven times as much artillery, and six times as many planes. The German defenses collapsed.

On January 17, the Red Army entered Warsaw, occupied by the Germans for 64 months. Two days later they were in Lodz, and a week later around Breslau (Wroclaw) on the river Oder, 180 miles from where they had started. In the center of the front, the Soviet forces were commanded by Marshal Georgy Zhukov, who had defeated the Germans near Moscow in the winter of 1941–42 and crushed them at Stalingrad a year later. (The battle of Moscow is described in Chapter 3 and Stalingrad in Chapter 10.) Now Zhukov's armies drove the Germans back 220 miles in five weeks, until they stood 100 miles from Berlin. Some other Soviet units were only 50 miles from the suburbs of the German capital.

German civilians and the Red Army

As the Soviet offensive swept across the German province of East Prussia, the civilian population was swept by panic. Two million people abandoned their homes and fled west, trying to escape the Red Army.

Many Germans believed that the Red Army would slaughter them in revenge for what Germany had done in Russia. German forces had murdered millions of Russian civilians. Three million Soviet soldiers had been shot or had starved or frozen to death after being captured by the Germans.

The Germans' fears turned out to be accurate. Some units of the Red Army, usually carefully disciplined, turned into murderous gangs once they entered German territory. They set entire villages on fire, as the Germans had done to Russian villages. They raped thousands of German women and girls. They shot whole families, especially if the Soviet soldiers saw some Nazi symbol or a picture of Hitler in their house.

The refugees clogged the roads. Thousands of people died in the winter cold, crushed by advancing tanks, blown up by artillery shells, machine-gunned by troops rushing by on trucks. Some units of the German army fought with great heroism to hold off the Soviets long enough to allow columns of refugees to escape.

Apart from its human cost, the Red Army's rampage in East Prussia also had military and political effects. From then until the end of the war, it was clear that the German army would fight harder in the east than in the west. German troops were much more willing to surrender to the Americans or British than to the Soviets.

The pause

In the middle of February 1945, the Soviet advance came to a halt. The Red Army had outrun its supplies again, which were stockpiled behind the Vistula. In addition, the German retreat narrowed the front from north to south. It was easier for the remaining German troops to defend the shorter front. But the area they were defending was also shrinking in another way, which showed that defeat would come soon: the Red Army was now only 400 miles from the Americans and British.

Southeast Europe, 1942.

During their advance, Red Army troops freed the Auschwitz concentration camp on January 27, 1945. Only about 6,000 prisoners were still there, many near death from disease and starvation. A week earlier, the Nazi guards had forced 60,000 others on a death march, in subzero weather, to other concentration camps farther west. Before that, more than 1 million men, women, and children, most of them Jews, had been murdered at Auschwitz. (Auschwitz is described in Chapter 7.)

The western front: Crossing the Rhine

Back on the western front, the months after the Battle of the Bulge saw a series of Allied operations that cleared all

The German Defeat in Southeastern Europe

Although the Red Army's advance in Poland had been stopped, it continued to move forward on the southern end of the eastern front. One advantage of the Red Armiy's moving in this direction was that it put pressure on Germany's allies to abandon Germany and the war.

The first to collapse was Romania. The Romanians had been Germany's most important ally in the invasion of the Soviet Union, sending large numbers of troops to fight alongside the Germans. They had also engaged in a series of brutal massacres in the Soviet Union, especially of Jews. In August 1944, large Red Army forces entered Romania, threatening to overwhelm its army. The pro-German government was overthrown, and the king arrested its leader. In response, German planes bombed Bucharest, the Romanian capital. Romania then declared war on Germany and sent its troops west to attack Hungary, Germany's remaining ally and Romania's traditional enemy. This series of events also led to the capture of 200,000 more German troops.

While Romanian troops joined the Red Army's attack on Hungary, another part of the Red Army headed toward Bulgaria. Bulgaria had helped Germany invade Yugoslavia and Greece, but it had not joined the German invasion of the Soviet Union and had never declared war on the Soviets. (The German attacks on Yugoslavia and Greece are described in Chapter 3.) On September 5, 1944, the Soviet Union declared war on Bulgaria. But almost no one in Bulgaria wanted to fight the Red Army. There were mutinies in the Bulgarian army, and pro-Soviet groups

German resistance from the west bank of the Rhine River, the last major obstacle in Germany. After this, the Allies could cross the river along the entire front, as General Dwight D. Eisenhower, the supreme commander of the Allied forces, had wanted. On March 8, 1945, American troops at Remagen, near Bonn, captured the only bridge over the Rhine that the Germans had not yet blown up. Soon, three American divisions had reached the other side of the river. Elsewhere, the crossing was more difficult. The first troops might go across in small boats and then hold the other shore while combat engineers, under German fire, constructed new bridges.

On March 22, troops of General George S. Patton's Third Army crossed the Rhine. The next day, farther north, took over the streets of Sofia, the Bulgarian capital. After Soviet troops entered Sofia on September 18, Bulgaria declared war on Germany and sent 150,000 troops to fight against their former ally.

West of Romania and Bulgaria was Yugoslavia, conquered and split up by Germany and its allies in April 1941. (See Chapter 3.) Aside from the Soviet Union, Yugoslavia had the largest partisan movement in Europe. Partisans or guerrillas are troops operating behind enemy lines, usually employing hit-and-run tactics. (See Chapter 5.) After the Red Army entered Yugoslavia, German forces in Greece and Yugoslavia were in danger of being cut off. The Red Army could block the overland routes back to Germany, and the British navy could prevent evacuation by sea. The Germans began withdrawing from both countries in the middle of October. On October 20, the Yugoslav partisans and the Red Army together entered Yugoslavia's capital, Belgrade. The partisan army continued to free the rest of the country while the Soviets turned north to join the attack on Hungary.

By mid-October, the Red Army was within 50 miles of Budapest, the Hungarian capital. But German leader Adolf Hitler was determined to keep control of Hungary to prevent a Soviet advance into Austria and Germany. After two months of fighting, the Red Army surrounded Budapest the day after Christmas, bombarding it with artillery. It took until mid-January for the Soviets to enter the city, and it was not until February 13, 1945, after a month of savage street fighting, that German resistance in the city finally ended.

British, Canadian, and American troops commanded by General Bernard Montgomery crossed the river in force and began their attack on the Ruhr, Germany's most important industrial region. Soon the American Seventh Army and the French First Army had crossed the river, their tanks striking into southern Germany.

By April 1, 1945, nine Allied armies with 90 divisions, 25 of them armored, were either across the Rhine or waiting their turn. There were no more natural barriers. From now until Germany surrendered five weeks later, they pushed the retreating Germans ever eastward. Although the Germans often fought hard, there were increasing cases of mass surrenders. As the end of the war approached, German troops some-

times did everything possible to surrender to the British or Americans rather than be captured by the Red Army. German soldiers knew that the Nazies had murdered Soviet prisoners by the millions, and they feared the same treatment if they were captured.

British and Americans troops soon saw examples of Nazi mass murder as well. On April 11, American soldiers liberated the Buchenwald concentration camp. Four days later, the British freed Bergen-Belsen. In these and many other places, the battle-hardened soldiers and officers of the Allied armies came face to face with scenes of human cruelty beyond anything they had experienced on the battlefield. General Patton, seeing Buchenwald, vomited.

The Nazis had continued trying to murder as many of their enemies, especially Jews, as they could, even when the Allied armies were only a few miles away and they had obviously lost the war. One example of this occurred at Dachau, near Munich, the first concentration camp. The Americans reached Dachau on April 29, only ten days before Germany surrendered. Just before the Americans arrived, the SS guards had evacuated the camp. By this time, however, there was no place left to transfer the prisoners. So the Nazis marched 15,000 to 20,000 people aimlessly around the countryside to keep the American troops from freeing them. Exhausted, starving, and sick, many of them died before the GIs could find them. (The Nazi effort to kill the Jews of Europe, known as the Holocaust, is described in Chapter 7.)

Western Germany, spring 1945, showing the approximate locations of western Allied armies as they crossed the Rhine and moved into the heart of Germany.

The battle of Berlin

The Allied leaders had already decided that when Germany was defeated they would divide that country into different occupation zones. The Soviet zone, in the east, would run roughly to the river Elbe. That put Berlin within the Soviet area and meant that the Red Army would make the final attack against Hitler's capital. The final push began on April 16, 1945. This last battle of the war against Germany was as large as the other terrible struggles on the eastern front. Two-and-a-half million Soviet soldiers moved against Berlin; a million German troops defended it.

A U.S. Army tank drives through the streets in Aachen, Germany, firing at the enemy. (Reproduced by permission of AP/Wide World Photos)

By April 22, the fighting reached the streets of Berlin. Block after block was destroyed and thousands of men died. The Germans fought ferociously. Among them were hard-core veterans of countless battles, as well as men too old and boys too young to fight. Among them also were groups of foreign Nazis, who fought for Germany because they believed in Hitler and his ideas, which had brought so much suffering to the

The Death of Hitler

German leader Adolf Hitler lived the last three-and-a-half months of his life in a series of small rooms buried 55 feet below the center of Berlin, issuing orders to his armies by radio and telephone. His companions included some high Nazi officials, secretaries and assistants, and Eva Braun, his longtime lover, whom he married just before both committed suicide.

At first the underground bunker was the center of the German government. But as the weeks passed, the atmosphere inside became more and more unreal. Increasingly, Hitler's orders could no longer be obeyed; the armies to which he issued them no longer existed. Almost to the end, Hitler sometimes believed that Germany might not lose the war. He thought the western Allies and the Soviet Union would split apart, as he had predicted for years.

When President Franklin D. Roosevelt died on April 12, 1945, some of the Nazi leaders were sure that his death would somehow change the course of the war.

At the same time as he seemed to be waiting for some miracle to save Germany from defeat, Hitler also seemed determined that the war would not end until Germany was completely destroyed. He insisted that the battle of Berlin continue, no matter the cost. Even as Soviet troops were fighting their way into the center of Berlin, squads of SS (Nazi Party military) men roamed the streets and hanged German soldiers who were trying to escape the battle.

Hitler's own escape came on April 30, 1945, when he took poison. In accordance with his instructions, his men doused his body with gasoline and burned it in the courtyard above the bunker.

people of Europe and so much destruction to its cities. Now Berlin was the scene of that suffering and destruction.

The remaining civilian population, short of food and water, crowded into cellars as hundreds of thousands of Soviet artillery shells exploded in the city. Fires raged everywhere. Behind the Soviet front-line troops there were thousands more Soviet soldiers, some of them recently freed prisoners of war. They spread terror among the German civilians, killing, looting, and raping. In all, more than 100,000 Berliners died in the battle.

On April 30, as the Red Army reached the government buildings above him, Hitler committed suicide in his under-

Toward the end of the war, young boys were recruited to fight in the German army. This boy was captured by U.S. forces in Germany. *(Reproduced by permission of the Corbis Corporation [Bellevue])*

ground bunker. (See Box.) The next day, the German military commander of Berlin asked for cease-fire terms from the Soviets. They told him the only terms they would accept were unconditional surrender. The following day, May 2, Berlin surrendered. A quarter of a million soldiers of the Red Army had been killed or wounded.

German troops still controlled sections of the country, and there were German forces in other parts of Europe that the Allies had bypassed in their advance. Fighting continued for several days, some of it extremely bloody. On May 8, 1945, Admiral Karl Dönitz, the man Hitler had appointed to replace him as Führer (leader) of Germany, sent representatives to General Eisenhower's headquarters at Reims in eastern France. There they signed the unconditional surrender of Germany. The next day, representatives of the German armed forces repeated the signing at Soviet headquarters in Berlin, amid the ruins of the war they had begun.

The War Against Japan   13

By the spring of 1942, Japan had conquered a vast territory. It stretched thousands of miles from the border between Burma (present-day Myanmar) and India east to the Gilbert Islands in the middle of the Pacific Ocean. The Japanese controlled most of the immense island of New Guinea, situated south of the equator near Australia, and small Arctic islands in the Aleutians, off the coast of Alaska. In all these places, battles raged from the time of the Battle of Midway in June 1942 (discussed in Chapter 4) and the final defeat of Japan in August 1945.

The largest Japanese force, by far, was in China, which was the scene of large battles and great human suffering. But for the most part, the Japanese army in China avoided major offensive actions. The Chinese armies—almost all poorly equipped, poorly trained, and poorly led—did the same. Despite pressure from the United States, which provided arms, supplies, and training to the best Chinese troops, the Chinese leaders never seriously threatened the Japanese. The battles fought in China did not decide the outcome of World War II in Asia. Neither did the attempts to retake Burma that cost the lives of many British and Indian troops, as well as their Japanese enemies.

The war in Asia becomes a Pacific war

Instead, the war against Japan was decided by events in the Pacific, a war fought almost entirely by the United States. In the western Pacific, it involved huge spaces—thousands of miles of open ocean dotted by groups of small islands, including the Gilberts, the Marshalls, the Carolines, and the Marianas. Farther south, nearer Australia, the islands were much larger and the distances between them shorter.

Month after month, from Australia northward and from Hawaii and Midway westward, the Americans pushed back the Japanese. From both directions, U.S. forces advanced slowly toward Japan. Protected by ships and airplanes, the marines and soldiers of the U.S. Army (and, in a few places, Australian soldiers) landed on island after island. After each landing they fought to overcome the Japanese troops, who usually resisted with tremendous determination—sometimes literally to the point of suicide. When the island, or one region of a large island, was secure, with airfields and facilities for warships established, the war would move farther north or west to a new island. Sometimes the next target was hundreds of miles away. Sometimes the Americans bypassed islands still held by the Japanese because the enemy forces there were now isolated and useless. For almost three years, the Americans conquered (or reconquered) one island after another. When the war in Europe ended in the spring of 1945, American forces were in the middle of the largest of these Pacific island battles, on Okinawa—less than 400 miles from Japan itself.

The Burma Road. Japan took control of this important trade route into China in May 1942. *(Reproduced by permission of the Corbis Corporation [Bellevue])*

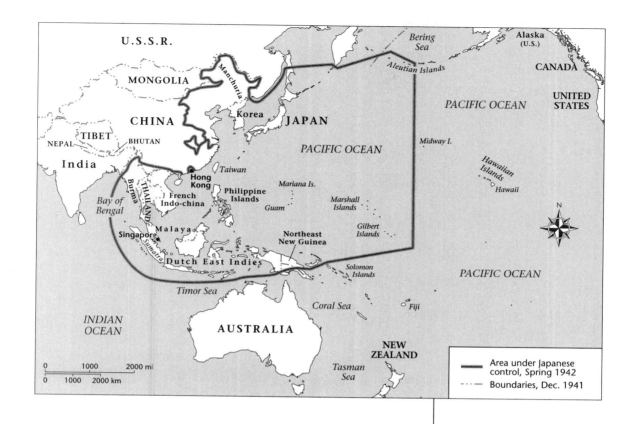

World War II and the Pacific strategy

Taking one island after another was the basic American strategy for the war against Japan—a Pacific war, where the navy used its power to protect an invasion of an island, usually involving relatively few soldiers. It was not the only way that a war against Japan might have been fought. For example, the Allies (Britain, the United States, and the other countries fighting on their side) could have sent armies to attack the large Japanese force that was stationed in China. Such a war might have been similar to the war in Europe, with large masses of soldiers led by tanks, supported by artillery, and protected by planes.

But a land war in Asia was not a real possibility because the United States had decided that the Allies should concentrate their forces and resources on defeating Nazi Germany first. Only after Germany surrendered would they forcefully pursue the war against Japan. In the meantime, the Allies

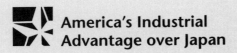

America's Industrial Advantage over Japan

A major reason that the Germany first strategy made sense was because of the huge economic—and especially industrial—advantage the United States had over Japan. This advantage meant that time was on America's side. The longer the war continued, with both sides producing weapons and ships, the greater the American advantage would become.

In the long run, as both American and Japanese leaders knew, Japan did not have the industrial power to defeat the United States. For example, Japan built and sent to sea a total of fourteen aircraft carriers during the years it was at war with the United States. During that same period, the United States built 104. Perhaps even more important, Japan constructed merchant ships weighing a total of 3.3 million tons during the war—and the United States built more than 50 million tons.

Japan built more than 28,000 planes in 1944, the most of any year. Its ally Germany built nearly 40,000. But the United States—without counting Soviet or British production—built more than 100,000 planes that year.

would prevent Japan from expanding further and, if possible, win back some of Japan's conquests.

The motive behind the Allied strategy was to prevent an immediate German victory in Europe. At the time the United States entered the war, in December 1941, both Britain and the Soviet Union were in serious danger. German submarines were winning the Battle of the Atlantic, threatening to cut off Britain's supplies. German leader Adolf Hitler's armies controlled almost all of Europe and had nearly reached Moscow, the Soviet capital. (These events are described in Chapter 3.) If America had concentrated on defeating Japan, then later it might have found itself facing Germany alone—with the Soviet Union conquered and destroyed by Germany, and with Britain having been forced to make peace.

A large navy and a small army

The Germany first decision was the driving force behind the way America fought the war against Japan. The Pacific strategy stressed the use of American naval power. Part of the reason for this involved the efficient use of valuable resources. American shipyards were building great warships in increasing numbers. These battleships, cruisers, and aircraft carriers could be spared more easily from Europe and the Atlantic than planes, tanks, and cannons. In the Atlantic, naval power was supreme. Navy ships were needed to protect merchant ships (civilian ships that carry freight) that were bringing food and weapons from the

United States to Britain. German submarines were a constant—and serious—threat. Generally, the type of escort ships needed in the Pacific were fast and relatively small. Small aircraft carriers, carrying planes designed for antisubmarine warfare, were useful in the Atlantic. But the great fleet carriers—with their fighters, bombers, and dive bombers—that were so important in the Pacific were far less useful in Europe and the Mediterranean, where air bases on land were usually close by.

Because of the island-hopping strategy chosen for the Pacific war and the huge distances the Americans crossed, the number of warships and planes involved was great. By the end of the war, the American fleet in the Pacific was the largest in the history of warfare. Three thousand planes based on aircraft carriers, and thousands of others based on land, dominated the air. But the actual number of soldiers, sailors, and airmen who fought the battles of the Pacific was small compared with the size of the armies that fought in Europe.

A relatively small number of American combat troops, like these Marines pinned down on a beach on the island of Iwo Jima, did most of the fighting in the Pacific. *(Reproduced by permission of the National Archives and Records Administration)*

The use of a relatively small number of combat troops was a key factor in the American Pacific strategy. The number of marines or soldiers who landed on a particular island might be fairly large, but only one or two battles were going on at the same time. The great majority of the battles in the Pacific were fought by six American army divisions and four marine divisions (a division is usually around 15,000 men). Although troops from some of the additional nineteen divisions in the area saw some action, the American combat force in the Pacific really amounted to an army of about 150,000 soldiers. The entire Japanese army outside Japan and China was about the same size.

In comparison, *millions* of soldiers were involved in the European war. In mid-1944, 300 divisions of the Soviet army were fighting the Germans in Russia, while another 70 British and American divisions fought in western Europe. Against them, Germany and its Axis partners in Europe had about 300 divisions.

Another benefit of the Pacific strategy was that it led to quick successes that the American people could read about and celebrate. This was especially important after the Japanese triumphs against the United States at Pearl Harbor and the Philippines, only a few months earlier. The American strategy allowed a comparatively small number of troops to attack an island and win a clear-cut victory. In contrast, it took almost a year after entering the war for American troops to fire a shot against the Germans. (This happened during the North Africa campaign in November 1942, described in Chapter 10.) Each island campaign in the Pacific meant another victory, usually within a short time. This was unlike the long, drawn-out fighting in Europe, where individual battles seemed to be part of a single, endless advance toward Germany.

Rivalry

Historians generally agree that another, related reason for the way the war in the Pacific was fought was the rivalry between the top admirals of the U.S. Navy and the generals of the army. Admiral Ernest King, the chief of staff of the navy, and other leaders were never really happy with the Germany first decision. Throughout the war, Admiral King argued for sending more resources to the Pacific. He knew that his opinion was shared by many Americans, who wanted revenge for Pearl Harbor.

Disputes about resources continued throughout the war. Probably the best-known example concerned the navy's not being willing to send landing craft to Europe, preferring that the craft be sent to the Pacific instead. Some historians believe the shortage of landing craft was a major factor in delaying the D-Day invasion of France. When the invasion finally came, naval support for the landings was vital—but it was still *support* for what was really an *army* operation. The ships, like the soldiers and the air forces, were all under the command of an army general, Dwight D. Eisenhower.

Although these developments occurred later, it was obvious as soon as the United States entered the war that the army would play the major role in Europe. The navy was determined to play that same role in the Pacific. If Germany first meant that the Pacific would not get as many resources as Europe, then at least the navy would run the operation.

The island-hopping strategy that the navy proposed was based on a plan that the navy had drawn up long before the war, in case of a Japanese attack. It involved landings on a series of islands, some of them tiny, located in the Solomon, Gilbert, Marshall, and Mariana Islands. The ground troops that attacked these islands would be under the command of Admiral Chester Nimitz. This force included army troops as well as marines, whom Nimitz preferred to use. (The Marine Corps is part of the Department of the Navy, not the army.) No army general would command any of the navy's ships. (In the European area, the

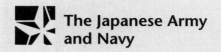 ## The Japanese Army and Navy

Rivalries between the American army and navy may have caused some problems, but they were not nearly as serious as what happened in Japan. The Japanese navy and army were like separate worlds. The top generals and admirals were each represented in the government. When they acted together, they controlled the government. But when they disagreed, there was no one who could break the deadlock. It was almost impossible for the government to order either the army or the navy to do something it did not want to do.

This meant that the army or the navy could carry out operations by itself without the other's agreement. For example, in April 1942, the Japanese navy attacked the British-controlled island of Ceylon (now the nation of Sri Lanka), off the southern tip of India. It looked like the first steps in an invasion, which would have been a serious threat to India. But the army refused to assign the two divisions needed to make a Japanese invasion of Ceylon possible.

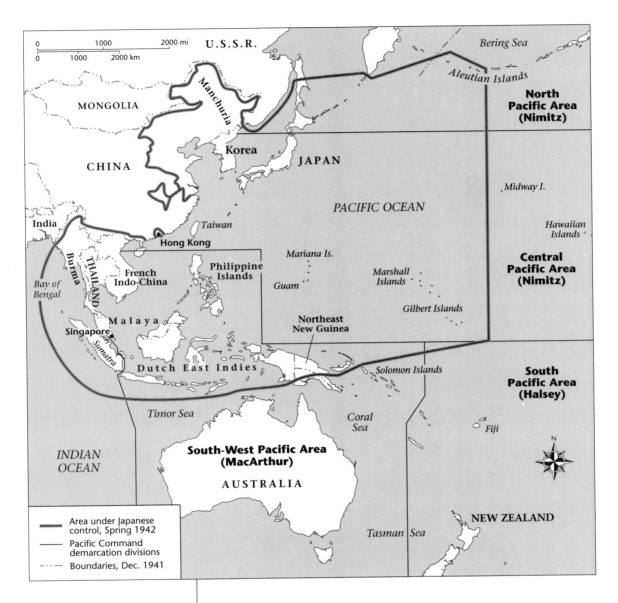

Pacific Command divisions, 1942.

commanding officer of an area, regardless of whether he were army or navy, controlled all forces in the region.)

The army was not happy with this arrangement. Especially unhappy was General Douglas MacArthur, who had commanded the defense of the Philippines and was now in Australia. The heroism of the American soldiers fighting in the Philippines in the early months of the war had made MacArthur very popular in the United States. (The Japanese attack on the Philippines is described in Chapter 4. MacArthur is described in a box in that chapter as well.) He and the army used his popularity to gain the advantage in disagreements with the navy. As part of a compromise between the army and navy, MacArthur was made commander of the Southwest Pacific, which included Australia, New Guinea, the Dutch East Indies, and the Philippines. Admiral Nimitz soon named Admiral William Halsey to command the South Pacific Area, east of Australia. The rest of the Pacific was under Nimitz's direct command.

A double strategy

The division of command between MacArthur and Nimitz, and between the army and the navy, meant that the American effort against Japan would take two different forms. MacArthur's soldiers would fight the Japanese on a series of large islands north of Australia. Often the Japanese outnumbered them, but the American forces defeated them anyway, through superior tactics and leadership.

Nimitz and the navy would drive west across the Pacific, attacking a series of small islands with overwhelming naval and air force. In one battle after another, they suffered heavy casualties, but they inflicted much heavier losses on the Japanese defenders.

This double strategy was originally an attempt to satisfy both the American army and navy—specifically MacArthur and Nimitz, both strong-willed men determined to get their way. By splitting the American attack along two routes, it might have made each one too weak to succeed. Instead, the opposite happened. Each of the campaigns was powerful enough to defeat the forces Japan placed in its path. The Japanese could never shift enough military and naval forces to stop one of the American advances without severely weakening their defenses against the other.

The United States strikes back: Guadalcanal

In August 1942, only two months after the great American naval victory at Midway (which is described in Chapter 4),

U.S. Marine Corps tanks in the jungles of Guadalcanal; the Allied strategy in the Pacific led to deadly fighting for places with little value.
(Reproduced by permission of AP/Wide World Photos)

Nimitz launched the first American offensive operation of the war. A relatively small force of U.S. Marines landed on the island of Guadalcanal, in the Solomon Islands. The Americans planned the operation very quickly, with little knowledge of the geography or conditions the marines would face. The island had rugged jungle terrain and it was incredibly hot and humid. Tropical diseases, especially malaria, were very common.

Guadalcanal had some military importance because the Americans could use an airfield there as a base for further advances. The Americans and Japanese each thought it would be a short fight, perhaps a week or two. But the battle that developed became much larger than the island's military value could justify.

The Japanese leaders understood that they could not defeat the United States in a long war because the United States' industrial power was so much greater. Japan's hope was that it might make the cost of victory so high—in American lives and in money—that the United States would agree to a compromise peace that would leave Japan in control of much of eastern Asia. (This topic is described in more detail in Chapter 4, in the section titled "Japan's strategy for the war.") The key for Japan was to make the war so difficult and so bloody that the American people would stop supporting it.

So the battle of Guadalcanal was the first test of America's island-hopping strategy, but it was also crucial for Japan's long-term plans. Each side threw more and more resources into the fight, as winning became increasingly important. At that time, the Japanese army had not yet given up an inch of conquered territory. American ground troops had not been involved in combat anywhere. The Americans were determined to prove that their soldiers could defeat the Japanese; the Japanese wanted to prove the opposite.

So the Japanese rushed reinforcements to Guadalcanal to drive the Americans away. The Japanese thought there were fewer marines than had actually landed and sent too few troops. When these reinforcements could not defeat the U.S. forces, more troops arrived. For a while, Japanese warships brought small numbers of Japanese troops and supplies every night. The Americans called the system the Tokyo Express.

In response, the Americans sent reinforcements of their own. Eventually, army troops joined the exhausted marines. For six months, the two sides fought dozens of small, bloody battles: for the airfield, for high ridges or little streams, and for a few hundred yards of jungle.

A series of five major sea battles also took place as part of the Guadalcanal campaign. In these battles, dozens of ships were lost to the guns and torpedoes of enemy warships and carrier-based planes. The Americans called the water between Guadalcanal and a nearby island Ironbottom Sound because so many ships had been sunk there. In the long run, the result of these battles was that Japan was unable to resupply its troops on the island or defend them from the growing number of American planes and soldiers.

By January 1943, it was clear that the United States would win control of Guadalcanal. Unlike in many later battles, the Japanese leadership in Tokyo decided to withdraw its remaining troops rather than fight to the last man. The Japan-

The key for Japan was to make the war so difficult and so bloody that the American people would stop supporting it.

Almost as many Japanese soldiers had been killed on the small island of Guadalcanal as had died conquering Japan's vast new empire in Asia less than a year earlier.

ese officers on the island obeyed this order, possibly because it was personally approved by the emperor. By early February, the last 13,000 Japanese soldiers boarded warships and escaped from Guadalcanal. Of the 36,000 Japanese troops who fought on the island, 14,000 had been killed and another 9,000 had died of tropical diseases. The dead included hundreds of trained pilots killed in the sea battles. Like the many experienced Japanese pilots who died at Midway, they could not be easily replaced. Almost as many Japanese soldiers had been killed on this single small island as had died conquering Japan's vast new empire in Asia less than a year earlier.

American casualties were also high, although they were much lower than the Japanese. This was a pattern that would be repeated again and again in the Pacific war. At its height, American strength on Guadalcanal was more than 50,000 men; 1,600 were killed and 4,300 wounded; thousands more developed malaria. The First Marine Division, the first to land on Guadalcanal, was temporarily destroyed as a fighting unit. It had lost 774 dead and nearly 2,000 wounded. More than 5,000 of its men—more than one-third—had become sick with malaria.

Suicide in the far north

At the time of the Battle of Midway in June 1942, the Japanese had captured islands in the Aleutian chain, which was part of Alaska. The islands were very cold, often battered by storms and high winds, and covered in fog, which meant they were not very useful as air bases. Even so, Admiral Nimitz decided to retake them.

In May 1943, Nimitz sent an army division and powerful naval forces, including battleships, to the island of Attu. The 2,500 Japanese troops on the island, although heavily outnumbered, strongly defended their positions, retreating slowly and inflicting serious losses on the American attackers. But after two weeks of fighting, the Japanese were at the end of their strength. Instead of surrendering, however, the Japanese commander led his troops in a bayonet charge against the Americans. Hundreds of Japanese soldiers then committed suicide rather than be captured. Almost all the Japanese defenders of Attu died; the Americans captured just twenty-eight

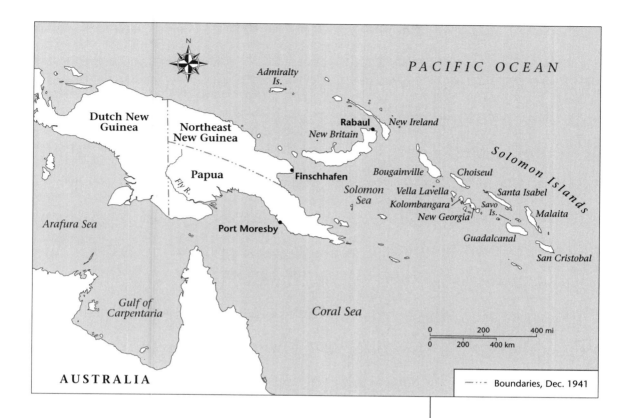

The following labels appear on the map:

PACIFIC OCEAN

Admiralty Is.

Dutch New Guinea

Northeast New Guinea

Rabaul

New Britain

New Ireland

Papua

Finschhafen

Fly R.

Bougainville

Choiseul

Solomon Islands

Solomon Sea

Vella Lavella

Santa Isabel

Kolombangara

Savo Is.

New Georgia

Malaita

Arafura Sea

Port Moresby

Guadalcanal

San Cristobal

Gulf of Carpentaria

Coral Sea

AUSTRALIA

| 0 | 200 | 400 mi |
| 0 | 200 | 400 km |

- - - - Boundaries, Dec. 1941

mapfile 14-3

The Solomon Islands and New Guinea, 1941.

alive. The Americans—despite having to attack strong defensive positions—lost about a third as many soldiers.

Two months later, Japanese warships evacuated more than 5,000 troops from the Aleutian island of Kiska under cover of fog. The waiting American invasion force of 34,000 men took the island without a fight.

Clearing the Solomons

The most important Japanese military and naval base in the southern Pacific was at Rabaul, on the large island of New Britain. Driving the powerful Japanese forces from Rabaul would be very difficult, but it became the first major goal of the combined American navy and army strategy.

After the victory on Guadalcanal, the navy continued west through the rest of the Solomon Islands. At the end of June 1943, troops landed on New Georgia, and on Vella Lavella in August. They skipped the island of Kolombangara, leaving the 10,000 Japanese troops there in control of the island but unable to play any part in the war because they were surrounded by American troops. This was an example of the island-hopping strategy. In November, a division of marines, soon joined by an army division, landed on Bougainville, at the northwestern end of the Solomons chain. They soon built an airfield and established a powerful defensive position. The 35,000 Japanese troops on the island could not crack this position, and American naval and air power prevented Japanese reinforcements from joining them. The American base on Bougainville was within striking distance of Rabaul.

Closing in on Rabaul: The fighting in New Guinea

Meanwhile, General MacArthur's Australian and American troops were fighting on New Guinea, just north of Australia. New Guinea is the second-largest island in the world, about twice the size of France, but with few roads, high mountains, and impassable rain forests. Before the war it was divided between the Dutch, who controlled the western half of the island, and Australia, which controlled the eastern half, including the southeastern quarter, called Papua. Japanese troops occupied the Dutch half as part of their conquest of the Dutch East Indies in early 1942. In May of that year, the Japanese tried to land troops on the southern coast of Papua, near its capital, Port Moresby. From there, they could threaten Australia itself. This attempt led to the Battle of the Coral Sea, the first great naval battle fought between aircraft carriers. (These events are described in Chapter 4.)

With their fleet driven off in the famous battle, the Japanese instead landed troops on the north shore in July and attempted to attack Port Moresby by crossing the mountains along a single jungle trail—something that MacArthur and his planners had thought was impossible. Australian troops defending the trail were pushed back. In mid-September, the Japanese were only 40 miles from Port Moresby, but they could no longer get enough reinforcements to make up for the men they had lost. By then, the Americans had landed on Guadalcanal. Japanese ships were being used to bring reinforcements and supplies there. Unlike the Allies, the Japanese did not have the resources to attack in New Guinea and Guadalcanal at the same time.

Now MacArthur went on the offensive. The Australians forced the Japanese back to the north shore of Papua. Meanwhile, American troops landed by boat at other points on the north shore. By the end of January 1943, the Allies had cleared Papua of Japanese forces. In six months of fighting, more than 12,000 Japanese soldiers died. The Allies lost almost 4,000 soldiers, more than three-quarters of them Australians. Another 7,500 Allied soldiers were wounded.

In a series of battles over the next eight months, MacArthur's forces moved farther west along the New Guinea coast. In October 1943, the Allies captured Finschhafen, a port across the strait from New Britain. On the other end of New Britain was the great Japanese base at Rabaul. A month later, with the success of the American operation on Bougainville, the Allies could threaten Rabaul from New Guinea to the south and from Bougainville to the east.

The attack on Rabaul might have been very costly. But the 100,000 Japanese troops on New Britain and New Ireland were now isolated. They had suffered constant American air raids, and many of their planes had been destroyed. American naval strength in the area was far greater than the Japanese. The forces at Rabaul did not have the air or sea power to support Japanese forces elsewhere. There was no American attack on Rabaul. The Japanese forces there could stay until the end of the war.

Nimitz moves west

Instead, Nimitz and MacArthur moved far beyond Rabaul. In November 1943, Nimitz's marines landed on the tiny island of Tarawa in the Gilbert Islands. Almost the entire Japanese force of 5,000 soldiers defending the island was killed, refusing to surrender even when further resistance was useless. But the marines lost 1,000 men and 2,000 were wounded.

In February 1944, the advance continued northwest to the Marshall Islands. Early in the month, after a tremendous

Unlike the Allies, the Japanese did not have the resources to attack in New Guinea and Guadalcanal at the same time.

The date that the Americans attacked Saipan shows how great Allied resources were: it was barely a week after the Allies had launched the invasion of Normandy.

naval bombardment, marine and army troops captured the island of Kwajalein in four days of fighting. They suffered far fewer casualties than at Tarawa. Within two weeks, American troops landed on Eniwetok, the farthest west of the Marshall Islands, and captured it in a battle that lasted five days. The Americans bypassed all the other islands between Kwajalein and Eniwetok because, without a powerful Japanese navy, the soldiers on those islands presented no threat.

The next target was the Mariana Islands, 1,000 miles across the Pacific from Eniwetok—and within striking distance of the Philippines. The new B-29 long-range bomber, known as the superfortress, could even reach the cities of Japan from the Marianas. The first island the Americans attacked was Saipan, on June 15, 1944. The date shows how great Allied resources were: it was barely a week after the Allies had launched the invasion of northwest Europe, landing hundreds of thousands of soldiers in Normandy in France. (The Normandy invasion is described in Chapter 11.)

Two marine divisions and one army division attacked Saipan, which was defended by 32,000 Japanese. As usual, the Americans had strong naval and air support to protect their landing. The fighting continued for three weeks. At the end, the remaining Japanese troops, running low on ammunition, charged the amazed Americans with bayonets. After that, hundreds committed suicide by jumping off cliffs. The Americans quickly followed up this bloody victory with much easier ones on Tinian and then on Guam, an American island that Japan had captured in December 1941, immediately after Pearl Harbor.

Meanwhile, in the two-day Battle of the Philippine Sea, American carriers thoroughly defeated a Japanese fleet. The Americans lost 29 planes while shooting down 243 enemy planes—almost two-thirds of the total Japanese strength. The Americans called it the Great Marianas Turkey Shoot. Three Japanese carriers were sunk and one was damaged. The battle confirmed that the United States now had higher-quality planes and better radar than the Japanese. In addition, Japan's pilots were increasingly inexperienced replacements, not nearly as skilled as the men who had won Japan's first great victories.

Closing in on the Philippines

While the battles for the Marshalls and Marianas were being fought, MacArthur's troops continued their advance northwest along the coast of New Guinea, avoiding most of the Japanese troops stationed on the island. In a series of carefully planned operations, large Allied forces landed at points along the coast, usually surprising the Japanese defenders. In each case, the American aim was to capture or build an airstrip and create a strong base that the Japanese could not eliminate. Planes from the new airfield would provide cover for the next operation. By July 1944, American troops had established bases in the extreme northwest corner of the giant island, the area known as Vogelkop ("bird's head" in Dutch, because of its shape). From here, the next step was the Philippines.

The Defeat of Japan

14

The war in the Pacific, which saw the United States face off against Japan, began on December 7, 1941, when Japan bombed the American naval base at Pearl Harbor in Hawaii. Events in the Pacific until mid-1944 and the American strategy for the war are discussed in Chapter 13.

The return to the Philippines

By the summer of 1944, the United States had bases in the Mariana Islands and in northwest New Guinea, both within range of the Philippines. Control of the Philippines was now the great prize of the Pacific war. If Japan lost those islands, it would be almost impossible for resource-poor Japan to import oil, tin, and other valuable products from the Dutch East Indies and Southeast Asia.

But the Philippines had great symbolic importance for the United States as well. America had controlled the islands since 1898 and had promised to make the Philippines an independent country in 1946. Many Filipinos admired and were

After losing the Phillipines to the Japanese in 1941, the U.S. Army's strategy when it returned in 1944 was to retake Leyte and use it as a base for attack on Luzon.

loyal to the United States. The army that fought the Japanese invasion of the islands in December 1941 included many Filipino as well as American soldiers. The Philippines was the only area outside China conquered by Japan where a significant guerrilla movement developed. (Guerrillas are people who fight behind enemy lines, usually employing hit-and-run tactics against a more powerful enemy. Guerrilla, or partisan, movements in Europe during World War II are described in Chapter 6.)

The Americans chose as a goal Leyte (pronounced lay-tee), a major island in the center of the Philippines. The plan was to retake Leyte and use it as a base for an attack on Luzon, the most important of the Philippine Islands. The overall commander of the operation was General Douglas MacArthur, who had commanded the defense of the Philippines at the beginning of the war. In early 1942, he had made a famous promise to the Filipino people when, on President Franklin D. Roosevelt's orders, he had left the Philippines to avoid capture by the Japanese. "I shall return," he had promised.

As the invasion force landed on the shores of Leyte Gulf on October 20, 1944, several large sections of the Japanese fleet steamed toward them. The Japanese admirals had developed a highly complicated plan involving large groups of ships coming from different directions and meeting near the American invasion beaches. The result was the Battle of Leyte Gulf, the largest naval battle in history.

The Battle of Leyte Gulf

Most of the other major naval battles of the Pacific war, such as Midway, were fought mainly between carrier-based planes. Although planes did play a major role at Leyte Gulf, they were not the deciding factor. In fact, the Japanese used their few remaining aircraft carriers as bait to lure away the primary American carrier force. The rest of the Japanese and American fleets fought it out the way navies had fought battles since the invention of the cannon. Warships fired their guns and torpedoes at one another, sometimes at close range. Among the ships involved were five American battleships that the Japanese had bombed at Pearl Harbor, including two, the *California* and *West Virginia,* that had been sunk and raised from the bottom of the harbor.

The Japanese intent was to destroy the transport ships that had brought the American forces to Leyte, effectively cutting off the American troops onshore from reinforcements and supplies. The Japanese troops on the island could then defeat them. The Japanese almost succeeded in catching the transports unprotected because the most powerful part of the American fleet had sailed north, chasing the Japanese carriers. But the Japanese did not account for the rest of the American ships fighting so desperately. The battle involved a series of often confused fights, with groups of ships racing from one engagement to another, sudden changes of direction, surprise confrontations between enemy forces, and leaders badly misinformed about what was happening. When it was all over, the Americans had smashed the Japanese navy.

During the battle, the Americans saw a new Japanese threat for the first time. Japanese pilots intentionally crashed their planes, loaded with bombs, into American ships. The pilots were all volunteers, although the Americans refused to believe this at the time. These suicide pilots were called kamikaze (komma-kozzy), or divine wind, a name for the sudden storm that had destroyed a Mongol invasion fleet heading for Japan hundreds of years earlier. This name implied that they were the last hope to save Japan from invasion, that only a miracle could now protect the country from defeat.

Leyte, Luzon, Manila

Onshore, the Japanese reinforced their troops with forces brought from other parts of the Philippines, and even with one division from China. (A division is usually around 15,000 soldiers.) Although it was also reinforced, the American

Japanese suicide pilots—kamikazes—intentionally crashed their planes, loaded with bombs, into American ships.

U.S.S.R.

Hokkaido

Sea of Japan

JAPAN

Yellow R.

Korea

Honshu

Yellow Sea

CHINA

Yangtze R.

Shikoku

Kyushu

Ryukyu Islands

Okinawa

Bonin Islands

Iwo Jima

Taiwan

Luzon

Philippine Islands

Philippine Sea

Mariana Islands

Saipan

Leyte

Palawan

Sulu Sea

Mindanao

0 250 500 mi
0 250 500 km

Islands of the eastern Pacific, 1941: the Marianas with Saipan, the Bonins with Iwo Jima, and the Ryukyus with Okinawa.

army made slow progress in fighting that sometimes resembled battles in World War I: bloody attacks against strong defensive positions to gain only a few hundred yards. In December, the Americans beat back a major Japanese counteroffensive aimed at the American airfields. Although some Japanese units continued fighting until April 1945, the Americans controlled most of Leyte by Christmas 1944. At least 50,000 Japanese troops had been killed.

On January 8, 1945, the American army landed on Luzon, the main Philippine island. The Philippine capital of Manila is located on Luzon. Near Manila is the Bataan Peninsula and the island of Corregidor, where the Americans held off the Japanese for several months before surrendering in the spring of 1942. Ninety-five thousand American and Filipino troops had become Japanese prisoners on Bataan and Corregidor. The Japanese had badly mistreated them in their years in captivity. Now, after almost three years, the Americans were returning, as MacArthur had promised.

The large Japanese force on Luzon did not try to prevent the American landings. Instead, it defended carefully prepared positions, trying to hold out as long as possible. The Japanese did not try to block the road to Manila either, and American troops entered the city's suburbs by early February. To destroy Manila's harbor, the Japanese set fires which spread through large sections of the city. In the southern part of Manila, Japanese troops went on a rampage of murder, looting, and rape against Filipino civilians, killing tens of thousands, much as the Japanese army had done in China during the 1930s. (The Japanese actions in China are described in Chapter 1.)

At the same time, the 20,000 Japanese defenders, mostly from the navy, fought the Americans for each street and building in Manila. House-to-house fighting in a major city with modern weapons is one of the bloodiest forms of war-

A Japanese prisoner, blindfolded, taken on Iwo Jima. Very few Japanese soldiers surrendered or were taken prisoner: most fought to the death. *(Reproduced by permission of the National Archives and Records Administration)*

fare, as had been shown in European cities like Stalingrad. (The Battle of Stalingrad is described in Chapter 10.) Sixteen thousand Japanese died fighting for Manila, as did 12,000 Americans. One hundred thousand civilians were killed, some in the battle and some in the Japanese massacres.

The Americans cleared Japanese troops out of the area around Manila, including Bataan, while the fighting in the capital continued. By March 1, the Americans raised their flag over Corregidor, and by the next day the fighting in Manila was over. Fighting continued in Luzon and other parts of the Philippines, some of it difficult. But the remaining Japanese forces, some of which were still fighting when Japan finally surrendered, presented no real danger to American control of the Philippines.

Iwo Jima: Death in a small place

The tiny island of Iwo Jima is a volcanic rock in the middle of the ocean. But it lies on the route that American B-29

An Image of Triumph and of Sacrifice

Iwo Jima has become one of the most famous battles fought by Americans in any war. Part of the reason is simply how bloody it was in comparison to its size. Another reason is the famous photograph of a group of marines planting the American flag on top of Mount Suribachi while the fighting was still going on. That photograph, taken by Joe Rosenthal, is the model for the Marine Corps Monument in Arlington National Cemetery and has been reproduced countless times.

Today, the picture seems to be an image of triumph, a tribute to fighting men who have won a great victory. But when it was first published, every American who saw the picture knew what was happening while the flag was being raised. At that time, the picture was also an image of sacrifice, a reminder of the terrible price the marines had paid on Iwo Jima.

long-range bombers flew from Saipan in the Marianas to bomb Japan. The B-29s had to avoid the island because it was under Japanese control, making their long trip to Japan even longer. In addition, the air force wanted to use Iwo Jima as an emergency landing field for damaged B-29s.

To gain these comparatively small advantages, however, the United States paid a very high price. On February 19, 1945, three marine divisions landed on Iwo Jima. The fighting continued almost a month, until March 16.

The Japanese had 21,000 soldiers on Iwo Jima, most of them dug into rocks, caves, and tunnels underground and determined to die rather than surrender. Almost all of them did. The marines lost 6,900 soldiers in the fighting and 20,000 were wounded.

The last Pacific island: Okinawa

The next target was Okinawa. At 80 miles long, Okinawa is the largest of the Ryukyus, a group of islands that lies about 400 miles from the closest of the main home islands of Japan. Despite this distance, Okinawa and the Ryukyus are often considered part of Japan itself. For the first time, the Japanese troops would be defending a part of their own homeland, not territory they had taken from another country.

The fight for Okinawa became the largest ground battle of the Pacific war. On the first day of the landings, 50,000 Americans came ashore; by the time the battle ended, 200,000 American troops were fighting on the island.

American ships bombarded Okinawa for a full week before the troops landed on April 1, 1945. There was no Japan-

ese opposition to the landings, which was very unusual. The Japanese troops usually attacked the Americans even before the invaders reached the beach. Instead, the Japanese had dug in and waited for the American troops to reach them. When they did, the Japanese resisted every yard of the American advance. There was no surrender. As on Saipan, the Japanese resistance was quite literally suicidal.

Offshore, Japanese planes attacked the American fleet. Many were kamikaze, suicide attackers trying to crash their planes into American ships. Sometimes the kamikaze came in waves—50, 100, even 300 planes at a time. It was almost impossible for the ships' antiaircraft guns and the fighter planes to shoot them all down before they could reach the American ships.

The Japanese also sent the battleship *Yamato*, the largest and most powerful in the world, against the American fleet on a suicide mission. Partly because of Japan's severe petroleum shortage, the *Yamato* was loaded with only

Marines on Okinawa surround a Japanese tunnel entrance.
(Reproduced by permission of AP/Wide World Photos)

enough fuel to reach the battle. It sailed directly toward the American fleet, hoping to use its huge guns. But American planes sank the *Yamato* with torpedoes before it could cause any damage. Almost all of its 2,300 sailors died when the ship went down.

The battle on Okinawa continued until the end of June. In the last days of fighting, 4,000 Japanese soldiers sur-

rendered, which brought the total who had given up to about 7,400. This number included many who were so badly wounded that they could not commit suicide. But another 110,000 Japanese troops had died—in combat or by suicide. Not a single senior officer was taken prisoner. The Japanese lost nearly 8,000 of their remaining planes, including 1,000 on kamikaze missions.

Kamikaze crashes into the USS *Bunker Hill* off Okinawa, May 1945. *(Reproduced by permission of the National Archives and Records Administration)*

With Okinawa as a base, the next major campaign would be against Japan itself.

Of the 450,000 civilians on the island, somewhere between one-sixth and one-third were also dead. Many had hidden in caves to avoid the fighting. They had been killed when Japanese troops used the caves as defensive positions and the American troops blew them up or fired flamethrowers into them.

Seven thousand U.S. soldiers and marines were killed on Okinawa, and more than 5,000 sailors died at sea, most of them as a result of kamikaze actions.

Defeating Japan

With Okinawa as a base, the next major campaign would be against Japan itself. A limited invasion of Kyushu, the southernmost of the main Japanese islands, was scheduled for November 1, 1945. Its purpose was to provide a base for the next operation: the invasion of Honshu, the main Japanese island. Honshu was scheduled for March 1, 1946. The American planners believed the invasion would require at least 25 divisions—a third of a million men.

Germany had surrendered in May 1945, and large forces could come from Europe. The American First Army, which had landed in Normandy in June 1944 and fought its way across France and Germany, would not be sent home. Instead, its soldiers would go to the Pacific and prepare for an invasion of Japan. One-and-a-half million American troops and another half-million British were scheduled to be sent to various parts of Asia when the European war ended. Neither the soldiers nor their families at home would be happy about that.

Worse, the planners believed that American deaths in the invasion would be very high. They were afraid that the Japanese would fight for every inch of Japan, as they had fought on Okinawa. Several thousand kamikaze were waiting to attack American ships. If Allied forces took casualties at the same rate as on Okinawa, then hundreds of thousands would be killed or wounded. Sometimes they used the figure of 1 million casualties, although apparently no Allied planner ever considered this a serious possibility.

Another part of the Allied plan was for the Soviet Union, which was still not at war with Japan, to enter the

The United States planned an invasion of Japan at the southern island of Kyushu for November 1945 and hoped to use this as a base to attack the main island Honshu in March 1946.

fighting. The Soviets had promised they would attack Japan after Germany surrendered. It was planned that several months before the scheduled American invasion of Japan the Soviet army would invade Manchuria in northern China and fight the 750,000 Japanese troops stationed there. The Japanese would then not be able to use these troops to defend Japan. The destruction of their army in China might also make the Japanese leaders see that continuing the war was hopeless, even before the Americans invaded.

But most American military planners did not believe it was possible to defeat Japan without invading it. Some navy and air force leaders, however, thought that the combination of the American submarine campaign and the bombing campaign might force Japan to surrender. The submarine campaign amounted to a blockade of Japan. Food was in short supply, as were the raw materials for war industries, including oil. Many Japanese factories had shut down even before American bombers destroyed them.

American submarine warfare against Japan was extremely effective. By the spring of 1945, Japan had less than 1 million tons of shipping left—not even enough to transport goods within Japan.

Japanese shipping and American submarines

American submarine warfare against Japan was extremely effective. As an island country with few natural resources, Japan depended on shipping more than any other industrial nation. In fact, because Japanese roads and railroads were poor, and because it is made up of several large islands with most major cities on the coasts, Japan even depended on ships for moving large quantities of goods inside the country.

Japan began the war with about 6 million tons of merchant ships (civilian ships that carry freight). It built around 3.3 million tons during the war. It also seized a substantial number of British, Dutch, and other enemy merchant ships in early 1942 soon after it went to war.

By the end of the war, the Allies (Britain, the United States, and the other countries fighting on their side) had sunk 9 million tons of Japanese shipping; submarines, almost all of them American, sank more than half of this total. Even worse for Japan, the rate was speeding up. American submarine captains and crews were becoming more skillful, and they were operating from bases much closer to Japan. In 1944 alone, they sank 600 ships totaling 2.7 million tons. American planes, both carrier and land-based, sank many more Japanese ships, including those used to carry or supply Japanese troops. Finally, large numbers of merchant ships were hitting mines (explosive devices floating in the water) that American planes had dropped in large quantities along the Japanese coast.

By the end of 1944, two-thirds of Japan's available oil tankers had been destroyed, and it was almost impossible to get fuel to Japan from the Dutch East Indies. In the spring of 1945, Japan had less than 1 million tons of shipping left—not even enough to transport goods within Japan.

The bombing of Japan

While the submarines were threatening to starve Japan's cities, the B-29 bombers were burning them down. This was part of the Allies' strategic bombing campaign. Strategic bombing is intended to have a long-term effect on the enemy's ability to wage war—for example, by destroying its steel industry. In contrast, tactical bombing involves battlefield support—attacking trains bringing reinforcements to a battle, for instance. (The role of strategic bombing in World War II is described in Chapter 8.) For months, the bombers had dropped high explosives onto Japanese factories and other targets in high-altitude daylight raids. This was the same method the United States had used to bomb Germany. But the raids were not accurate, rarely hitting their targets. At first they did not seem to have much effect on Japan's ability to fight. Then the United States changed the way it conducted the strategic bombing campaign. From now on, it would do in Japan what the British bombers had done in Germany.

On the night of March 9, 1945, 325 B-29s dropped many tons of incendiary (fire-starting) bombs from a low altitude on Tokyo. The wood-and-paper buildings of the Japanese capital were perfect material for a fire. By morning, more than 250,000 buildings had been destroyed, and 1 million people had lost their homes. Nearly 90,000 people—almost all of them civilians—had died in the flames and smoke.

Over the next three months, similar raids devastated almost every large city in Japan. A quarter of a million Japanese were killed and millions were homeless. Combined with the sea blockade, the Japanese economy was barely functioning. Malnutrition and even mass starvation were real possibilities.

From now on, U.S. bombers would do in Japan what the British bombers had done in Germany.

The future of the emperor

Still, the Japanese government did not surrender. In July 1945, the Allies issued a declaration at Potsdam, a city near the German capital of Berlin, where they were holding a conference to plan the postwar world. The declaration repeated the call for the unconditional surrender of Japan, the same demand that Germany had finally been forced to accept. Among other things, the Potsdam Declaration made it clear that Japan would be placed under military occupation (that is, Allied troops would be stationed in the country and the Allies would run the government). But it also assured the Japanese people that they would eventually be allowed to choose their own government. This seemed to indicate—as it was intended to—that Japan could keep its emperor.

Retaining an emperor was an issue of great importance to the Japanese. Although in reality Japanese emperors did not

British prime minister Winston Churchill, U.S. president Harry S. Truman, and Soviet leader Joseph Stalin (left to right) at the Potsdam conference, July 1945. *(Reproduced by permission of the Corbis Corporation [Bellevue])*

have much power, they were a symbol of the country and were considered godlike. While some Japanese leaders, especially military officers, wanted to continue the war regardless of the consequences, others wanted to end the slaughter. But very few were willing to agree to have Emperor Hirohito removed.

Some leaders in the United States strongly opposed leaving the emperor on his throne. They believed he was a symbol of the system that had started the war and committed terrible crimes—for example, against the people of China and Allied prisoners. They blamed the empire system for creating blind obedience to authority and for glorifying war. Allowing the emperor to keep his title, they thought, was the same as allowing a Nazi leader to remain the official head of Germany.

But most Allied leaders took this issue less seriously. They thought that at some point the defeated Japanese people should be allowed to choose whatever government they wanted—even if they wanted an emperor. More immediately, there would be a great advantage in having the emperor call for surrender. Japanese military and naval officers, with large forces still undefeated in Japan, China, and elsewhere, might not obey anyone else's order to end the war. The military occupation of Japan would also be much easier if the emperor cooperated with it.

Officially, the Allies stuck to the demand that Japan surrender without *any* conditions. But they hinted very strongly, in several different ways, that the Potsdam Declaration meant that surrender did not require removing the emperor. But the Japanese political leaders who favored surrendering were still afraid to try to end the war without Allied guarantees that the emperor could stay.

There would be a great advantage in having the emperor call for surrender. Japanese military and naval officers, with large forces still undefeated in Japan, China, and elsewhere, might not obey anyone else's order to end the war.

The destruction of Hiroshima and Nagasaki

While the two sides were passing hints and suggestions to each other through various go-betweens (especially the Soviet Union, which was still at peace with Japan), American planners continued to prepare for the invasion of Japan. But there would be no invasion. On August 6, 1945, the American bomber *Enola Gay* dropped a single bomb on the Japanese city of Hiroshima. It was an atomic bomb, a weapon developed in the United States in great secrecy. (The development of the atomic bomb is described in Chapter 15.) The Americans had chosen Hiroshima partly because it was one of the few Japanese cities with little bombing damage. As such, it would be possible to evaluate the effects of the atomic attack. The impact was greater than ever imagined.

A survivor of the bombing at Hiroshima bears permanent scars from burns caused by the bomb. *(Reproduced by permission of the Corbis Corporation [Bellevue])*

In a few moments, a four-square-mile area at the center of Hiroshima was obliterated. The air in that area reached 3,000 degrees Celsius. Not one building in central Hiroshima escaped destruction. Almost all of them simply disappeared; only the skeletons of a few buildings made from reinforced concrete survived. Overall, 80 percent of the buildings in the city were destroyed. Thousands of people were killed immediately, and thousands more died in the next few hours. This one explosion killed approximately 78,000 people and injured about the same number. Some of the survivors were blinded by the flash of the explosion. Almost all had horrible burns that caused their skin to fall off. Many became ill from radiation sickness and died slowly and in great pain for years after the bomb was dropped.

On August 9, 1945, the Americans dropped a second atomic bomb, of a different and even more powerful type, on Nagasaki. Because of a combination of factors—including geographical features and the fact that the bomb missed the city center—the effects were not as devastating as at Hiroshima.

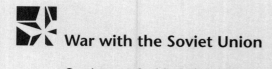

War with the Soviet Union

On August 8, 1945, between the first and second atomic bomb attacks on Japan, the Soviet Union declared war on Japan, as it had promised the United States it would. (The United States had not told the Soviets of its plan to drop the bomb.) The next day, huge Soviet armies invaded Manchuria from two directions, soon broke through the Japanese defenses, and captured Japanese troops by the thousands. The surrender of large numbers of Japanese soldiers, instead of a fight to the death, was something new. In ten days, the Soviets drove what was left of the Japanese army back into the northern part of Korea.

Many historians believe that the Soviet invasion of Manchuria played as large a role in persuading the Japanese to surrender as did the atomic bomb. Perhaps the large-scale surrender in China made the Japanese leaders less confident that their soldiers would continue to fight a hopeless war forever. Certainly it meant that it would be impossible for the Japanese army in China to defend Japan.

If this reasoning is true, it may indicate that the Japanese leaders simply did not understand how different atomic weapons were from conventional weapons. Like many Allied leaders when they were first informed about it, the Japanese may have thought the atomic bomb simply amounted to a more powerful version of a regular bomb.

But at least 35,000 more people died, and another Japanese city was effectively wiped out in a moment.

The United States had no more atomic bombs immediately available. But the Japanese did not know this. It looked as if the United States could wipe out another Japanese city every few days, or even more often. There was no possible defense against this weapon. Air raid shelters would make little difference. Yet even now, the top Japanese military and naval leaders did not want to surrender. Arguments in the government continued, as did the normal American air raids.

Japan surrenders

Finally, the emperor himself ended the argument. On August 15, the people of Japan heard something they had

Destruction in Nagasaki after the United States dropped an atom bomb on the city. *(Reproduced by permission of the Corbis Corporation [New York])*

never heard before: the voice of their emperor. A recording he had made the day before was broadcast over the radio. Although he never mentioned surrender, he told the Japanese people that they must prepare to "endure the unendurable."

The decision to drop the atomic bomb

Why the United States dropped the atomic bomb on Japan, and whether it was right to do so, is probably the single greatest controversy surrounding World War II. This argument has not been limited to historians or military experts. It is a subject that many ordinary people have felt very strongly about. All over the world, the anniversary of the bombing of Hiroshima is observed as a day of mourning and of reflection on the possibility of nuclear war.

Even at the time of the bombing, there were disagreements in the United States, though they were not known to the public. General Dwight D. Eisenhower, supreme commander of Allied forces in Europe, did not believe the bomb should be used. Apparently, neither did General Douglas MacArthur, who was to command the invasion of Japan and who only found out about the bomb shortly before it was dropped. A few of the scientists who had helped build the bomb opposed using it against Japan.

Avoiding an invasion

The man who made the decision, President Harry S. Truman, claimed that it had been an easy one and that he never lost a single night's sleep over it. To Truman, the choice was between using the bomb and invading Japan. The way he figured it, the bomb saved the lives of tens of thousands, perhaps hundreds of thousands, of American soldiers. Most people in the United States certainly agreed with him at the time. In addition, some historians have pointed out that an invasion would almost surely have caused the deaths of even more Japanese—both soldiers and civilians—than did the atomic bomb.

Winston Churchill, the British prime minister (head of the government), was one of the few leaders who knew about the bomb project. He remembered the decision to use the bomb as something that was hardly debated at all. It was assumed that atomic weapons, like any other powerful new weapon, would be used as soon as possible. Most political leaders did not fully understand the difference between the atomic bomb and previous weapons. They thought it was just a more powerful version of a regular bomb. This may be the way Truman understood it. He had no idea of the existence of the bomb project until he became president after President Franklin D. Roosevelt's death in April 1945.

Other possible motives

Other reasons have been suggested for why the bomb was dropped. Building it was probably the most expensive pro-

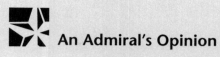

An Admiral's Opinion

"My own feeling was that, in being the first to use it, we had adopted an ethical standard common to the barbarians of the Dark Age. I was not taught to make war in that fashion, and wars cannot be won by destroying women and children."

—Admiral William D. Leahy, chief of staff to President Franklin D. Roosevelt and President Harry S. Truman, on the use of the atomic bomb.

Many historians argue that part of the reason the United States dropped the bomb was to demonstrate the power of this superweapon to the Soviet Union.

ject that the United States government had ever attempted—as well as the most secret. It was natural that the people involved in this massive project would want to use the bomb, to show that the project had helped win the war and that the money had not been wasted.

Many historians have emphasized that by the time the bomb was dropped, serious conflicts were developing between the United States and the Soviet Union. (Some of the wartime conflicts are described in Chapter 9; events after the war are discussed in Chapter 17.) They argue that at least part of the reason for using the bomb was to demonstrate the power of this superweapon to the Soviet Union.

The deteriorating American-Soviet relations are one explanation for the timing of the Hiroshima and Nagasaki attacks. For years, the United States had wanted the Soviet Union to declare war on Japan and invade Manchuria. However, when they successfully tested the first atomic bomb in New Mexico in July 1945, top American officials felt that they no longer needed Soviet help against Japan. Instead, they now feared that a Soviet invasion would ensure Soviet control of Manchuria and great influence in the rest of China after the war.

Although it was too late to call off the Soviet invasion, as top American military officials wanted, the sooner Japan surrendered, the less influence the Soviets would have in eastern Asia after the war. This is one reason, according to these historians, why the United States did not wait a few more weeks or even months to see if Japan would surrender without an invasion.

Question of timing, or a warning shot

In some ways, the question of timing is the most troubling aspect of the use of the atomic bomb. Some historians are convinced from the records of secret discussions in the Japanese government that Japan would soon have accepted the same terms even if Hiroshima and Nagasaki had not been bombed. American leaders knew the details of many of these discussions at the time because the United States had broken the secret codes used by the Japanese.

In addition, critics have argued that the United States could have informed the Japanese government of the exis-

tence of the bomb, or even demonstrated it on an uninhabited island in the Pacific in the presence of Japanese observers. This idea was apparently considered but rejected at the time. One reason was that American officials were afraid of what would happen if the bomb were a dud. Apart from that problem, such an approach was completely different from the way countries at war behaved. It probably just didn't seem very realistic to American officials.

Japanese leaders sign surrender documents aboard the USS *Missouri*, September 2, 1945.
(Reproduced by permission of AP/Wide World Photos)

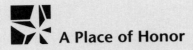

A Place of Honor

As General Douglas MacArthur signed the Japanese surrender aboard the USS *Missouri,* two men stood directly behind him in a place of honor. Both looked too thin for the uniforms they were wearing. They had lost weight in the years they had spent as prisoners of the Japanese. One was Arthur Percival, the British general who had surrendered the island fortress of Singapore in February 1942. The other was Jonathan Wainwright, the American general who had surrendered Corregidor and the

No one will ever know whether Japan would have surrendered without the atomic attack and without an invasion. When the emperor told his people on the radio that they must accept defeat, most of the Allies did not care why.

The end of the war

In every great city of the Allied countries, deliriously happy crowds cheered the news of victory. In America, soldiers and sailors home from Europe now knew they would not have to ship out again. The GIs (ordinary soldiers) celebrated because they would not have to die on the shores of Kyushu and Honshu, as their friends had died at Anzio in Italy and Omaha beach in France. They would not have to fight their way through Japan, as they had fought through Germany. They would not have to die in the streets of Tokyo, as GIs had died in Manila and as the Russians had died in Berlin.

Two weeks after the emperor's broadcast, an immense Allied fleet gathered in Tokyo Bay. Aboard the American battleship *Missouri,* military representatives of the United States, Britain, China, the Soviet Union, and France waited. Representatives of the Japanese army and navy, and of the Japanese government, approached a small table on the *Missouri*'s deck, bent forward, and signed their names to the surrender. MacArthur signed for the Allies. It was September 2, 1945—six years and one day after Germany's armies had invaded Poland and begun World War II. The war was over.

Spies and Scientists

15

A country at war wants to find out how strong the enemy is, what its weaknesses are, and what its plans are. And each country does everything possible to keep this information secret. Gathering information, in all its forms, is called intelligence; preventing the enemy from learning information is called counterintelligence. Countries at war also try to develop technology and weapons that are better than those of the enemy. Scientists play a major role in developing new technology or enhancing existing equipment that will help win the war, creating anything from drugs to heal wounded soldiers to stronger or more accurate bombs to drop on the enemy.

Sneak attacks

One of the most important secrets in any war setting is where and when an attack is coming. Countries in World War II used every way they could to protect this information. When the Japanese fleet sailed to attack Pearl Harbor in December 1941, its orders were hand-delivered by courier. (The Japanese attack on Pearl Harbor is described in Chapter 4.) At sea, the

Gathering information, in all its forms, is called intelligence; preventing the enemy from learning information is called counterintelligence.

ships did not use their radios to communicate with one another or with Japan. This radio silence prevented the Americans from knowing where the Japanese ships were—or even that they had sailed. The fleet also used natural conditions to conceal its movements. It sailed across the Pacific on the edge of an advancing weather front. Heavy clouds and constant rain made it much less likely that the fleet would be seen by American reconnaissance planes sent ahead to gather intelligence.

The Germans also kept careful radio silence and used fog and the heavily wooded terrain of the Ardennes Forest to keep Allied planes from seeing their preparations for the Battle of the Bulge. (See Chapter 12.) Despite German precautions, however, there were strong hints that there might be a major attack in the Ardennes. For example, the Allies knew that the Germans were moving some tough armored (tank) divisions into the area. Unfortunately, the top American generals were convinced that the German army was then too weak to launch a major offensive and that even if one came, it would not be in the Ardennes. So they explained away the information they had learned. They came to the conclusion that the Germans were sending new divisions to the area to let them rest in a quiet section of the battlefront.

Decoys and deceptions

Even better than concealing the location and timing of an attack is making the enemy think it is coming somewhere else. One famous example of this occurred before the Allied invasion of Sicily in July 1943 (described in Chapter 10). The Allies had just finished clearing North Africa of German and Italian troops. Nearby Sicily was the obvious next target, or so it seemed.

"The man who never was"

British intelligence officers in England found a man who had died of pneumonia—which can look as if the cause of death were drowning. They dressed the body in a British officer's uniform, took it by submarine to the coast of Spain, and released it where they knew it would float to shore. It looked like the body of a soldier who had drowned after his plane had crashed into the sea.

Spain was officially neutral in the war, but it was unofficially pro-German. The body of the British "officer" attracted the attention of German agents in Spain—just as the British wanted. The officer carried various papers in his wallet and in the briefcase chained to his waist. These documents identified him as a captain in the British marines, an expert on landing craft on his way to North Africa to join the staff of the British commanding general there. He also carried various personal items that confirmed his identity. All of these were fake, part of the British plan.

Most important, he carried a top-secret personal letter from one British general to another. This letter made it clear that the next Allied invasion would not be in Sicily but in Greece and the island of Sardinia. The letter also said that the British should continue to try to make the Germans think Sicily was the target.

The letter included some negative comments about other top generals as well. That explained why it was being hand delivered, instead of being sent through official (and coded) radio messages. The Germans were not sure whether all this information was authentic. Being handed a personal letter from a top British general explaining invasion plans seemed too good to be true. Even so, probably on German leader Adolf Hitler's personal orders, the Germans sent reinforcements to Greece and Sardinia. Because of "the man who never was" (as both the book and movie about this deception are titled), one of Germany's best armored divisions and a mechanized infantry division were not in Sicily when the Allies attacked it.

Operation Fortitude

A much more considerable deception occurred in connection with the D-Day invasion of Normandy in June 1944. (See Chapter 11.) Code-named Operation Fortitude, it was by far the most successful counterintelligence operation conducted by any country in the war.

The Germans knew the invasion of Europe was coming soon. The most likely place for it was the area of northeastern France called the Pas de Calais. It is the closest part of Europe to England, and the Germans had placed many of their best troops nearby, armored divisions ready to rush to the coast and drive an invasion back into the sea.

Operation Fortitude was by far the most successful counterintelligence operation conducted by any country in the war.

The photographs showed tanks, trucks, jeeps, and tents for soldiers. But it was all fake.

The Allies developed an elaborate plan to convince the Germans that the invasion force would land at the Pas de Calais. And they wanted to keep the German generals guessing as to whether the real invasion were at Pas de Calais even after troops were already landing in Normandy on D-Day. If the German leaders believed that Normandy might be a decoy and that the real invasion would soon take place at Pas de Calais—they would be afraid to send their tanks and best troops to Normandy. If they could be fooled, even for a few days, the German tanks and reinforcements might arrive in Normandy too late to defeat the Allies.

A real commander and a cardboard army The Allies created a make-believe army, the First United States Army Group, known as FUSAG. FUSAG was commanded by a real American general, George S. Patton, whom the Germans knew as one of the best American tank commanders. Just as the Allies wanted, the Germans believed that Patton was a logical choice to command the ground troops in the invasion.

Patton had a headquarters, as did the various army divisions and army corps that were supposedly part of FUSAG. There were constant radio messages sent between them and between FUSAG and other Allied military commands. The Germans could not understand the encoded radio messages, but they could tell that there were a great many of them. The number of messages made the Germans believe that FUSAG must be a very large force.

FUSAG headquarters was in southeastern England, across from the Pas de Calais, and German planes photographed it from high above. The photographs showed tanks, trucks, jeeps, and tents for soldiers. German spies in England confirmed the evidence from the planes. But it was all fake.

The tents were empty, and the tanks were made of cardboard. The Allies purposely allowed the Germans to hear the radio messages and let the German planes fly over and escape back to German-held France. (Any German plane that came near the *real* bases was shot down.)

Using double-crossers The German "spies" in England were actually working for the Allies. Every one of them had been arrested long before, and only those who had agreed to work for the Allies had been released. The British called this the

Double-Cross System. For years, they carefully allowed the spies to report certain information back to the Germans, to make the Germans believe the spies were still loyal to them. But the information, although accurate, was always unimportant or arrived too late to do the Germans any good. Now the spies sent false information to Germany, helping to convince the German high command that FUSAG was real, that it was the invasion army, and that therefore the invasion would come at the Pas de Calais.

The information, although accurate, was always unimportant or arrived too late to do the Germans any good.

The deception continued right up to D-Day itself. Out of 92 German radar stations on the coast, the Allies successfully jammed almost all of them by electronic interference. However, they purposely allowed the 18 radar installations around the Pas de Calais to keep operating. As the great invasion fleet approached the Normandy beaches, a much smaller number of Allied ships sailed toward the Pas de Calais. Each boat towed balloons behind it. From each balloon, specially shaped strips of aluminum dangled. Just as intended, the German radar at the Pas de Calais "saw" a huge invasion fleet approaching.

Operation Fortitude helped keep the German tanks far from Normandy until it was too late. Even as hundreds of thousands of American and British troops were already in Normandy, Hitler refused to allow the armored divisions from the Pas de Calais to go there. Instead, they waited for the real invasion.

Spies

One of the ways to learn about an enemy's plans is from spies. But there are many dangers in relying on spies. As the British Double-Cross System showed, spies can be "turned," sending false information supplied by the enemy. The Germans, as well as the Allies, succeeded in turning spies several times. One major spy network in the Netherlands sent the British a great deal of information that was in fact created by the Gestapo, the German secret police.

Equally important, even an honest spy rarely has a complete picture of what is really going on. He or she is privy to usually only a small piece of information, which in itself may be misleading.

There was one source of information that might have changed the war itself.

There are two ways to use spies in determining the accuracy of information. One way is to employ spies who do have access to important military or political leaders in the enemy country. This is the image of the secret agents whom people have learned about from spy novels and movies. But these spies were very rare in World War II. A second way is to employ a large number of spies, each sending back small bits of information. When all the pieces are put together and analyzed, an accurate picture unfolds.

A powerful double agent: Admiral Wilhelm Canaris

There was one source of information that might have changed not just a battle but even the war itself. At various times during the war, Allied intelligence agencies had secret contacts with Admiral Wilhelm Canaris, the head of German military intelligence, called the *Abwehr*. By the nature of his job, he knew almost all German military plans and secrets. Canaris, whom Germany eventually executed for his part in the plot to kill Hitler (described in Chapter 12), apparently quietly opposed Hitler's war plans right from the beginning. But he was also playing complicated political games inside the German military. In fact, historians are still not sure about Canaris's goals, or even about what he actually did or didn't do.

Canaris and other *Abwehr* agents seem to have given away some—but certainly not all—military secrets for years. In fact, there was a ring of anti-Hitler spies inside the *Abwehr*. *Abwehr* agents—possibly with Canaris's knowledge—apparently warned the Dutch about Germany's plan to invade their country in 1940. The Dutch ignored this information because they had no reason to trust its source.

It is also possible that the *Abwehr* was the original source of the Oslo Report, a document given to the British in Norway in 1940. It was a list of all the secret weapons being developed by Germany. (German secret weapons are described later in this chapter.) Once again, the British didn't believe this document at first, thinking it might be a bluff intended to frighten them.

Spy for the Soviets: Richard Sorge

Canaris was in a position to make a real difference in the war, but as far as is known, he never did. The spy who probably had the greatest effect was Richard Sorge. Sorge was a German journalist in Tokyo—but he was also a spy for the Soviet Union. He became a trusted friend of German diplomats in Japan and of important Japanese officials. Unknown to any of them, and like most Soviet spies in World War II, Sorge was a communist who was secretly loyal to the Soviet Union because it was the first communist country. (Communism is a political and economic system based on government control of the production and distribution of goods and the abolition of private ownership of factories, banks, and most other businesses.)

Sorge and his small ring, which included Japanese communists, passed a great deal of information to the Soviet Union. But he is best remembered for two reports, one that was not believed, and one that was. In the spring of 1941, Sorge warned that Germany was preparing to invade the Soviet Union. He even gave the exact date, June 22, on which the Germans would attack. But this information made no difference, despite many other indications that it was true. Joseph Stalin, the Soviet dictator, simply did not want to believe that Germany was planning a war against him.

German journalist Richard Sorge provided crucial information to the Soviets during the war. *(Reproduced by permission of AP/Wide World Photos)*

A few months later, Sorge told the Soviets that Japan would not invade the Soviet Union, as the Soviets feared. Instead, Japan would attack the United States and Britain. This information, confirmed by Soviet observations of Japanese troop movements, was believed. It allowed the Soviet army to transfer a large number of troops from the border between the Soviet Union and Japanese-occupied northern China, where they had been stationed. These troops, including some of the best in the Soviet army, went west to fight the German invasion. It was a crucial moment in the war because the German army had almost reached Moscow, the Soviet capital. The reinforcements helped stop the German advance and then played

Much espionage work involves gathering information that might seem unimportant but when collected and analyzed reveals a great deal.

a major role in the Soviet counterattack. (These events are described in Chapter 3.) By the time of the Soviet victory near Moscow, however, the Japanese secret police had arrested Sorge. After nearly three years as a prisoner, he was executed in July 1944.

The networks

Unlike Canaris or Sorge, most spies are not in a position to learn top-level secrets. But spies who gather small pieces of information about the enemy can be very important if there are enough of them. The Allies had an enormous advantage in this kind of intelligence gathering. Throughout Europe, thousands of people were willing to risk their lives to defeat the Germans who occupied their countries. (An occupation is when one country stations military forces in another to control it.) They joined together secretly in resistance movements, groups opposing the occupation.

Resistance movements spy for Allies

Resistance movements engaged in a wide variety of anti-German activities, from secretly publishing newspapers to blowing up railroad lines. (See Chapter 6 for more information on resistance movements.) They also spied on the Germans and sent their information to the Allies.

Much espionage work involves gathering information that might seem unimportant but when collected and analyzed reveals a great deal. For example, a member of a resistance organization might note the insignia worn by German soldiers coming to the town cafe. The insignia would show which units were stationed in the area. If one unit left or a new armored division arrived, it was almost always known to local resistance groups, who sent the information to England by radio. To radio was extremely dangerous because the Germans had detecting devices to find radio transmitters. Radio sets were carefully hidden, often in suitcases, and sometimes moved from one attic hideout to another. They were taken out only for short transmissions. Sometimes information and agents got to England aboard a plane that landed at night in a field, guided by resistance flashlights.

Sometimes the information was very valuable. Members of the Polish resistance recovered key parts of a secret German V-1 flying bomb that crashed during tests and got them to England. Information from resistance networks also helped ensure the success of the Normandy invasion. (See Chapter 11.) The Germans created a system of fortifications, obstacles, and mines along the coast of Europe to protect against Allied invasion. It was called the Atlantic Wall. French resistance groups learned every detail about the construction in each area and passed this knowledge to Britain. These details helped the Allies choose where to land. In addition, the resistance built scale models of the landing beaches, showing the location of the German fortifications. With the help of these models, Allied troops could practice attacking German positions, knowing where the enemy troops were located, how well they were protected, and what kind of equipment they had.

British spy network: The SOE

In addition to the resistance groups that engaged in espionage, the Allies set up their own intelligence networks. In July 1940, less than a month after France surrendered to the Germans, Britain began creating an organization called the Special Operations Executive, known as the SOE. It was in charge of both intelligence activities and sabotage (destruction of military or industrial facilities) for Europe and had sections responsible for each occupied country. The SOE recruited agents from among the thousands of foreign refugees who had fled their homes and made their way to Britain and still wanted to fight the Germans. It also recruited English people who spoke other European languages.

Invisible ink and hand-to-hand combat In the English countryside, the SOE created training centers, usually in a large country house. There, the newly recruited agents were taught to be spies. They learned how to encode their messages to make them secure. They learned Morse code to transmit messages, how to assemble and operate their secret radio transmitters, even how to use invisible ink. Training sergeants from the British army gave them lessons in hand-to-hand combat and how to kill an enemy silently. Then the SOE sent them into Europe, by parachute or sometimes by submarine.

American OSS agent Allen Dulles had secret contacts with German military intelligence officer Admiral Wilhelm Canaris.
(Reproduced by permission of the Corbis Corporation [Bellevue])

American spy network: The OSS

The American Office of Strategic Services (OSS) had the same mission as the British SOE: intelligence and sabatoge. The OSS was run by Colonel William J. Donovan, a millionaire lawyer who had gotten the nickname "Wild Bill" during his service in World War I. Sometimes OSS operations lived up to this nickname. OSS agents such as Allen Dulles (later the longtime director of the Central Intelligence Agency), working in neutral Switzerland, had important secret contacts with men such as Admiral Canaris in Germany. Later, OSS agents helped armed resistance groups fighting the Germans. But most of the spying networks in western Europe were already in existence when the OSS was created. Especially in France, the largest and most important country in the area, the spying networks reported to the British SOE.

Marie-Madeleine Fourcade and the Alliance

One of the key groups working with the SOE was called the Alliance. The Gestapo called it Noah's Ark because each agent's code name was the name of an animal. Its leader was a young woman named Marie-Madeleine Fourcade, code-named Hedgehog. The Alliance received most of its funds and equipment from the SOE and reported its intelligence findings to it, but its members and leaders were all French.

The Alliance organized a network of spies in every part of France. Its agents included people from all sections of French society. There were French military officers who were supposedly working for the pro-German government, naval engineers, and salesmen. One of the most valuable agents was a young woman whose job as a seamstress in the French port of Brest included sewing damaged life vests for the crews of German submarines. By listening to the crews' conversations, she learned which submarines were leaving port and on exactly what date—which meant that British warships would often be waiting for them. Information on German submarine bases and other naval facilities was one of the network's specialties.

Although France was the SOE's most important area of operation, there were also 35 networks in Belgium with a total of 10,000 people, including about 300 who had parachuted in. Networks in the Netherlands, Belgium, and France cooperated in setting up escape routes for Allied air crews who had been shot down.

The Red Orchestra

The largest spy network, and one of the most successful, was probably the Red Orchestra. Many of its most important members already had experience in secret activity because they were communists, and communist parties had often been illegal in pre-war Europe. The Red Orchestra did not report to the British SOE but instead sent its information to the Soviet Union.

The Red Orchestra had agents in France, Belgium, and the Netherlands. But what made it unique was that it also had a substantial network in Germany itself. In some ways, the Red Orchestra resembled other resistance networks. It distributed anti-Nazi pamphlets and posters, helped fugitives escape from the Gestapo (the German secret police), and even engaged in small-scale sabotage of war industry. Amazingly, however, it did these things in Germany.

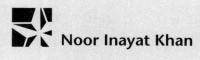 **Noor Inayat Khan**

One SOE agent who has become famous is Noor Inayat Khan, the daughter of an Indian father and an American mother, who was born in Russia but raised in France. Escaping to England when Germany conquered France, she volunteered to be an SOE agent. She parachuted back into France in June 1943 and became a radio operator for an intelligence network in Paris. The network was destroyed by a Gestapo raid just after Khan arrived; she was the only member not captured. Instead of escaping to England, as she could have, she stayed in Paris. For the next three months, she handled almost all the radio work from Paris to England. Several times she was almost captured, such as when a German soldier inspected her suitcase-carried radio transmitter on the subway. She convinced him it was part of a movie projector. But in October, an informer betrayed her to the Gestapo. Arrested and tortured, she refused to reveal any information. After an escape attempt, Khan was kept in solitary confinement, chained to a wall, for ten months. Eventually, she was transferred to the concentration camp at Dachau in southern Germany, where she was executed at the age of thirty.

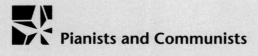

Pianists and Communists

The Red Orchestra received its name from the Gestapo, the Nazi agents who hunted it. The secret radio transmitters used in World War II, like old-fashioned telegraphs, had keys that were pressed to tap out a message. The women and men who sent these messages were known as "pianists" because they "played the keys," and the radio sets themselves were called "pianos." So the Gestapo called a network of spies an "orchestra." Just like real pianists, every radio operator's touch was different, like a signature, and an experienced listener could recognize a sender from his or her touch.

The "red" part of the Red Orchestra's name came from the fact that the network reported to the Communist Soviet Union, whose flag was a brilliant red. Thus communists are often called "reds." (This is also why the army of the Soviet Union was called the "Red Army.")

Much of the Red Orchestra's work, however, and what it is mostly remembered for today, was in intelligence activities. It concentrated mostly on giving the Soviet Union an accurate, day-to-day picture of the German forces. Between 1940 and 1943, the members of the Red Orchestra sent about 1,500 radio messages back to the Soviet Union. For a time, one of its sources was an intelligence officer in the German air force. In August 1942, the Gestapo arrested about 100 Red Orchestra members and tortured them to make them reveal information about the network. Germany then tried and executed many of them, a result that was guaranteed by the fact that Hitler took a personal interest in the procedures.

Eavesdropping on the enemy

The most important and dependable source of intelligence in World War II was not spies but the interception of secret messages sent by the enemy. This was true both in Europe and the Pacific.

Japan's codes broken

In 1940, even before the United States went to war, American experts broke the code, called the Purple Code, used by the Japanese government to communicate with its ambassadors and other diplomats around the world. Japan never discovered that the code had been broken and continued to use the same code, which the Americans continued to intercept, until 1945. These diplomatic messages gave a good picture of Japanese intentions in general, though not of Japanese military or naval plans. However, the Allies learned *German* military secrets from these messages because Japanese diplomats in Germany used the Purple Code to send reports to the Japanese government, including information about new German weapons and how effective the Allied bombing of Germany was.

By the spring of 1942, the United States could also read many of the most important Japanese navy codes. Beginning a year later, the Americans also began to break the codes used by the Japanese army. The United States called the system of breaking and reading Japanese military and naval codes Magic.

Magic influenced the outcome of the war in the Pacific in both large and small ways. The Japanese probably lost hundreds of ships because Magic intercepts (intercepted and decoded messages) were used to send American submarines to sink them.

The most significatn use was at the Battle of Midway in June 1942, considered the turning point of the Pacific war. (Midway is described in Chapter 4.) Partly because Magic revealed the Japanese attack plan, the outnumbered American aircraft carriers won a decisive victory.

In April 1943, Admiral Isoroku Yamamoto, Japan's most prominent naval commander, who had planned the attack on Pearl Harbor, was flying to the island of Bougainville in the South Pacific. The Japanese transmitted, in code, the exact route and time of his flight. A squadron of American fighter planes, specially outfitted with extra gas tanks for this mission, waited for Yamamoto's plane and shot it down, killing him.

German Code Breaking

The Germans were also successful at breaking codes. During parts of the Battle of the Atlantic, the German navy was reading decoded British naval messages that were being used to direct convoys of cargo ships from America to Britain. The Germans sent packs of submarines to intercept and destroy the ships.

The American Black Code, named after the color of its binder, was stolen by the Germans in August 1941, before American entry into the war. This code was used by the military experts (called attachés) in U.S. embassies. Knowledge of the Black Code gave the Germans a strategic advantage in the battles of North Africa. (See Chapter 3.) For many months, German General Erwin Rommel, the famous "Desert Fox," knew everything about British military plans because they were discussed with the American military attaché in the Egyptian capital of Cairo. In July 1942, the British captured some German documents that gave away the source of the German knowledge, and America changed the code.

The Code Talkers

One of the most successful codes in World War II was also one of the simplest. Beginning at the battle of Guadalcanal and continuing through many campaigns in the Pacific, some battlefield messages were transmitted by Native American soldiers speaking the Navajo language. The Navajo language is very complex and it was estimated that at the time there were less than ten non-native speakers who could understand the language. A relatively simple code was created using Navajo words. Since the code relied more on translation than on coding and decoding, orders could be sent and understood much more quickly and were as safe as if they had been put into an elaborate code.

Ultra: Breaking the German code

The vast ocean distances of the Pacific meant that both the Americans and Japanese relied on radio messages, which can be intercepted by the enemy's radios. In Europe, the Germans could communicate by telephone and telegraph (land lines), which at the time were more difficult to intercept than radio messages. The Germans could also use messengers traveling by train or car. Even in Europe, however, orders to ships or submarines had to be by radio. As the war continued, sabotage of land lines and the bombing of railroads increased German reliance on radio messages.

Unknown to the Germans, using land lines or messengers was the only sure way of keeping their communications secret. Germany developed its code long before the war and military intelligence agents from Poland, France, and Britain had been working to break the code since before the war. An anti-Nazi German helped the allies break the code by turning over key information to the French.

The organization that decoded, evaluated, and distributed German messages was called Ultra. Its headquarters at Bletchley Park in the English countryside was called the Government Code and Cipher School. The staff at Bletchley Park included mathematicians from nearby Oxford and Cambridge Universities. One of them, Max Norman, designed the world's first electronic computer, which was built at Bletchley specifically to help break the German codes.

The Germans used an encoding machine called Enigma that looked like a typewriter. Using information from the intelligence agents, the code breakers at Bletchley reconstructed a version of an Enigma machine, but this alone did not break the German codes. Special gears inside the Enigma allowed trillions of possible code combinations, and the codebreakers at Bletchley had to figure out which combination was being used for each message. And they had to do it quickly enough for it to be useful. The person sending the message from the Enigma machine had to let the person receiving it know how to decode it, so at the start of each message was a key. The keys established a pattern that the mathematicians at Bletchly could use to break the coded messages.

For most of the war, the Allies could decode many German radio transmissions. Eventually, they could be decoded so rapidly that Allied generals knew their contents as quickly as the German generals to whom they were addressed. The Americans and British often knew exactly what the Germans would do. Probably the most important example was during the last stages of the Battle of Normandy, in August 1944. Hitler ordered a surprise counteroffensive centered on the town of Mortain and committed all available armored divisions to this attack. But the Allies knew about this plan and positioned their own armored divisions to stop it. The German defeat at Mortain opened the way for the Allied breakout from Normandy and across France to the German border.

Navajo code talkers on Guadalcanal. *(Reproduced by permission of Archive Photos, Inc.)*

The Germans did not know that any Enigma messages could be read, and the Allies took extraordinary precautions to prevent them from finding out. Sometimes the Allies did not act on secret information because that would have alerted the Germans that their code had been broken. When the British warned the Soviet Union that Germany was about to invade, they did not tell the Soviets that this information had come from reading top-secret German messages. Like Richard Sorge's similar warning (described earlier in this chapter), it was not believed.

Science and secret weapons

Bletchley's computer was only one example of the greatly increased role of science in World War II. Perhaps the most important scientific development was radar, originated by the British. Secret work on radar was conducted beginning in 1935, and the first radar station on the coast was ready two years later. By the time of the Battle of Britain in 1940, there was a chain of 50 radar stations operating on the coasts of England. These stations gave the British a vital early warning of the number, direction, speed, and altitude of the attacking German planes. This knowledge allowed the outnumbered British to send planes from other areas to defend that day's targets. (The Battle of Britain is described in Chapter 2.)

But scientists everywhere were working on the same idea, and the Germans soon had radar too. Radar technology kept improving throughout the war. At first, radar required large sensing devices (dishes) mounted on towers. Eventually, instruments were made small enough to fit into planes, allowing bombers to hit targets they could not see and letting fighter planes find and attack bombers at night. Special British planes had radar that spotted submarines 30 miles away. Another development based on the same principle as radar was the proximity fuse for artillery shells. The fuse caused antiaircraft shells to explode when they came near their target, destroying planes even if they weren't hit. The British were using these to shoot down V-1s in August 1944, but the Germans never developed this technology.

Hitler's secret weapons: The V-1 and V-2

The V-1 was a pilotless jet plane that could travel a maximum of about 250 miles, reaching speeds of 375 miles an hour, about the same as the fastest regular fighter planes of that time. It made a buzzing sound, and Londoners named them buzz bombs. When the buzzing stopped, it meant the V-1 had run out of fuel—making it fall to earth and detonate the nearly one ton of explosives that it carried. The V-1 caused greater damage than regular bombs because the angle at which it fell caused more of the force of the explosion to remain near the surface instead of underground.

The first V-1s Germany launched against England on June 12, 1944, a few days after the Normandy invasion, catapulted from portable ramps on the coast of France. The V-1s

V-2 rocket in flight.
(Reproduced by permission of AP/Wide World Photos)

were not accurate enough to be aimed against specific targets. Instead, their target was anywhere in the city of London.

A total of 35,000 V-1s were produced, and more than 9,000 were fired at London. About a third of these were defective and never reached their targets or were shot down by British fighter planes and antiaircraft guns. Because they still exploded when they hit the ground, it was paramount that they be destroyed over the countryside before they reached the city. Before long, the Allied armies in northern France pushed the Germans away from the coast and the V-1s could no longer reach London. About 10,000 were fired at the Belgian port of Antwerp after the Allies captured it in September 1944. Altogether about 2,500 V-1s exploded in London, the same number as in Antwerp.

The V-2 was another type of German bomb. It was a 50-foot-long rocket powered by liquid fuel that was launched straight up and then flew at more than 2,000 miles per hour.

The V-1 and V-2 were weapons meant to terrorize civilians.

This is faster than the speed of sound, so people on the ground could not hear the missile coming before it landed. The lack of any warning made it especially frightening. The V-2 also caused many people to be blinded because shattered window glass flew into their eyes before they could raise their arms to protect their faces.

The Germans fired the first V-2s at England in early September 1944. Because their development had been so rushed, many were defective, with up to 25 percent crashing immediately after launch. More than half of the rest disintegrated as they came to earth, but the explosives they carried would still explode. Although some radio-controlled correction of its course was possible, the V-2 was hardly more accurate than the V-1.

About 3,200 V-2s were launched during the war, more than half at Antwerp. They killed a total of about 15,000 people, about 2,500 of them in London, and injured perhaps 50,000. The Allies finally captured the German's last launching sites in March 1945.

Both the V-1 and V-2 caused extensive damage to homes and other buildings. But because of their lack of accuracy, they had very limited military value. As used in World War II, they were weapons meant to terrorize civilians.

Jet planes

Jet engines allow planes to fly much faster and higher than propeller planes. The pilotless V-1 used a jet engine, and the German air force also developed jet-powered planes for combat. The first German jet had its test flight just before the war began, in 1939. But the project was not considered high priority, probably because Hitler and most German generals were convinced the war would be a short one and long-term projects would not be ready in time. Later, it seemed more important to devote Germany's limited resources to producing more tanks and submarines.

In the summer of 1944, however, jet-powered German fighters began to appear in the air battles over France. By this time, the Allies had complete control of the skies, and each jet was vastly outnumbered by Allied planes. The Allies also

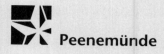

Peenemünde

V-1 and V-2 were not the official German designations for these weapons; they were nicknames used in German radio broadcasts meant to encourage German civilians and frighten the Allies. The "V" stood for the German word *Vergeltung,* which means "retribution" or "revenge." The idea was that these weapons would pay back the Allies for the devastation their bombers had caused in Germany.

The V-1 and V-2 might have been ready earlier and played a much greater part in the war if the British had not learned of the projects from spies. The jet-powered flying bomb (the V-1) was developed by the German air force at a secret base on Peenemünde, an island in the Baltic Sea. At the other end of the island, the German army was working on a rocket project, which became the V-2. The weapons were built and tested on the island, and the scientists and engineers running the projects were also on Peenemünde.

In August 1943, a giant force of 330 British bombers attacked the small island and caused severe damage to the weapons projects, especially the V-2. Several hundred technicians were killed, and construction of the weapons had to be shifted to other locations. The debuts of both the V-1 and V-2 were delayed by at least several months.

attacked the jets on the ground. Jets require much longer runways, and so it was easy to find their bases. Germany also had a severe shortage of aviation fuel. In fact, half the 2,000 jets Germany built by the end of the war never flew because there was not enough fuel. The fuel shortage also made it impossible to properly train pilots to fly them. In any case, British and American jets were also beginning to fly and would soon have become available if needed to challenge the Germans.

The atomic bomb

The largest scientific project of World War II—and the most secret—was the building of the atomic bomb. It is also the military development that has had the greatest impact on the world since then. But the bomb played a small role in the war

It is ironic that the bomb was used against Japan, since the main reason the Allies built the bomb was that they were afraid Germany would produce one first.

itself because it was completed only at the very end. By that time, Germany had surrendered, and the Allies dropped the bomb on an almost-defeated Japan. (The use of the atomic bomb against Japan is described in Chapter 15.) It is ironic that the bomb was used against Japan, since the main reason the Allies built the bomb was that they were afraid Germany would produce one first. Many of the scientists who built the bomb were refugees from Hitler's Germany who hated and feared the Nazis. (See box on p. 366.) They also believed that Germany, with its outstanding scientists, would have a head start.

The German bomb project

By the beginning of World War II, every top physicist in the world knew the theory of atomic weapons. But no one was sure that a bomb could actually be built. And even if it were possible, the process might be so expensive and time-consuming that it was not worth trying. The German scientists who explored the possibility of building an atomic bomb—including Werner Heisenberg, one of the greatest physicists of the century—made some vital errors in their theoretical calculations. These errors made them think that building a bomb would be more difficult and expensive than it really was. Because of this, the Germans never considered the project a top priority. There was no single agency in charge to ensure that it got the people, equipment, and money it needed. When Germany surrendered in May 1945, its atomic weapons program was at about the same stage that the Allies had reached in 1940—before the American program had even started.

The science behind the bomb

When a certain kind of uranium is bombarded with neutrons (one of the particles that make up the atom), its nucleus (center) splits in two, releasing energy. It also frees other neutrons, which in turn collide with nearby uranium atoms, causing them to split. If there is enough of this uranium "fuel," the process continues until all the uranium atoms have been split, something that takes only a fraction of a second. The result is a nuclear chain reaction that releases previously unimaginable amounts of energy—energy that can take the form of an explosive blast.

The particular type of uranium needed, U-235, exists only in tiny quantities in uranium ore dug from the earth. Separating the U-235 from the rest of the uranium is a very complicated and expensive process. In fact, in 1940 no one was sure how to do it in large quantities. The German scientists miscalculated how much U-235 would be needed. They thought a chain reaction, and therefore a bomb, would require about two tons of U-235. This meant that building an atomic bomb, if it were possible at all, would take many years and be incredibly expensive. Since Germany's political and military leaders all expected the war to be short, they concluded that even an all-out effort to build an atomic weapon would not succeed in time to make a difference.

The error the German team made was not a small one. At the beginning of the war, in April 1940, two refugees from Nazi Germany working at the University of Birmingham in England, Otto Frisch and Rudolf Peierls, were studying the same problem. They calculated that a much smaller amount of U-235 was needed for a chain reaction: not two tons, but less than one pound. Frisch and Peierls then sent a letter explaining that "a radioactive superbomb" could be produced to the British government's leading scientific adviser. Although, like the Germans, the British first thought such a project would probably take too many resources, they appointed a committee of scientists to recommend action. The group studied the problem for more than a year and came to the conclusion that a bomb could be built in two years and that work should begin immediately. Late in 1941, Britain launched the Directorate of Tube Alloys, giving the project charged with building an atomic bomb a name that purposely made it sound as if it were studying new and better metals to make pipes.

Since Germany's political and military leaders all expected the war to be short, they concluded that even an all-out effort to build an atomic weapon would not succeed in time to make a difference.

The Manhattan Project

At first the British made greater progress than the United States on building an atom bomb and—although no one knew it—much greater progress than the Germans. But in June 1942, six months after the United States entered the war, President Franklin D. Roosevelt gave the go-ahead for a full-scale American atomic project. The Americans soon caught up with and then passed the British.

Refugees Play Key Role in Creating Atomic Bomb

The reason Otto Frisch and Rudolf Peierls were working on atomic theory in early 1940 was because the British did not trust enemy scientists, even those who had fled from Germany to escape the Nazis, to work on military projects like radar.

Luckily for the Allies, the British altered this position. Many of the scientists responsible for the atomic bomb were originally from countries fighting the Allies, including Germany, Hungary, and Italy. A large number were Jews, forced to leave Europe by Nazi hatred and persecution.

In fact, the first steps in the American project to build the bomb came because of a letter President Franklin D. Roosevelt received in October 1939 from a Jewish refugee from Germany. The refugee was Albert Einstein, the most famous scientist in the world, and his letter warned Roosevelt of the possibility that Nazi Germany might be building atomic weapons and urged the United States to study the issue.

When the Manhattan Project got under way, foreign scientists played a crucial part. Enrico Fermi, who had won a Nobel Prize for his work on radioactivity in Italy before the war, led the team that produced the first self-sustaining nuclear chain reaction in Chicago in December 1942. Hans Bethe from Germany and Leo Szilard from Hungary were among the most important of the many anti-Hitler Europeans working on the atom bomb.

The organization that controlled all aspects of research, construction, and testing had the deceptive name of the Manhattan District of the Army Corps of Engineers, and became known as the Manhattan Project. The project cost $2.5 billion, an enormous amount at that time.

Eventually, 120,000 people were involved with the Manhattan Project. The Americans built secret factories in Oak Ridge, Tennessee, to work on separating U-235 from uranium. Since no one was sure which of three possible methods was the best way to do this, the project tried all three, despite the expense. In addition, another huge facility was built in Hanford, Washington, to produce plutonium, another element that scientists correctly thought could be used as fuel for an atomic bomb. In both places, workers and their families lived in newly built housing, surrounded by fences and armed guards to keep the work secret.

J. Robert Oppenheimer, with characteristic pork-pie hat, and General Leslie Groves inspect twisted metal, remains of an atomic bomb test, July 1945.
(Reproduced by permission of Archive Photos, Inc.)

The heart of the Manhattan Project, however, was at Los Alamos, New Mexico. There were gathered 4,000 physicists, mathematicians, chemists, engineers, skilled metalworkers—experts in every aspect of the complex process of designing and building the new weapon. The head of the project was J. Robert Oppenheimer, himself a brilliant young physicist, who somehow managed to keep all the different personalities working together.

"I am become Death, the destroyer of worlds."

On July 16, 1945, in the desert near Alamogordo, New Mexico, the first atomic explosion in history sent a blinding light through the predawn darkness. As Oppenheimer watched the test, he thought of words from the Bhagavad-Gita, a Hindu holy book: "I am become Death, the destroyer of worlds." Within a month, America dropped two atomic bombs on Japan, killing 120,000 people and obliterating the cities of Hiroshima and Nagasaki.

Art, Entertainment, and Propaganda

16

For a long time it has been thought that soldiers fight better when they believe they are fighting for a good reason. So every government in World War II wanted to convince its soldiers that they were risking their lives to protect their country—and their own families—from being conquered by a cruel enemy, that they had been forced to go to war to defend themselves, and that the world would be a much better place after the war than it had been before.

The nature of World War II also made it important for each government to rally its civilian population at home around these same causes. This was because World War II was a total war, in which victory depended on devoting all the resources of a country to the war effort. (Other aspects of total war are described in Chapter 8.)

The most obvious example of devoting resources concerned jobs. Millions of women in the United States and Britain worked outside the home for the first time during World War II. Both women and men were doing jobs, such as working in factories, that were harder, dirtier, noisier, and often more dangerous than anything they had experienced

Enemy communications were always described as "propaganda," while one's own side offered "information" or "news."

before. If people believed that their work helped preserve their country's freedom, they would work harder, with fewer complaints, and do a better job. The same was true for all the other hardships and inconveniences that the war brought, such as crowded housing, product shortages, and, of course, separation from loved ones in the armed forces. In countries like Britain and Germany, the civilians also had to endure deadly air raids. All these things were easier to tolerate if people believed in the goals of the war.

Propaganda

Convincing people that their cause is righteous is the job of propaganda. Propaganda is information, usually officially communicated by the government, that is aimed at large numbers of people to influence their opinions. Originally the word applied whether the information was true or false. By the time of World War II, however, propaganda usually implied that the information was one-sided, distorted, or even an outright lie. Enemy communications were always described as "propaganda," while one's own side offered "information" or "news."

In countries that Germany had defeated and taken over (occupied), the governments did not control the information the people received. Instead, there were two opposite sets of messages, one from the Germans and one from the Allies (the countries fighting Germany). There was also information from resistance movements, secret and illegal networks that opposed the Germans in each conquered country (see Chapter 6).

The Allies reached the people of these occupied countries mainly by radio, especially the programs of the BBC, the British Broadcasting Corporation. The BBC broadcast in twenty-three languages. Millions of Europeans listened every night, even though they risked severe punishment if they were caught. The BBC developed the best reputation that any source of information can have, especially in wartime: people believed that it told the truth. This was because the BBC rarely exaggerated Allied victories or underplayed their defeats.

The BBC did not need to explain the purpose of the war when it broadcast to countries under German occupation. Getting rid of the Germans and restoring their independence was enough for most people. This became increasingly true as the occupation became harsher and living conditions worse. (Life in occupied Europe is described in Chapter 6.) Instead, the BBC's message to those countries was that the war was continuing, that Germany would eventually be defeated, and that people who cooperated with the Germans would later pay for their actions.

German foreign propaganda

At the beginning of World War II, German political and military leaders were sure the war would be short. Because of this, they did not try to convince citizens of occupied countries that a German victory was a good thing. Instead, they just wanted to convince them that a German victory was certain, that there was no point in resisting, and that they should cooperate with the German occupation.

Later, when it became clear that the war would be a long one, some German authorities wanted to persuade people to actively support the German side. Germany was depicted as building a New Order and creating a united Europe. According to German propaganda, Germany was defending European civilization against the Communist Soviet Union. (Communism is a political and economic system based on government —not private—ownership of most businesses.) Posters showed a handsome German soldier protecting a helpless child.

A few people responded to these ideas, as well as to German propaganda that blamed the war on the Jews. But for the most part, these efforts came too late to have much effect.

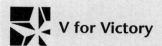 **V for Victory**

The British used the capital letter V as a symbol for "victory." Throughout German-occupied Europe, a quickly painted V on a wall was used to show defiance of the Germans and faith that the Allies would eventually win the war. People everywhere flashed the V sign by holding up their first two fingers, a gesture made famous by Winston Churchill, the British prime minister (head of the government).

But how could the BBC use the V for victory symbol on the radio, in broadcasts to occupied Europe? In Morse code, v is three dots and a dash. Someone realized that the opening four notes of Beethoven's Fifth Symphony, one of the most famous works of classical music, fit this pattern. Soon Beethoven's "da-da-da-DUM" was heard whenever the BBC broadcast to Europe, becoming the best-known use of classical music in the war—even though it was only four notes.

No matter what they saw on posters, hungry people blamed the Germans for stealing their country's food.

Even if it had been more skillful, German propaganda could not have overcome the reality of the occupation. Germany was using each conquered country's wealth for itself. No matter what they saw on posters, hungry people blamed the Germans for stealing their country's food. They knew they were forced to work harder for longer hours and less pay. They knew they could not speak freely, read what they wished, or vote.

Psychological warfare: Speaking to the enemy

Just as each country tried to convince its own people that it was necessary to fight, it tried to convince the enemy's people of the opposite. Each side used radio broadcasts, leaflets dropped from planes, and other methods to try to demoralize enemy troops and civilians, to try to discourage them and weaken their determination to fight. This was often called psychological warfare, and its backers claimed it would make a major difference in the war. Most historians now believe these efforts had very little effect.

One example of psychological warfare was Germany's use of a pro-Nazi Englishman named William Joyce on their radio. For years, Joyce told the British troops that they were losing the war, that they were fighting for no reason, that their leaders were getting rich while they died. The British troops called him Lord Haw Haw because of his exaggerated upper-class accent, and thought he was funny. There is no evidence that anyone ever believed anything he said. Even so, Britain tried Joyce and hanged him for treason after the war.

American troops in Europe often listened to an all-night program on the German radio that played the latest jazz and swing recordings. They called the show's host Axis Sally. (The Axis was the name for Germany and the countries fighting on its side.) Axis Sally was really Mildred Gillars, an American who had worked as an actress in prewar Germany. In between records, she tried to demoralize the troops by talking about how the GIs (ordinary soldiers) must be lonely, how their wives and girlfriends back home were probably cheating on them. Sometimes she read the serial numbers of American soldiers who had been killed or captured. In one of her programs, aimed at the troops preparing for the invasion of France, she and other actors dramatized the death and horror that awaited them. Gillars was one of only twelve Americans convicted of treason for their actions during World War II. Sentenced to ten to thirty years in prison, she was paroled after serving twelve years.

One of the other Americans convicted of treason was also a radio propagandist for the enemy. She was Iva Toguri Ikoku, an American woman whose parents were Japanese. She was the best-known of several women who broadcast to Allied troops on Japanese radio, all of whom were called Tokyo Rose. Like Gillars, Tokyo Rose mixed popular music with talk that was supposed to demoralize her soldier audience. Just as with Gillars, the soldiers listened to the music and apparently ignored the talk. Ikoku served six years of her seven-year sentence and was later pardoned.

Mildred Gillars, also known as "Axis Sally," was convicted of treason for hosting an anti-Allied radio show broadcast from Germany during the war. *(Reproduced by permission of AP/Wide World Photos)*

German propaganda at home

Although German propaganda did not have much impact on enemy soldiers or the people of occupied Europe, it was much more effective when directed at Germans. Propaganda had been an important tool for the Nazis both before and after Adolf Hitler came to power in 1933. The man most responsible was Joseph Goebbels (pronounced Ger-bulls). Goebbels developed the technique of the big lie, repeating the same outlandish accusations again and again until people believed them. It was he who arranged that the Nazis' uniformed parades, banners, posters, speeches, and songs all worked together to produce a powerful effect. Goebbels had also organized the book burnings in the first days of the Nazi government. Books written by Jews, by opponents of the Nazis, or by anyone whose ideas the Nazis hated were publicly thrown on bonfires.

Goebbels understood the power of radio and used it in a way that no one had ever done before.

But most of all, Goebbels became a master at using two relatively new ways of presenting information and entertainment: radio and film. As an increasingly powerful member of the government, whose official title was Minister (Secretary) of Public Enlightenment and Propaganda, he controlled all radio broadcasts and film production in Germany. By the beginning of the war, about 70 percent of German households owned a radio. Never before had a government been able to reach such a large proportion of its people at one time. Goebbels understood the power of radio and used it in a way that no one had ever done before.

Nazi Germany's films

Goebbels also understood the importance of film. Movie theaters in Germany never closed down during the war, even after 1943, when the government ordered that museums, concert halls, and sports arenas be shut down. In cities where Allied bombing had destroyed the available theaters, the government arranged special outdoor showings.

Some of the films that Goebbels sponsored before the war have remained famous. Chief among these were the films of Leni Riefenstahl, a young actress turned movie director. Her *Triumph of the Will* was a documentary that celebrated the Nazi Party's rally in Nuremberg, a city in southern Germany, in 1934. Riefenstahl filmed the massed Nazis marching in intricate formations at torchlight ceremonies. Even today, when everyone watching the film knows that it glorifies a political movement that led to mass murder, it still has the ability to stir and frighten audiences. Similarly, Riefenstahl's film on the 1936 Olympic Games, held in Berlin, glorified youth, strength, and athletic excellence—but also Hitler and the Nazis. Almost every documentary film made about sports competitions, especially later Olympic Games, was strongly influenced by Riefenstahl.

Entertainment and lies

As these examples show, Goebbels knew that artistic works were often the most effective propaganda. He also understood that most people did not want to be reminded of the war every minute of their lives, that they sometimes

Film director Leni Reifenstahl created *Triumph of the Will*, a documentary that celebrated the Nazi party and its leader Adolf Hitler.
(Reproduced by permission of the Kobal Collection)

needed to relax. He knew entertainment was necessary, and he tried to cloak his political message in entertaining forms.

Goebbels' propaganda machine had a major success with *Jud Süss* ("The Jew Süss"). This supposedly historical movie was intended to stir anti-Jewish hatred by telling the story of a Jew who became an important adviser to a German duke in the early eighteenth century. The movie portrays Süss

Documentaries, Newsreels, and Censorship

Once World War II started, Germany produced a series of full-length documentary films showing the German army's early victories, with titles such as *Victory in the West*, which showed the defeat of France. The German army even created propaganda companies that went into combat with regular troops and filmed each campaign. There were also eighty "war artists," painters who produced "combat art."

Like all countries, Germany also produced newsreels, short films about the week's current events that movie theaters showed with the main film. They were an important source of pictorial information before television. Although in countries like the United States newsreels were made by private film companies instead of the government, they still reported the "official" government war news—since the military controlled all information in war zones.

Government censorship of news affected all war reporting, not just films. The stories that reporters sent to their newspapers had to be read and cleared by military censors before they could be printed. Everyone agreed that some information had to be kept secret—for example, the location of Allied troops or ships could not be revealed without endangering them. But the military censors often went much further than this. They killed any stories that they thought might hurt the morale of soldiers or civilians. For the first several years of the war, for example, no American newspaper or magazine could publish a photograph of a dead American soldier. No one denied that Americans were dying in the war. But the government thought that seeing dead bodies on a beach would weaken American support for the war.

as a rapist who plots with his fellow Jews to take over a city. The film apparently succeeded because German audiences accepted it as dramatic entertainment rather than propaganda. It was shown throughout occupied Europe in an attempt to persuade other countries to support the Germans' anti-Jewish actions. It was also shown to concentration camp guards.

Another historical drama—in fact, an epic—was *Kolberg,* a project that Goebbels insisted on completing even though it drained increasingly scarce resources. Thousands of real German soldiers—180,000, according to its director—were used in the film, made in the final years of the war. *Kolberg* tells the story

✶ Music and Literature

Governments did not rely just on films, radio, and other popular art forms to build support. They used literary and musical classics whenever they thought it might be useful. For example, the Russians distributed 500,000 copies of Leo Tolstoy's great nineteenth-century Russian novel *War and Peace* to the people of Leningrad while that city was surrounded by the Germans and its citizens were starving and freezing to death. *War and Peace* is about an earlier invasion of Russia and how the Russian people resisted and eventually defeated the forces of French Emperor Napoleon Bonaparte in 1812. (The siege of Leningrad is described in Chapter 3.)

The ordeal of the people of Leningrad was also the inspiration for the best-known piece of classical music written during World War II. This was the Seventh Symphony, also known as the Leningrad Symphony, by the Russian composer Dmitry Shostakovich. Composed in the surrounded city in 1941 and first performed the following year, it soon became the most played piece of classical music in the world, both in concerts and on the radio. Although today it is not considered one of Shostakovich's better compositions, at the time it moved listeners with its dramatic and stirring melodies. For Soviet listeners, it was a musical tribute to the heroism of Leningrad's citizens. In the United States, the piece was a way of showing support for and a sense of unity with America's Soviet ally.

Germany also used classical music to stress patriotism, especially the nineteenth-century operas of Richard Wagner, which often use stories from German folk tales or the mythology of the ancient Germanic tribes. For these reasons, and because Wagner had been strongly prejudiced against Jews, his music was a particular favorite of Adolf Hitler.

of how the people of a German town resisted French Emperor Napoleon Bonaparte's army in 1807 until the arrival of a German army saved it at the last minute. Obviously Goebbels hoped the film would inspire the German people to resist the invading Allies. The film opened in bomb-devastated Berlin at the end of January 1945—just as the Allied armies were preparing to advance into the heart of Germany.

Other popular German films of the period were made purely for entertainment. The most successful German film of the war years—in fact, the most successful German film ever

During the war, Hollywood provided all its films for free showings to troops overseas and sailors aboard ships; it was the only industry that gave its products to the government.

up to that time—was *Die Grosse Liebe* ("The Great Love"), released in 1942 and seen by 28 million people, more than one-third of the population. The film, about the stormy romance and marriage between a German singer, played by Swedish star Zarah Leander, and an air force fighter pilot, was set against a war background. In it, Leander sang a song called "I Know Someday a Miracle Will Happen," which became a kind of theme song for German civilians during the war years. Another extremely popular production, made in 1943, was *Münchausen*, a color film depicting the fantastic adventures of Baron Münchausen, including a balloon trip to the moon.

American films

The American film industry was by far the biggest in the world, both before and during the war. In 1940, it produced more than 500 feature films. During the war, Hollywood provided all its films for free showings to troops overseas and sailors aboard ships; it was the only industry that gave its products to the government. But Hollywood could afford to be generous with the government: Americans were going to the movies like never before. In 1944, nearly 100 million tickets were sold every week in the United States—at a time when the U.S. population was about 130 million.

Nonfiction films

Before the United States entered the war, the film industry formed the Motion Picture Committee Cooperating for National Defense to distribute and show, without charge, national defense films made by the government. These films included so-called recruitment films made by the different branches of the armed services used to persuade people to enlist. It also made *Women in Defense,* written by First Lady Eleanor Roosevelt and narrated by the movie star Katharine Hepburn, which encouraged women to work in defense factories or to join the armed services.

After Japan attacked Pearl Harbor in December 1941 and the United States entered the war, the government produced documentaries on various aspects of the war. Typical examples include *The Fighting Lady* (the "life story" of an aircraft carrier), *With the Marines at Tarawa,* and *The Liberation of Rome.*

One important American documentary series was *Why We Fight,* seven films produced by the U.S. Army Signal Corps. The series was conceived by Frank Capra, the star Hollywood director whose films, like *It's a Wonderful Life,* are still shown. Capra himself directed the first film in the series, *Prelude to War.* The purpose of the series was to explain the events in Europe and Asia leading up to the war, the kind of governments the United States was fighting, and the purposes of the war. Originally, the audience was supposed to be limited to members of the armed forces. When President Franklin D. Roosevelt saw *Prelude to War* at a special White House screening, however, he said that "every man, woman, and child must see this film." Despite heavy promotion, these films were not box-office favorites, though apparently American soldiers liked them more than they did most war films.

Hollywood and the war in Europe

The great majority of American films made during World War II were fiction. They were supposed to be entertaining, and they were supposed to make money. In 1940, 95 percent of Hollywood films had nothing to do with political themes or the war. The big American studios (film companies) earned a significant part of their profits by showing their films in foreign countries, where, just as today, American films were very popular. Fear of offending foreign governments, which might strike back by banning a studio's films, was one reason that American films usually did not address controversial world issues.

Even so, even before World War II began a few films dealt with the rising threat of Nazism. One of the most important was *Confessions of a Nazi Spy,* released early in 1939 and directed by the German-born Anatole Litvak. A fictionalized version of the activities of a real German spy ring operating in the United States, the movie was the first openly anti-Nazi American film. It was a major commercial hit, but it was banned in Germany and countries that supported Germany— or that were afraid of offending it.

More typical in some ways was 1938's *The Lady Vanishes,* which, although it was a British movie directed by Alfred Hitch-

Fear of offending foreign governments was one reason that American films usually did not address controversial world issues.

A scene from the 1941 film *Sergeant York,* one of many Hollywood films that seemed to be aimed at winning support for entering the war.
(Reproduced by permission of The Kobal Collection)

cock, was very popular in the United States. The bad guys in that film are from some unnamed country apparently in central Europe. However, the message of the movie, that ignoring evil in foreign countries will never bring safety, is clearly referring to Germany.

During the more than two years between the beginning of the war and the attack on Pearl Harbor, many Hollywood films seemed to be aimed at winning support for United States entry into the war. *Sergeant York* was based on the life of Alvin York, an American soldier who became America's greatest war hero fighting the Germans in 1918 during World War I. The story revolves around York's early opposition to serving in the army because killing violates his religious beliefs. But York is finally convinced that fighting a war is sometimes the only way to prevent even more killing. An American audience seeing *Sergeant York* when it was released in 1941 would almost certainly have understood this message to refer to World War II as well.

Even more obvious was *A Yank in the RAF,* which told about an American pilot who joined Britain's Royal Air Force to fight the Nazis. The film was made by 20th Century-Fox, whose top executive, Darryl F. Zanuck, was strongly in favor of American entry into the war.

Support for allies

A Yank in the RAF illustrates one of the most common themes in Hollywood films of the period: creating sympathy for the countries fighting Germany, especially Britain, as a way of building support for the war. This theme continued even after the United States entered the war.

Perhaps the most effective and certainly the most popular pro-British movie was *Mrs. Miniver,* the 1942 film that

Jews and Hollywood

Many film historians say that one reason Hollywood hesitated so long in making anti-Nazi films was because many important leaders of the industry were Jews. This seems surprising, because Jews had been the Nazis' special target since the beginning, and every Jew had plenty of justification to oppose them.

For that very reason, however, Jews in Hollywood were afraid that they would be accused of trying to provoke the United States into entering the war against Germany. Men like the Warner brothers were worried that they would be accused of putting their feelings as Jews ahead of their duties as Americans—a difference that did not really exist. But this was the kind of accusation that was used to stir up anti-Jewish feelings in America. Similar accusations were made against Darryl F. Zanuck, head of 20th Century-Fox, for producing *A Yank in the RAF*. Unlike other important producers, however, Zanuck was not Jewish.

Even when Hollywood did make anti-Nazi films—in fact, even after the United States was at war with Germany and anti-Nazi films were expected—they tended to avoid any mention of the word "Jew." Although anyone who read a newspaper knew about the Nazis' special hatred of Jews, the American film industry almost always played it down during the war.

won five Academy Awards, including best picture. Set at the beginning of the war, it tells the story of an average English middle-class family (though, since they have two live-in servants, they probably would have seemed somewhat wealthier than average to American audiences). The film shows the increasing hardships and dangers of the war, including German bombing of their village. The title character, played by Academy Award-winning actress Greer Garson, displays quiet strength and determination, even capturing a downed German pilot. Each person in the village puts aside his or her own selfish concerns in an increasing sense of national unity. The final scene takes place in the badly damaged village church, after a heavy air raid that killed several people in the village, including a lovable old stationmaster, a choirboy, and the beautiful young bride of the Minivers' son (Teresa Wright, who also won an Oscar). The minister explains that these vic-

Claude Rains (in dark uniform), Humphrey Bogart (in trench coat), and Ingrid Bergman in a scene from the 1942 film *Casablanca*. *(Reproduced by permission of AP/Wide World Photos)*

tims are all part of the fight because this is a "people's war. It is our war. We *are* the fighters."

Mrs. Miniver was used as an example of the movies Hollywood should be making by the Office of War Information (OWI), the government agency created in June 1942 to oversee American propaganda efforts. The OWI was different from military censors, who kept information secret because they were worried it would hurt military and civilian morale. Instead, the OWI was more concerned with making sure that certain messages got into movies, books, and newspapers— messages like the one in *Mrs. Miniver*.

The British were not the only people that Hollywood idealized. Many American films portrayed the activities of resistance movements in different parts of Europe, often in a completely unrealistic way. The French resistance was a favorite theme, with the classic 1942 film *Casablanca*, starring Humphrey Bogart and Ingrid Bergman, being the most successful. *Casablanca* also included one of Hollywood's favorite character types of the war—the American (Bogart) who does not want to get involved, but who comes to see the need to put aside his personal desires and join with others to fight the Nazis.

In a single year, beginning in September 1942, Hollywood released five movies describing the resistance in Norway. One of them, *The Moon Is Down,* based on a book and play by leading American writer John Steinbeck, Hollywood bought for $300,000, a record amount at the time. It was expected to be a major hit, and prints were even dropped by parachute into German-occupied Norway.

The Moon Is Down was not a hit, probably because audiences were tired of seeing gloomy films about the war. But it did create a major controversy because it portrayed the German colonel in charge of the Norwegian town not as a violent brute but as a complicated man who was partly motivated by a desire to be respected and liked. Actually, although it was unusual to show a German officer this way, the "good German" was a common character in many American World War II films, especially those set before the war. The idea was that most German people had fallen under the spell of the Nazis but were themselves were not necessarily evil.

This attitude is not surprising, since there were many Germans who had fled Hitler—writers, directors, and actors—now working in Hollywood. One of these directors, Fritz Lang, had even been offered the top job in the German film industry by Goebbels in 1933, shortly after the Nazis came to power. Instead, Lang went to Hollywood.

The same is not true for portrayals of Japanese people in American movies. Almost without exception, the Japanese were shown as sneaky and dishonest, or as savages who enjoyed inflicting pain. Most historians believe that these differences can be explained by racist feelings toward the Japanese. (The treatment of Japanese Americans in the United States is described in Chapter 5.) Whether Hollywood helped create those feelings or simply reflected the way people already felt is impossible to know.

The "good German" was a common character in many American World War II films that seemed to reflect the idea that most German people had fallen under the spell of the Nazis but were themselves were not necessarily evil.

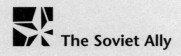

The Soviet Ally

Sometimes, showing an ally in an approving way was harder than attacking an enemy. For many years before the war, the United States had been on unfriendly terms with the Soviet Union. At the beginning of World War II, the Soviet Union signed a treaty with Nazi Germany, which outraged many Americans, and then it attacked its neighbor, Finland, which fought back bravely and won the support of most Americans.

After Germany invaded it, however, the Soviet Union had carried the heaviest burden of fighting Hitler's armies. The United States was sending huge amounts of supplies to help the Soviets. It was important to get the American public to support this action.

At President Franklin D. Roosevelt's direct request, in 1942 the Warner Brothers studio made a film version of Joseph E. Davies' book *Mission to Moscow*. Davies had been the American ambassador to the Soviet Union from 1936 to 1938, and both the book and the movie portrayed the Soviet Union and its leader Joseph Stalin as great champions of democracy. Stalin was in fact a brutal dictator, and the film's defense of his methods became a great embarrassment after the war.

Some films were embarrassing even at the time. *Song of Russia* used a love story between a famous American orchestra conductor and a young Russian pianist to paint a picture of a happy country where everyone sings and dances until the German invasion turns them into heroic fighters for freedom. Some audiences actually laughed out loud.

Other films made their point in less obvious ways. In *Action in the North Atlantic,* American merchant seamen risk their lives by sailing through submarine-infested waters to bring desperately needed supplies to Russia. By the end of the film, when Soviet planes appear overhead, the American sailors refer to them as "ours."

Combat films

Once the United States entered the war, Hollywood began turning out hundreds of features with a war theme. The new Tarzan movie had Nazis for the enemy, and Sherlock Holmes now hunted German spies in modern London. Even Donald Duck collected scrap metal for the war. At the same time, Hollywood never stopped making musicals, romantic comedies, and other films that had nothing to do with the war.

Some of them were far more popular than most war pictures—especially among the soldiers, who actually had to fight and considered most combat films unrealistic.

The earliest of these combat films was *Wake Island*, released in September 1942, less than nine months after the events it described. Dozens of others followed, depicting specific battles or particular branches of the armed services. *Action in the North Atlantic* portrayed the bravery and sacrifice of the sailors of the merchant marine. *The Fighting Seabees* was about the navy construction companies that built airfields on Pacific islands, often while fighting was still going on. *Destination Tokyo* was about submarines, *Sahara* and *The Immortal Sergeant* were set in the desert battles of North Africa, and *The Purple Heart* and *Thirty Seconds over Tokyo* were both about the American bombing raid on Tokyo in April 1942.

One of the best of these films was *Guadalcanal Diary*, released in late 1943. It was based on the best-selling book of the same name by Richard Tregaskis, a twenty-six-year-old reporter who was with the marines on Guadalcanal in August and September 1942. The book originated with the notes he wrote for his daily reports. Although his criticisms of the navy's failure to adequately supply the marines were censored by the military, the book and the movie both seemed to provide a realistic picture of the day-to-day experiences of combat troops, even though the film included invented scenes not found in the book.

War correspondents

The publication of *Guadalcanal Diary* made Richard Tregaskis famous, but he was only one of many well-known American war correspondents who reported on the war. For the first time, many of the correspondents were women. But they were not readily accepted: the women had to fight against the prejudices of top military and naval officers, whose permission was necessary to enter a war zone, as well as their own editors and publishers.

One of the most successful American correspondents in Nazi Germany before the war was Sigrid Schultz of the *Chicago Tribune*. She sometimes published under a false name

For the first time, many war correspondents were women.

so that the Nazis would not throw her out of Germany. Her articles gave American readers an idea of the ambitions and goals of the German leaders—who were not pleased. Hermann Göring, the second most important Nazi, called her the "dragon lady from Chicago." Schultz continued to report from Berlin, the German capital, for the first year of the war. She left Germany for a visit home in January 1941, and the Nazis refused to allow her to come back.

By reporting on war plans and preparations and covering war news from Berlin, Schultz helped open the door for other women reporters. But she did not travel with armies, sail on warships, or report on battles as an eyewitness.

Despite opposition, however, many women were soon doing just that. Helen Kirkpatrick, the London correspondent for the *Chicago Daily News,* covered the Blitz, the German air raids on London, riding through the city in ambulances and fire trucks. Later she accompanied Allied troops in North Africa, Italy, France, and Germany. In one famous story, she wrote an eyewitness account of gunfire erupting inside Notre Dame Cathedral in Paris during a service to celebrate the liberation of the French capital. Kirkpatrick became so popular that the *Daily News* featured her in promotions, including placing her picture on the sides of Chicago buses.

Some of the women correspondents reported from areas that were more difficult for reporters to cover than the European theater (area of operations). Sonia Tomara of the *New York Herald-Tribune,* for example, covered the China-Burma-India theater, flying in combat missions over the high mountains. The pictures of Margaret Bourke-White, one of a group of brilliant photographers for *Life* magazine, spanned many areas of the war, but she was one of the few Americans who covered the war in the Soviet Union.

Ernie Pyle and the GIs' war

The most famous American war correspondent was Ernie Pyle. Pyle was very successful at home, where almost 400 daily newspapers and 300 weeklies around the country carried his reports. He was respected by everyone in his profession, winning a Pulitzer Prize in 1944.

Besides these achievements, Pyle was unique in one respect. He was immensely popular with, and even loved by, the troops. Whenever a GI met a reporter, the most common question was, "Do you know Ernie Pyle?" In his early forties, Pyle was significantly older than typical GIs, but he often shared their hardships. His writing was not flashy, and his subjects were rarely glamorous. Perhaps because of this, many GIs felt that Pyle expressed what the war—their war—was really like.

Ernie Pyle's writing was not flashy, and his subjects were rarely glamorous. Perhaps because of this, many GIs felt that Pyle expressed what the war—their war—was really like.

Ernie Pyle working on a column. *(Reproduced by permission of Archive Photos, Inc.)*

Pyle was with the GIs through North Africa, Sicily, and Italy, and then in France from the Normandy beaches to the liberation of Paris. He returned home to America but then decided to go to the Pacific, to cover the war against Japan. Pyle said he was not seeking more fame or glory. "I'm going simply because there's a war on and I'm part of it," he said. "I'm going simply because I've got to, and I hate it." In other words, he felt very much like the GIs felt about the war. On April 18, 1945, Pyle was killed by Japanese fire on the little island of Ie Shima, near Okinawa. The GIs put up a wooden sign. Above Ernie Pyle's name and the date on which he died, they wrote: "At this spot, the 77th Infantry Division lost a buddy."

Willie and Joe

Another war correspondent who was extremely popular with the soldiers—and who also won a Pulitzer Prize—was

Bill Mauldin. Mauldin was not a writer or photographer, but a cartoonist. He drew a cartoon called *Willie and Joe.* Unlike Pyle, Mauldin was the same age as many of the soldiers he pictured. In fact, he had started the war as a regular soldier, who drew cartoons for his division's newspaper as a part-time assignment. Before long, Mauldin's fame had spread to soldiers in other divisions, and eventually he was transferred to the staff of *Stars and Stripes,* the daily newspaper published by the army and distributed to the troops. When Ernie Pyle wrote a column praising Mauldin, newspapers back home also began to carry his cartoons.

Like Pyle, Mauldin told the story of the GIs' war, but he told it humorously. He saw it through the eyes of two infantrymen named Willie and Joe whose feet always hurt and who thought officers led an easy life while the GIs did all the work. In Mauldin's cartoons, the soldiers were always unshaven, with their shirts hanging out. Willie and Joe did not have much use for army rules about neatness. It was always muddy

Cartoonist Bill Mauldin's *Willie and Joe cartoon was popular among GIs.* *(Reproduced by permission of AP/World Wide Photos)*

GI Joe

Just after the end of the war, Hollywood released a film based on Ernie Pyle's war reporting. Set in Italy and called *The Story of G.I. Joe,* it was directed by William Wellman and starred Burgess Meredith as Pyle. Many critics think it is the best American combat film of World War II. *Time* magazine praised how authentic it was and called it "the least glamorous war picture ever made," words that Pyle would probably have appreciated. Others have pointed out that the Italian civilians whom the soldiers encounter in the film seem like real people, something quite rare in war movies. And although Pyle's greatest fans were the lowly infantrymen who traveled on foot and slept in the holes they dug, he might also have been pleased to hear what was said about *The Story of G.I. Joe* by General Dwight D. Eisenhower, the supreme commander of Allied forces in Europe. Eisenhower called it "the greatest war picture I've ever seen."

and miserable where they slept, and keeping dry seemed more important than capturing Berlin.

Willie and Joe were no heroes, but they did their job. They did not talk about the purpose of the war, and they often expressed doubts about the way it was being run—but they never questioned that it was necessary. Some top officers did not appreciate the way Mauldin kept poking fun at them and thought Willie and Joe set a poor example of discipline and the proper behavior for a soldier. General George S. Patton, commander of the U.S. Third Army, threatened to ban *Stars and Stripes* from his area if Mauldin continued to publish his cartoons. General Dwight D. Eisenhower, Patton's boss, instead arranged for Patton and Mauldin to meet face to face and discuss the problem. Mauldin defended his cartoons, saying they made soldiers laugh at their own problems. Patton was not convinced, but *Stars and Stripes,* with Mauldin's cartoons, continued to be read by GIs throughout Europe—including the soldiers of Patton's Third Army.

The World After the War 17

The world in 1945 was very different from the one before World War II. The terror and mass murder of Nazi Germany had been eliminated, and Japan's attempt to conquer much of Asia had been defeated. If these two things had not happened, the history of the rest of the twentieth century would have been very different. The end of the war brought many changes in the way people lived and the way they looked at their world. Some of those changes were a result of what the war had cost the world. The most obvious cost was the loss of life.

Millions die in Europe

The exact number of people killed during the war is not known, but the losses were staggering. Fifty or perhaps sixty million people died throughout the world, more than in any other war—more than for *any* reason in such a short time in human history. In Europe, only about half these deaths were soldiers, sailors, and airmen. The rest were civilians. By comparison, in World War I only 5 percent of war casualties were civilians.

But no people in western Europe were treated as savagely as the people of eastern and southeastern Europe.

These men, women, and children died in many ways. They were crushed by the roofs and walls of their houses when air raids shattered their cities. They were blown up by mines on the roads as they tried to escape advancing armies, or died hiding in fields and forests in winter without enough food. Many thousands were hanged or shot by the Germans in retaliation for attacks on German forces. Millions, including nearly 6 million Jews, were deliberately murdered by the Nazis, machine-gunned and dumped into mass graves or gassed in death camps specially created for this purpose. (Nazi persecution of Jews is described in Chapter 7.)

In some places, the proportion of civilian deaths was especially high. The Netherlands (often called Holland; in English, the people are called Dutch) lost 200,000 people out of a population of less than 9 million during the German occupation. An occupation is when foreign military forces are stationed in a country to control it. Though the German occupation of the Netherlands was harsher than in other parts of western Europe, the citizens of many of the countries that Germany occupied during the war suffered greatly. (German occupation is discussed in Chapter 6.) Ninety-five percent of the people killed were civilians. The French lost 600,000 people, two-thirds of them civilians.

But no people in western Europe were treated as savagely as the people of eastern and southeastern Europe. In Yugoslavia, about 1.5 million people died. Only about 300,000 were soldiers. In neighboring Greece, about 250,000 died, the overwhelming majority civilians.

Poland lost approximately 300,000 soldiers in the war. Some died when Germany first invaded in 1939. Others died later while fighting the Germans with the British and American armies in western Europe and with the Soviet army in eastern Europe. This figure, however, is only a small part of the cost to Poland. All told, 6 million Poles, including 3 million Jews, died in World War II. More than one out of every five Poles was killed. If the United States lost the same proportion of its 1999 population, that would be more than 55 million people.

The Soviet Union (Russia) lost still more. At least 20 million, possibly as many as 40 million, Soviet citizens died from June 1941 to May 1945, including more than 7 million soldiers. One million Russian civilians died just in the city of Leningrad, surrounded by the Germans for two-and-a-half years.

British and American losses

The other two major Allies who fought against Germany, Britain and the United States, were far less devastated. Britain fought the war from the first day to the last, for a while almost alone. In that long struggle, 250,000 of its soldiers died. Another 100,000 troops from the countries of the British Commonwealth (independent countries that had been British colonies and still had close ties to Britain) and from British colonies also died. Among these were 37,000 from Canada, 24,000 from India, and 23,000 from Australia.

But there was no fighting in Britain itself, no invading army to burn its villages, no occupation force that arrested and murdered its citizens. But this did not mean all its people were safe. German planes bombed its large cities, killing 60,000 people, half of them in London.

Almost 300,000 American men died fighting Germany and Japan. But no enemy soldier set foot on the American mainland except as a prisoner. No enemy plane dropped a single bomb on the United States. (Alaska and Hawaii were not yet states.)

Axis powers pay a high price

The Axis powers (Germany and its allies) also suffered terrible losses. Italian deaths were around 400,000, about half of them civilians. Hungary lost 400,000 soldiers and Romania probably almost as many. Civilian deaths, especially in Hungary, were very high.

Germany, the country that began the war, paid one of the highest prices. Only the Soviet Union lost more soldiers; only the Soviet Union and Poland lost more civilians. More than 4 million men died fighting in Germany's armed forces. Six hundred thousand Germans, including 150,000 children, were killed by Allied bombing raids. An unknown number of civilians, perhaps 1 million more, died trying to escape the Soviet Union's Red Army as it moved into Germany from the east in the last months of the war. Some of these civilians died due to exposure (being stranded out in the cold), or drowned in half-frozen rivers while trying to cross to safety. But Soviet troops purposely killed many in revenge for the German army's brutal treatment of Russia's soldiers and citizens when it invaded Russia in June 1941.

Germany, the country that began the war, paid one of the highest prices. Only the Soviet Union lost more soldiers; only the Soviet Union and Poland lost more civilians.

The psychological effects of being a prisoner were also often very serious. This was even more true for the survivors of concentration camps.

Physical and psychological wounds

In addition to the millions of deaths, there were at least as many soldiers and civilians wounded during the war, many of them permanently disabled. For most countries, the number of wounded soldiers was higher than the number of dead. This was usually true of civilians as well. For example, in Germany, 800,000 civilians were seriously injured in air raids.

Millions of soldiers had been held as prisoners of war. Prisoners faced hunger and malnutrition. In some cases they were treated inhumanely by their captors. Even those who had been treated humanely, such as Axis prisoners of the Allies, were sometimes weakened for the rest of their lives. The psychological effects of being a prisoner were also often very serious. This was even more true for the survivors of concentration camps.

The effects of hunger and malnutrition were not limited to prisoners. Much of the population of occupied Europe never received adequate food. Sometimes, as in the still occupied Netherlands in the last winter of the war, people starved. Wartime conditions, including malnutrition, inadequate sanitation, and a lack of medical care, also increased the incidence of disease. There were 1.5 million cases of tuberculosis in Poland in 1945.

Villages, towns, cities, and countries destroyed

The physical destruction caused by the war was even easier to see than the human loss. Some examples from a few countries make the extent of these losses clear. In the Soviet Union, 28 million people had their homes destroyed. Forty thousand miles of Soviet railroads were wrecked. Seven million horses and 17 million head of cattle had been taken by the Germans. Almost every town and city in this vast region—1,710 of them—suffered serious damage, and many were in ruins. The same was true for 70,000 villages.

In France, 1 million buildings were damaged or completely destroyed. Sixty percent of the country's machine tools and almost all its coal and iron supplies had been taken to Germany. The railroads, roads, bridges, and harbor facilities had

all suffered extensive damage, much of it from Allied bombing during the German occupation of France.

Germany itself had been the scene of great land battles at the end of the war and had also been the target of the largest air attacks for the longest period of the war. About 15 percent of the country's houses had been destroyed and another 25 percent damaged. Only the smaller towns and villages had escaped the bombing. The transportation system had collapsed, which meant that even the factories that had not been destroyed could not get raw materials and had to shut down. Mass starvation was avoided only because the conquering Allied armies brought in food.

It would be misleading to downplay the extent of the human misery that Europe suffered as a result of World War II. But the most surprising aspect is how quickly Europe recovered economically. In part, this was due to the help of the United States who provided extensive economic aid. Also per-

A street in Berlin after an attack from the Allies in February 1945. Fifteen percent of Germany's homes were destroyed during the war.
(Reproduced by permission of AP/Wide World Photos)

The Soviet Union, which was officially communist, began to turn the eastern zone of Germany into a communist country. The western Allies began to see the rest of Germany as a valuable partner in the conflict with communism.

haps, it was because more European leaders and their people saw a need to put aside the old rivalries that had led to war and work together to rebuild Europe.

Even before the war was over, Belgium, Luxembourg, and the Netherlands agreed to form an economic union. Before too long, these three small countries and France joined with two of their World War II enemies, Italy and West Germany, in what eventually became the Common Market. (West Germany was the part of Germany that did not become communist; this development is described later in this chapter.) The Common Market grew until most western European countries were members. At the end of the twentieth century, it looked possible that the old dream of a united Europe might at last become a reality.

The division of Germany

Unity, however, came after many years of division. Before the war ended, the Allied leaders decided that Germany would be divided into four zones, each occupied by one of the four great powers that had fought Germany. These four were the United States, Britain, and France, usually called the western Allies, and the Soviet Union. The four powers had not decided on Germany's long-term future. Some Allied leaders believed Germany should be kept divided forever, to prevent the country from becoming powerful enough to start another war. For the same reason, a few even wanted to turn Germany back into a farming country, without the industry necessary to fight a modern war.

There had always been significant disagreements between the Soviets and the western Allies. (These issues are described in Chapter 9.) In general, these had been put aside to win the war. But they became paramount once the war was over. The division of Germany was one of the major points of conflict. The Soviet Union, which was officially communist, began to turn the eastern zone of Germany into a communist country. (Communism is a political and economic system based on government control of the production and distribution of goods and the abolition of private ownership of factories, banks, and most other businesses.) The western Allies began to see the rest of Germany as a valuable partner in the conflict with communism.

The entrance to the American zone of Berlin, Germany. *(Reproduced by permission of the Corbis Corporation [Bellevue])*

Increasingly, this conflict interfered with every attempt at four-power cooperation. Within a few years, the conflict became a Cold War, a worldwide struggle between the United States and its supporters on one side and the Soviet Union and its allies on the other. All the countries of eastern Europe, controlled by the Soviet army, would become communist. All the countries of western Europe would reject communism; many would join the United States in a permanent military alliance called NATO (the North Atlantic Treaty Organization). Germany would be one of the main focal points of the conflict. But, especially at the beginning of the occupation, there were still times when the four powers worked together.

Denazification and war crimes trials

For many of the people in the Allied nations, the war in Europe was not only—or even mainly—a war against Ger-

Germany's border in 1939 and in 1945. The four post-war power zones are indicated.

many. It was a war against Nazism, the brutal system based on race hatred that had turned Europe into a vast prison camp and slaughterhouse. (The special nature of the Nazi system, and how it affected World War II, is discussed in Chapter 1.)

Many people had known, in a general way, about the crimes the Nazis were committing. The Soviets publicized the fact that German forces massacred thousands of people in each area they conquered. Rumors about the Nazi treatment of Jews and of Soviet prisoners of war were widespread. During the war, the Allies publicly stated that the Nazis would be held responsible for these crimes and that their punishment was one of the aims of the war against Germany.

Later, Allied leaders and ordinary people throughout the world began to learn of the enormous scale of Nazi crimes. As Allied soldiers reached the concentration camps of Germany, they found the remains of hundreds of thousands of victims and thousands more barely alive. As survivors and witnesses began to talk, as Nazi documents and records came to light, it became clear that Nazi Germany was not just a normal country. Its leaders had planned and carried out the murder of millions of civilians, including an attempt to kill all the Jews of Europe.

Perhaps even more than punishing the guilty, the Allies were determined to destroy the entire Nazi system. In the words of the high command of the American armed forces, "Nazism must be completely and finally removed from all aspects of German life." This meant barring active Nazis from official posts and removing their supporters from important positions in the press and broadcasting, in the arts, in education. The plan was to completely wipe out Nazi teachings and doctrines. The entire process was called denazification.

At the beginning of the Allied occupation, the Allied military authorities arrested and investigated thousands of Germans. Thousands more were questioned about their activities during the Nazi era. They were classified as major offenders, offenders, lesser offenders, followers, or non-Nazis. The denazification process caused great resentment among many Germans. People who had played a minor part in the government during the Nazi years and told the truth were sometimes treated more harshly than those who had been fanatical Nazis but lied. In addition, the system worked differently in the four zones of Germany. The western occupation authorities soon began to overlook some Germans' Nazi pasts if they could help rebuild the German economy or help them in the growing conflict with the Soviet Union. The most famous example of this is the German scientists who developed the American missile and space programs. During the war, these men had worked on the German rocket program, which depended heavily on the use of slave labor.

In all three western zones, many judges, lawyers, and police officials who had served throughout the Nazi period continued in office. In the Soviet zone as well, former Nazis who cooperated with the new communist setup were often allowed to remain in positions of authority.

The Nuremberg trials

The Allies believed punishing war criminals would help accomplish denazification, and they decided to create a

The Allies were determined to destroy the entire Nazi system.

Defendants dock at the Nuremberg trials.
(Reproduced by permission of the National Archives and Records Administration)

special international court, called the International Military Tribunal, to put the Nazi leaders on trial. The four occupying powers were represented. The trial was held at Nuremberg in southern Germany, where the Nazi Party had held its rallies and proclaimed the racial laws against the Jews.

The defendants included twenty-two high officials of the German government, Nazi Party, and German military. The first set of charges was that they had committed crimes against peace. Basically, this meant the Nazis were charged with planning and waging wars of conquest. Some observers at the time, and some historians afterward, argued that the winners of any war might claim the same about their defeated enemies. The four countries that put the German leaders on trial could all be accused of having started a war to conquer territory sometime in their history.

The second set of charges involved war crimes. These are acts that are against the laws and customs of war. They include the use of civilian populations of conquered countries as slave workers, killing hostages, mistreating prisoners of war, and the unjustified "destruction of cities, towns, or villages." Many of these actions violated treaties that Germany had signed.

But the Nazi leaders were also charged with a third set of actions, described as crimes against humanity. This was a new idea. These crimes included "murder, extermination, enslavement, deportation, and other inhumane acts committed against any civilian population, before or during the war." They also included "persecution on political, racial or religious grounds," whether or not this violated the laws in force in that country at the time the crimes were committed.

The Allies were essentially saying that the Nazis had done things that had to be considered crimes in all circumstances and at all times—even if the actions were considered legal by the government in power at that time. This idea is often considered the major accomplishment of the Nuremberg trials. It is closely related to the idea that following orders, even legal orders, cannot be an excuse for committing such crimes.

At the first Nuremberg trial, twelve of the defendants were sentenced to death and seven to prison terms, and three were found not guilty. A series of twelve other trials followed. Together, the evidence showed how every department of the German government, the military, and large sections of private industry were all involved in the crimes that the top Nazis had planned.

In this sense, the Nuremberg trials were show trials. While they were fair, their purpose was not simply to punish individual criminals. It was also to educate the public, including the German public, about what had happened and how it had happened.

The last wave of killing

While the first Nuremberg trial showed the world the extent of Nazi crimes, other terrible events took place on Germany's borders that received comparatively little attention—except in Germany. These events were a result of the border

After Nuremberg, following orders, even legal orders, cannot be considered an excuse for committing such crimes against humanity.

National border changes at the end of World War II led to massive deportation of Germans living in areas that no longer belonged to Germany. This map indicates areas that changed hands and the new Polish-Soviet-German borders.

changes that the Allies had agreed to, giving Poland land that had long been German, in some cases for hundreds of years. (See box on p. 403.)

The Allies were afraid that Germany would never stop trying to get these areas back from Poland if large numbers of Germans continued to live there. The same was true of the German minorities in Czechoslovakia, in the regions bordering the Baltic Sea, and other parts of eastern Europe.

Two million Germans had already fled from East Prussia in early 1945, trying to escape from the advancing Soviet army. (These events are described in Chapter 12.) The following winter, as the Allies had agreed, there was a massive expulsion of the remaining Germans from eastern Europe. They were forced to leave their homes and move to western Germany.

From Silesia in southwest Poland and Pomerania farther north, from the Sudetenland and other areas of Czechoslovakia, from throughout eastern Europe, some 14 million

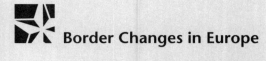

Border Changes in Europe

The map of Europe after World War II was surprisingly similar to that of 1937. At the end of World War I in 1918, many new independent countries were created that were then destroyed by German conquest during World War II and the years immediately before. At the end of World War II in 1945, these countries were restored, with most of their borders as they had been.

Austria became a separate country again, instead of being part of Germany. Czechoslovakia lost its eastern tip to the Soviet Union, but it was restored as an independent nation, reuniting Slovakia with the Czech areas. Nazi Germany had created an independent Slovakia that was really controlled by Germany and had made the Czech areas a part of Germany. Yugoslavia, which Germany, Italy, and their allies had invaded and split up, was again unified.

The three small Baltic countries of Lithuania, Latvia, and Estonia did not regain the independence they had lost, first to the Soviets in 1939 to 1940 and then to the invading Germans in 1941. Instead, they became part of the Soviet Union and remained so until 1991.

The major European border changes involved Poland and Germany. Large parts of eastern Poland became part of the Soviet Union. At the same time, it gained territory from Germany on the west and the north, where half of East Prussia became Polish. The other half became part of the Soviet Union. The effect of these changes was to shrink Germany and to move Polish territory westward by 100 miles.

Germans were forcibly deported. Like so many refugees throughout the war—a war that had now been over for almost a year—many of them were weak from hunger and cold, and they were often treated with great brutality. Historians estimate that 2 million people died during the expulsions.

The United States at the end of the war

The experience of the United States was very different from the devastation and exhaustion of Europe. American factories, railroads, and mines had not been damaged. During the war, American industry doubled its production. The American

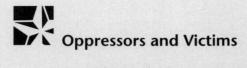

Oppressors and Victims

Considering how many people were involved and how many died, it is remarkable how little attention the expulsion in 1946 of Germans from eastern Europe received, except in Germany. The reason for this is simple, though it may not be admirable.

At the end of the war, very few people were ready to sympathize with Germans being oppressed by Poles and Czechs. Germany had terrorized, brutalized, and murdered these and other eastern Europeans, for the past five years or longer. Most Germans in the Sudetenland, for example, had apparently welcomed it when Adolf Hitler tore Czechoslovakia apart, using the supposed bad treatment of the Sudeten Germans as his excuse. (Hitler's destruction of Czechoslovakia is described in Chapter 1.)

To many people, and certainly to the Czechs, it seemed that the Germans were now getting what they deserved. Similarly, the treatment of the Germans in Poland, as terrible as it was, could not compare with what the Nazis had done to the Poles.

The problem was that all Germans in eastern Europe were being expelled, not just those who had been Nazis, committed war crimes, or taken over their neighbors' land. Certainly, many thought of themselves as Germans and did not want to become Poles or Czechoslovakians. But they were not given a choice. Instead, they were expelled because they were born into a particular nationality. Because of that, it was thought, they could never be fully loyal citizens. It is not surprising that this idea was common in Europe in 1945: it was the same one the Nazis had proclaimed for many years.

aircraft industry had employed 46,000 people before the war; now there were fifty times as many. They built 275,000 planes during the war. American factories produced the requirements of war in seemingly unlimited quantities—enough to supply the British army with most of its tanks and with 86,000 jeeps. In the Soviet Union, the soldiers and supplies of the Red Army traveled to the battlefront on American trucks. To protect their feet in the Russian winter, the United States sent millions of pairs of felt boot liners, made in American factories to Soviet specifications.

In 1945, the United States produced one-half of the world's coal and two-thirds of its crude oil. Sixty percent of the world's gold reserves were in the United States. The American merchant marine was now three times larger than Britain's, which had been the largest in the world before the war. The United States had provided $30 billion in aid to its allies, including $13.5 billion to Britain and $9 billion to the Soviet Union. (These amounts were worth far more then than they would be today.)

Both in total amounts and compared with other countries, the United States was far stronger economically at the end of the war than at the beginning. It was the only major country for which this was true. The experience of World War II changed the United States as deeply as it changed the countries of Europe, but in very different ways. Many of these developments were already under way during the war and only sped up when it ended. (Life in America during the war is described in Chapter 5.)

One set of changes was directly related to these economic developments. At the beginning of the war in Europe, the United States was still feeling the effects of the Great Depression (1929–39), a severe economic downturn marked by falling industrial production and very high unemployment. The war created jobs for everyone, and despite the fears of many experts, these jobs did not disappear when the war ended.

One reason the American economy was able to convert to peacetime conditions was that Europe now depended on American farms and factories to supply its needs. Another was the sudden increase in demand for a wide variety of products. During the war, consumer goods were hard to buy, even though people earned enough money. For example, no passenger cars were built for several years. Instead the auto plants built tanks and army trucks. When the war ended, many Americans wanted a car and had saved the money to buy one. The same was true for many other products.

America booms: The GI Bill

Millions of Americans felt that they needed to make up for lost time. Sixteen million Americans had been in the armed forces. Almost all had been sent away from home, even if they

The experience of World War II changed the United States as deeply as it changed the countries of Europe, but in very different ways.

never left the country. Men had been separated from their wives and girlfriends, sometimes for many years. They wanted to get married, buy houses, start families, and do it all right away.

On June 22, 1944, a new law that was usually called the GI Bill went into effect. (GI, which stands for "government issue," is the nickname for ordinary American soldiers.)

Almost all veterans (people who had been in the armed forces) were eligible. The law paid for their college tuition and provided some money to live on while they were in school. Millions of veterans took advantage of the bill, and there was a very large increase in enrollment in American universities, junior colleges, and community colleges. Other veterans finished their high school educations. The GI Bill was one of the major reasons why Americans became much better educated after the war than before the war.

Education became more important to Americans for another reason, too: they were having more children. The end of the war was the beginning of the baby boom, a large increase in the birthrate that continued for twenty years. Generally, a veteran with a good education could earn better money to support his growing family.

The GI Bill also allowed veterans to buy homes without a down payment and with low-interest loans. This meant that veterans could buy a house for a monthly payment lower than their rent. One million former servicemen and servicewomen took advantage of this provision by 1947. This section of the bill accounted for part of the large increase in home ownership. The war had created a housing shortage because so many people had moved into urban areas to work in war industries and very few resources were used to build residential housing during the war. In 1944, only 114,000 new houses were begun in America. The number exploded once the war ended, and it kept growing. In 1950, construction began on about 1.7 million homes.

Many of these houses were not in cities or existing towns. Instead, they were built in newly created suburbs. Large communities were developed outside cities, often consisting of hundreds or even thousands of quickly built, identical homes. The places where they were built had no indus-

try or office buildings nearby. Instead, people lived in the suburbs and commuted—increasingly by private cars instead of trains or buses—on newly built highways to jobs in the cities. The new suburban areas rarely had enough existing stores for their rapidly expanding populations. Soon, malls would be created that drew shoppers from many surrounding suburbs. All of these things together changed the way average Americans lived.

A boom in housing led to the rapid growth of suburbs like Levittown, NY, America's first mass-produced suburb.
(Reproduced by permission of AP/Wide World Photos)

As the war ended and Americans found out about the scale of Nazi crimes, opinions changed and the idea grew that the United States had to remain involved in world affairs to prevent future wars and to protect itself.

America and the world

The United States was not only the largest economy in the world in 1945, but it was also the greatest military power. As tensions increased with the Soviet Union, the other great military power, Americans debated the proper role for the United States in world affairs.

World War II began only twenty-one years after the end of World War I. It was clear that Europe, and the world, could not afford to go through this terrible destruction once every generation. The leaders of the Allies, especially American President Franklin D. Roosevelt, were determined to establish some way of dealing with future threats to peace before they turned into wars. The key, in Roosevelt's opinion, was for the major nations of the world to act together.

In 1918, at the end of World War I, an organization called the League of Nations had been created, with some of the same ideas. All the countries of the world were supposed to meet, argue, and settle their disputes peacefully. If necessary, its members would use their economic and even their military power to enforce its decisions. (The League is explained in a box in Chapter 1, on p.6.)

But the League had failed; World War II was the final proof of that. Most historians believe one of the major reasons for the League's failure was that the United States refused to join it, despite the fact that it was the idea of Woodrow Wilson, the president during and after World War I.

Throughout American history, many Americans had believed that the United States should stay out of Europe's quarrels. They thought that America, protected by two great oceans, should remain safely isolated from Europe's troubles and Europe's wars. These ideas, usually called isolationism, were losing their attraction to Americans in 1945. The United States had no choice but to go to war after Japan attacked Pearl Harbor and Germany declared war in December 1941. But even before this, more and more Americans had believed that a victory by Adolf Hitler's Germany would threaten their own freedom. As the war ended and Americans found out about the scale of Nazi crimes, opinions changed and the idea grew that the United States had to remain involved in world affairs to prevent future wars and to protect itself.

The United Nations meets in London, 1946.
(Reproduced by permission of the Corbis Corporation)

The United Nations

So when Roosevelt proposed the creation of a new world body, called the United Nations Organization, most Americans supported it. (The United Nations was the official name for all the countries fighting Germany and Japan in World War II.) Roosevelt thought the League of Nations had been ruined by endless debates because each member nation

As in Germany, the Americans were determined to destroy the Japanese political system and way of thinking, called militarism, that they believed had caused the war.

had its own interests. He believed that maintaining peace required the most powerful nations to agree on important matters and then work together—without the interference of smaller countries. So in Roosevelt's plan for the United Nations, the decision to use armed force would not belong to the whole organization but to a small committee that included the United States, the Soviet Union, Britain, and China. (China was included at Roosevelt's insistence, and France was also added.) The great alliance that was fighting and winning the war would remain together and act as a police force for the world, as Roosevelt himself described it.

On April 25, 1945, only two weeks after Roosevelt's death, the United Nations Conference on International Organization met in San Francisco. A charter, or constitution, for the new United Nations Organization was signed on June 26. A month later, the United States Senate approved the charter by a vote of 89 to 2.

Japan in defeat

In some ways World War II had even more dramatic effects on Asia than on Europe. In Japan, 2 million people were dead, about 800,000 of them civilians. Its cities suffered more destruction from air attacks than those of any other country, partly because their wooden construction allowed the bombers to ignite huge fires.

Like Germany, Japan was placed under military occupation and run by the American military commander, General Douglas MacArthur, and his staff. As in Germany, the Americans were determined to destroy the Japanese political system and way of thinking, called militarism, that they believed had caused the war. Indeed, before the war, Japan was controlled by the army, war and conquest were glorified, and much of Japanese society was organized on military principles. Absolute loyalty and obedience were considered the highest virtues. (Japanese militarism is described in Chapter 1.)

The major wartime leaders of Japan were put on trial in Tokyo. Twenty-five were convicted, and seven were sentenced to death. Thousands of other Japanese, especially military men, were tried in various places that the Japanese army had ruled during the war. Many of them were charged with mistreating Allied prisoners of war, and 900 were executed.

Japan received a new constitution, secretly written by General MacArthur's staff. It said the emperor was a symbol of the nation, rather than a godlike person who had to be obeyed absolutely. It said that Japan would never again wage war, and it abolished the army; Japan would only have a small self-defense force. The constitution proclaimed equal rights for women and protected the workers' right to form labor unions.

Japan also lost all its colonies. Manchuria and Taiwan were returned to China, and Korea became an independent country. The militarists had argued that Japan needed to conquer territory in Asia in order to prosper. Now, without the militarists, without colonies, and despite the devastation of the war, Japan soon became more prosperous than ever before, eventually developing into the second-largest economy in the world, after the United States. Instead of aircraft carriers, its shipyards built giant oil tankers; instead of tanks, its factories built automobiles. It is hard to avoid the conclusion that defeat in World War II led to a much better life for the people of Japan than would have come from victory.

Without the militarists, without colonies, and despite the devastation of the war, Japan soon became more prosperous than ever before.

China

In most of the rest of Asia, the civilian casualties were relatively low because most of the actual fighting took place in areas where very few people lived, such as New Guinea and the Pacific islands. There were exceptions to this, such as the destruction caused in Manila, the capital of the Philippines. (See Chapter 13.)

By far the greatest exception was China. No one has a clear idea of how many Chinese were killed during the years that Japan was waging war against their country. Historians give figures ranging from 2 million all the way to 15 million people.

The surrender of Japan did not bring peace to China. There had long been a civil war between the official Chinese government, run by the Nationalist Party (the Kuomintang in Chinese), and the Chinese Communist Party. It had been pushed into the background while both sides fought Japan, but it had never completely ended. (See the box on p. 33) Although there

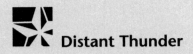

Distant Thunder

One of the things that makes it difficult to count civilian casualties in World War II is deciding who ought to be included. There was fighting in China both before and after the war with Japan. Disease and even starvation were widespread. When conditions such as these occur in wartime, it is hard to know what caused them. One example, from India rather than China, illustrates this problem.

In 1943 there was a famine in Bengal, in the eastern part of India. One-and-a-half million people starved to death, five times more people than all the American dead of World War II. These people are rarely considered victims of World War II.

However, the Bengal famine was not due to natural causes, such as a shortage of rain for crops to grow. Instead, in the words of historian Gerhard Weinberg, it was caused by the "disruption of trade, shipping shortages, and the extraordinary incompetence of the British administration" that ruled India. In other words, the normal ways that food was produced, transported, and sold to the people of Bengal were disrupted. Because of British wartime needs, the price of food in Bengal rose, and poor people could not afford to buy it. Almost certainly, the famine would not have occurred if there had been no war.

Everyone agrees that the Russian civilians who starved to death in Leningrad because it was surrounded by German troops are victims of the war. But no enemy troops attacked Bengal, no artillery shells or bombs fell there. The Bengalis died, as the title of Satyajit Ray's great film about the famine calls it, because of "distant thunder."

were attempts to negotiate a truce, the fighting grew worse once the war was over. By July 1946, within a year of Japan's defeat, full-scale civil war raged in China. It continued until 1949, when the Communists won complete control of the country.

Asian empires

One of the most important long-term effects of World War II was its impact on the Asian colonies controlled by European countries. Three of these colonial powers—Britain, France, and the Netherlands—were on the winning side in

Mao Zedong was the leader of the communist movement in China. After the end of World War II, the communists took control of the country from the Nationalist Party. *(Reproduced by permission of the Corbis Corporation [Bellevue])*

World War II. But the war weakened all three and destroyed their ability to hold on to their empires.

One reason the colonials lost their status was that Japanese victories early in the war showed the native people of the colonies that Asians could defeat Europeans. The prestige of the colonial powers, which was partly based on their superior technology and military strength, had been seriously weakened.

France and the Netherlands, among others, had just regained their own freedom after German domination. Reimposing French or Dutch rule in other countries seemed inconsistent with the reasons they had fought the war.

Independence movements of varying sizes existed throughout the area before the war. The colonial powers, determined to retain their control, often made these movements illegal and jailed many of their leaders. In many places, Japan's defeat of the Europeans was welcomed, and in some cases, these movements cooperated with the Japanese authorities. Pro-Japanese attitudes usually did not last long, however, because Japanese rule was very harsh. It became obvious that Japan wanted to treat these countries as its own colonies, not to set them free. Even so, Japan's slogan of "Asia for the Asians" was not forgotten. (See the box on p. 100 entitled "The Greater East Asia Coprosperity Sphere.")

The future of the European empires was also influenced by the attitude of the United States. In 1941, even before the United States was at war, the United States and Britain issued a declaration called the Atlantic Charter. It committed the Allies to oppose territorial changes unless they were the "freely expressed" desire of the people involved. (The Atlantic Charter is described in Chapter 9.) This seemed to mean that the British, French, and Dutch should not get their colonies back unless the natives voted for their return.

This language reflected President Roosevelt's strong opposition to colonies, an attitude that most Americans shared. Critics of American policy have often argued that the United States opposed colonies because it could influence and even dominate other countries through its economic power, without having to use its army or run a country directly. Whether or not this is true, Roosevelt's attitude and American public opinion encouraged colonized people to seek independence.

The language of the Atlantic Charter and the general attitudes it reflected also had an influence on the people of the European colonial powers. After all, France and the Netherlands, among others, had just regained their own freedom after German domination. Reimposing French or Dutch rule in other countries seemed inconsistent with the reasons they had fought the war.

Restoring control

Despite all these considerations, and despite their concern about displeasing the United States, on which they

depended for economic aid, the colonial powers still did not want to give up their colonies. In some cases they used armed force—even the defeated Japanese army— to restore their control.

On August 17, 1945, two days after Japan announced its surrender, the Indonesian National Party declared that the Dutch East Indies was now the independent country of Indonesia. They refused to return control of the government to Dutch officials, who were now being released from Japanese prisons. British troops soon arrived to accept the surrender of Japanese troops, disarm them, and put them in prisoner-of-war camps. But the British also tried to put the Dutch back in control. They found that they were outnumbered by Indonesian soldiers loyal to the independence movement. So the British released the Japanese troops, rearmed them, and, with British officers commanding them, used them to restore the Dutch to power.

The last British Viceroy of India, Lord Louis Mountbatten, seated at right of table, facing camera, meets with Indian leaders to discuss India's independence from England. To Mountbatten's right is Jawaharlal Nehru, who became the first prime minister in independent India. (Reproduced by permission of AP/ Wide World Photos)

By the end of the war, almost every British politician realized that Britain could not hold on to India.

Losing control

Something very similar happened in the French colony of Indochina (the present-day countries of North and South Vietnam, Cambodia, and Laos). The Allies had agreed that British troops should temporarily occupy the southern part of Vietnam, the largest of the three countries of Indochina. In Vietnam, an independence movement called the Viet Minh was taking over the country from the Japanese. When the small force of British troops arrived in September 1945, they used released Japanese prisoners of war to control the Viet Minh. In October, French troops arrived and reestablished French control, despite the Atlantic Charter. Before long war broke out between the Viet Minh and the French, lasting until the French were defeated in 1954.

The largest and most important European colony was India, the jewel in the crown of the British Empire. The Indian independence movement, led by Mohandas Gandhi and Jawaharlal Nehru, was committed to nonviolence, but it had used massive demonstrations to push for Britain to "quit India" even during the war. (Some of the developments in wartime India are described in Chapter 9.) By the end of the war, almost every British politician realized that Britain could not hold on to India. Britain was financially exhausted, and using force to crush the independence movement would be expensive, unpopular at home, anger the Americans, and might cause the Indians to abandon nonviolence.

British India was split into four countries: India, Pakistan (East Pakistan is now Bangladesh), Burma (present-day Myanmar), and Ceylon (now called Sri Lanka). India became independent on August 15, 1947, exactly two years after Emperor Hirohito told the Japanese people that Japan had lost the war.

Where to Learn More

The following list of resources focuses on material appropriate for middle school or high school students. The list is divided into sections, separating general sources from those that cover specific aspects of World War II; certain titles are applicable to more than one subject area and are repeated under different headings. Please note that web site addresses, though verified prior to publication, are subject to change.

General Sources:

Awesome Library. *World War II.* [Online] http://www.awesomelibrary.org/Classroom/Social_Studies/History/World_War_II.html (accessed on August 13, 1999).

Canadian Forces College. "Military History: World War II (1939-1945)." *War, Peace and Security Guide.* [Online] http://www.cfcsc.dnd.ca/links/milhist/ (accessed on August 13, 1999).

Clancey, Patrick. *Hyperwar: A Hypertext History of the Second World War.* [Online] http://metalab.unc.edu/hyperwar (accessed on August 13, 1999).

Freeman, Michael, and Tim Mason, eds. *Atlas of Nazi Germany.* New York: Macmillan, 1987.

Graff, Stewart. *The Story of World War II*. New York: E. P. Dutton, 1978.

Krull, Kathleen. *V is for Victory*. New York: Knopf, 1995.

Lawson, Don. *Great Air Battles: World War I and II*. New York: Lothrop, Lee & Shepard Co., 1968.

Marrin, Albert, *The Airmen's War: World War II in the Sky*. New York; Atheneum, 1982.

National Archives and Records Administration. *A People at War*. [Online] http://www.nara.gov/exhall/people/people.html (accessed on August 13, 1999).

Reynoldson, Floria. *Women and War*. New York: Thomson Learning, 1993.

Ross, Stewart. *Propaganda*. New York: Thomson Learning, 1993.

Snyder, Louis L. *World War II*. New York: Franklin Watts, 1981.

Sullivan, George. *The Day Pearl Harbor Was Bombed: A Photo History of World War II*. New York: Scholastic, 1991.

Yale Law School. "World War II: Documents." *The Avalon Project at Yale Law School: Documents in Law, History, and Diplomacy*. [Online] http://www.yale.edu/lawweb/avalon/wwii/wwii.htm (accessed on August 12, 1999).

Young, Peter. *Atlas of the Second World War*. New York: Berkley Windhover, 1974.

Asia and the Pacific:

Blassingame, Wyatt. *The U.S. Frogmen of World War II*. New York: Random House, 1964.

Castello, Edmund L. *Midway: Battle for the Pacific*. New York: Random House, 1968.

Conroy, Robert. *The Battle of Bataan: America's Greatest Defeat*. New York: Macmillan, 1969.

Dolan, Edward F. *America in World War II: 1942*. Brookfield, Conn.: Millbrook Press, 1991.

Dolan, Edward F. *America in World War II: 1943*. Brookfield, Conn.: Millbrook Press, 1992.

Grant, R.G. *Hiroshima and Nagasaki*. Austin: Raintree, Steck-Vaughn, 1988.

Harris, Nathaniel. *Pearl Harbor*. N. Pomfret, Vt.: Dryad Press, 1986

Marrin, Albert. *Victory in the Pacific*. New York: Atheneum, 1983.

Morin, Isobel V. *Days of Judgment*. Brookfield, Conn.: Millbrook Press, 1995.

Nicholson, Dorinda. *Pearl Harbor Child: A Child's View of Pearl Harbor—from Attack to Peace*. Honolulu: Arizona Memorial Museum Assn., 1993.

Rich, Earle. *The Attack on Pearl Harbor*. San Diego: Lucent, 1998.

Sauvrain, Philip. *Midway*. New York: New Discovery Books, 1993.

Sherrow, Victoria. *Hiroshima*. New York: New Discovery Books, 1994.

Skipper, G.C. *Battle of Leyte Gulf.* Chicago: Children's Press, 1981.

Skipper, G.C. *Submarines in the Pacific.* Chicago: Children's Press, 1980.

Stein, R. Conrad. *The Battle of Guadalcanal.* Chicago: Children's Press, 1983.

Stein, R. Conrad. *The Battle of Okinawa.* Chicago: Children's Press, 1985.

Stein, R. Conrad. *Fall of Singapore.* Chicago: Children's Press, 1982.

Stein, R. Conrad. *Hiroshima.* Chicago: Children's Press, 1982.

Taylor, Theodore. *The Battle off Midway Island.* New York: Avon Books, 1981.

See also: Japan

Europe, the Atlantic, and Africa, 1939-43:

Blanco, Richard L. *Rommel, the Desert Warrior: The Afrika Korps in World War II.* New York: J. Mesmer, 1982.

Barnett, Correlli Barnett. *The Battle of El Alamein; Decision in the Desert.* New York: Macmillan, 1964.

Hoobler, Dorothy, and Thomas Hoobler. *Joseph Stalin.* New York: Chelsea House, 1985.

Humble, Richard. *U-Boat.* New York: Franklin Watts, 1990.

Kronenwetter, Michael. *Cities at War: London.* New York: New Discovery Books, 1992.

Marrin, Albert. *Stalin.* New York: Viking Kestrel 1988.

Reynolds, Quentin James. *The Battle of Britain.* New York: Random House, 1953.

Severance, John B. *Winston Churchill: Soldier, Statesman, Artist.* New York: Clarion Books, 1996.

Skipper, G.C. *The Battle of the Atlantic.* Chicago: Children's Press, 1981.

Skipper, G.C. *The Battle of Britain.* Chicago: Children's Press, 1980.

Skipper, G.C. *Battle of Stalingrad.* Chicago: Children's Press, 1981.

Skipper, G.C. *Fall of the Fox, Rommel,* Chicago: Children's Press, 1980.

Skipper, G.C. *Goering and the Luftwaffe.* Chicago: Children's Press, 1980.

Skipper, G.C. *Invasion of Sicily.* Chicago: Children's Press, 1981.

Sloan, Frank. *Bismark!* New York: Franklin Watts, 1991.

Stein, R. Conrad. *Dunkirk.* Chicago: Children's Press, 1982.

Stein, R. Conrad. *Invasion of Russia.* Chicago: Children's Press, 1985.

Stein, R. Conrad. *Siege of Leningrad.* Chicago: Children's Press, 1983.

Taylor, Theodore. *Battle of the Arctic Seas: The Story of Convoy PQ 17.* New York: Crowell, 1976.

Whitelaw, Nancy. *Joseph Stalin; from Peasant to Premier,* New York: Dillon Press, 1992.

Germany:

Ayer, Eleanor. *Adolf Hitler.* San Diego: Lucent, 1996.

Ayer, Eleanor. *Cities at War: Berlin.* New York: New Discovery Books, 1992.

Berman, Russell A. *Paul von Hindenburg.* New York: Chelsea House, 1987.

Eimerl, Sarel. *Hitler Over Europe; The Road to World War II.* Boston: Little, Brown, 1972.

Emmerich, Elizabeth. *My Childhood in Nazi Germany.* New York: Bookwright, 1991.

Friedman, Ina R., *The Other Victims: First-Person Stories of Non-Jews Persecuted by the Nazis.* Boston: Houghton Mifflin, 1990.

Fuller, Barbara. *Germany* New York: Marshall Cavendish, 1996.

Goldston, Robert C. *The Life and Death of Nazi Germany.* Indianopolis: Bobbs-Merrill, 1967.

Heyes, Eileen. *Adolf Hitler.* Brookfield, CT: Millbrook Press, 1994.

Heyes, Eileen. *Children of the Swastika: The Hitler Youth.* Brookfield, CT: Millbrook Press, 1993.

Marrin, Albert. *Hitler.* New York: Viking, 1987.

Nevelle, Peter. *Life in the Third Reich: World War II.* North Pomfret, VT: Batsford, 1992.

Shirer, William L. *The Rise and Fall of Adolf Hitler.* New York: Random House, 1961.

Spence, William. *Germany Then and Now.* New York: Franklin Watts, 1994.

Stein, R. Conrad. *Hitler Youth.* Chicago: Children's Press, 1985.

Steward, Gail B. *Hitler's Reich.* San Diego: Lucent Books, 1994.

Tames, Richard. *Nazi Germany.* North Pomfret, VT: Batsford, 1992.

Wepman, Dennis. *Adolf Hitler.* New York: Chelsea House, 1989.

Williamson, David. *The Third Reich.* New York: Bookwright Press, 1989.

Italy and Fascism:

Crisp, Peter. *The Rise of Fascism.* New York: Bookwright, 1991.

Hartenian, Lawrence R. *Benito Mussolini.* New York: Chelsea House, 1988.

Leeds, Christopher. *Italy Under Mussolini.* New York: Putnam, 1972.

Lyttle, Richard. *Il Duce: The Rise and Fall of Benito Mussolini.* New York: Atheneum, 1987.

Japan:

Behr, Edward. *Hirohito: Beyond the Myth.* New York: Villard Books, 1989.

Black, Wallace B., and Jean F. Blashfield, *Hiroshima and the Atomic Bomb.* New York: Crestwood House, 1993.

Grant, R.G. *Hiroshima and Nagasaki.* Austin: Raintree, Steck-Vaughn, 1988.

Hoobler, Dorothy, and Thomas Hoobler *Showa; The Age of Hirohito.* New York: Walker & Co., 1990.

Severns, Karen. *Hirohito*. New York: Chelsea House, 1988.

Sherrow, Victoria. *Hiroshima*. New York: New Discovery Nooks, 1994.

Stein, R. Conrad. *Hiroshima*. Chicago: Children's Press, 1982.

The United States:

Brimner, Larry Dane. *Voices form the Camps*. New York: Franklin Watts, 1994.

Cannon, Marian. *Dwight David Eisenhower: War Hero and President*. New York: Franklin Watts, 1990.

Coleman, Penny. *Rosie the Riveter; Women Workers on the Home Front in World War II*. New York: Crown, 1995.

Darby, Jean. *Douglas MacArthur*. Minneapolis, MN: Lerner, 1989.

Devaney, John. *Franklin Delano Roosevelt, President*. New York: Walker and Co., 1987.

Dolan, Edward F. *America in World War II: 1942*. Brookfield, CT: Millbrook Press, 1991.

Dolan, Edward F. *America in World War II: 1943*. Brookfield, CT.: Millbrook Press, 1992.

Duden, Jane. *1940s*. New York: Crestwood, 1989.

Freedman, Russell. *Franklin Delano Roosevelt*. New York: Clarion Books, 1990.

Hacker, Jeffrey H. *Franklin D. Roosevelt*. New York: Franklin Watts, 1983.

Harris, Jacqueline L. *The Tuskegee Airmen: Black Heroes of World War II*. Parsippany, NJ: Dillon Press, 1995.

Levine, Ellen. *A Fence Away From Freedom*. New York: G.P. Putnam, 1995.

McKissack, Pat. *Red-tail Angels: the Story of the Tuskegee Airmen of World War II*. New York: Walker & Co., 1995.

O'Connor, Barbara. *The Soldier's Voice: The Story of Ernie Pyle*. Minneapolis, MN: Cardrhoda Books, 1996.

Oleksy, Walter. *Military Leaders of World War II*. New York: Facts on File, 1994.

Pfeifer, Kathryn Browne. *The 761st Tank Battalion*. New York: Henry Holt, 1994.

Sinott, Susan. *Doing Our Part: American Women on the Home Front During World War II*. New York: Franklin Watts, 1995.

Spies, Karen Bornemamm. *Franklin D. Roosevelt*. Springfield, NJ: Enslow Pub. Inc., 1999.

Stanley, Jerry. *I Am an American*. New York: Crown, 1994.

Stein, R. Conrad. *The Home Front*. Chicago: Children's Press, 1986.

Stein, R. Conrad. *Nisei Regiment*. Chicago: Children's Press, 1985.

Sweeney, James B. *Famous Aviators of World War II*. New York: Franklin Watts, 1987.

Tunnell, Michael O., and George W. Chilcoat, *The Children of Topaz*. New York: Holiday House, 1996.

Uchida, Yoshika. *Desert Exile; The Uprooting of a Japanese-American *Family*. Seattle: University of Washington Press, 1982.

Whitman, Sylvia. *Uncle Sam Wants You: Military Men and Women in World War II*. Minneapolis, MN: Lerner Publications Co., 1993.

Whitman, Sylvia. *V is for Victory*. Minneapolis, MN: Lerner Publications Co., 1993.

Wings Across America. *WASP on the Web*. [Online] http://www.wasp.wwii.org (accessed on August 12, 1999).

Woodrow, Martin. *The World War II GI*. New York, Franklin Watts, 1986.

Zeinert, Karen, *Those Incredible Women of World War II*. Brookfield, CT: Millbrook Press, 1994.

Children in the war:

Asscher-Pinkoff, Clara. *Star Children*. Detroit: Wayne State University Press, 1986.

Besson, Jean-Louis. *October `45: Childhood Memories of the War*. Mankato, MN: Creative Editions, 1995.

Butterworth, Emma Macalik. *As the Waltz Was Ending*. New York: Four Winds, 1982.

Cross, Robin. *Children and War*. New York: Thomson Learning, 1994.

Drucker, Olga Levy. *Kindertransport*. New York: Henry Holt, 1992.

Foreman, Michael. *War Boy: A Country Childhood*. New York: Arcade, 1990. (England)

Gelman, Charles. *Do Not Go Gentle: A Memoir of Jewish Resistance in Poland 1941-1945*. North Haven, CT: Archon Books, 1989.

Holliday, Laurel. *Children in the Holocaust and World War II*. New York: Pocket Books, 1995.

Isaacman, Clara. *Clara's Story*. Philadelphia: Jewish Publication Society, 1984.

Marx, Trish. *Echoes of World War II*. Minneapolis, MN: Lerner, 1994.

Roth-Hano, Renée. *Touch Wood: A Girlhood in Occupied France*. Portland, OR: Four Winds Press, 1988.

Stalcup, Ann. *On the Home Front; Growing Up in Wartime England*. North Haven, CT.: Linnet Books, 1998.

Ungerer, Tomi. *A Childhood Under the Nazis*. Niwot, CO: Tomic, 1998.

Wassiljewa, Tatjana. *Hostage to War*. New York: Scholastic Press, 1997.

Wojciechowska, Maia. *Till the Break of Day*. New York, Harcourt, Brace Jovanovitch, 1972.

Events in Europe, 1944 and later:

Banfield, Susan. *Charles de Gaulle*. New York: Chelsea House, 1985.

Black, Wallace B. *Battle of the Bulge*. New York: Crestwood House, 1993.

Black, Wallace B. *Victory in Europe*. New York: Crestwood House, 1993

Bliven, Bruce. *The Story of D-Day: June 6, 1944*. New York: Random House, 1956.

Dolan, Edward F. *The Fall of Hitler's Germany*. New York: Franklin Watts, 1988.

Hine, Al. *D-Day: The Invasion of Europe*. New York: American Heritage Publishing Co., 1962.

Marrin, Albert. *Overlord: D-Day and the Invasion of Europe*. New York: Atheneum, 1982.

Morin, Isobel V. *Days of Judgment*. Brookfield, Conn.: Millbrook Press, 1995.

Rice, Earle. *The Nuremberg Trials*. San Diego: Lucent Books, 1997.

Skipper, G.C. *Death of Hitler*. Chicago: Children's Press, 1980.

Skipper, G.C. *Mussolini: A Dictator Dies*. Chicago: Children's Press, 1981.

Stein, R. Conrad. *The Story of D-Day*. Chicago: Children's Press, 1977.

Stein, R. Conrad. *World War II in Europe: America Goes to War*. Hillside NJ: Enslow Press, 1984.

Whitelaw, Nancy. *A Biography of General Charles de Gaulle*. New York: Dillon Press, 1991.

The Holocaust:

Arad, Yithak. *The Pictorial History of the Holocaust* New York: Macmillan, 1992.

Bachrach, Susan D. *Tell Them We Remember: The Story of the Holocaust*. Boston: Little, Brown, 1994.

Chaikin, Miriam. *A Nightmare in History: The Holocaust, 1933-1945*. New York: Clarion Books, 1987.

Feldman, George. *Understanding the Holocaust*. Detroit: UXL, 1998.

Frank, Anne. *The Diary of Anne Frank: The Definitive Edition*. New York, Bantam Books, 1997.

"The Holocaust." *The Jewish Student Online Research Center (JSOURCE)*. [Online] http://www.us-israel.org/jsource/holo.html (accessed on August 13, 1999).

Meltzer, Milton. *Never to Forget*. New York: Harper & Row, 1976.

Museum of Tolerance Online Multimedia Learning Center. *Auschwitz-Birkenau*. [Online] http://motlc.wiesenthal.org/pages/t003/t00315. (accessed on August 12, 1999).

Resnick, Abraham, *The Holocaust*. San Diego: Lucent Books, 1991.

Rogasky, Barbara. *Smoke and Ashes*. New York: Holiday House, 1988.

Rossel, Seymour. *The Holocaust: The Fire that Raged*. New York: Frank;in Watts, 1989.

Strahinich, Helen. *The Holocaust: Understanding and Remembering*, Springfield, NJ: Enslow, 1996.

United States Holocust Memorial Museum. *The Holocaust: A Learning Site for Students*. [Online] http://www.ushmm.org/outreach/nrule. (accessed on August 13, 1999).

Resistance

Bauer, Yehuda. *They Chose Life; Jewish Resistance in The Holocaust.* New York: American Jewish Committee, 1973.

Friedman, Ina R. *Flying Against the Wind: The Story of a Young Woman Who Defied the Nazis.* Brookline, MA: Lodge Pole Press, 1995.

Healey, Tim. *Secret Armies; Resistance Groups in World War II.* London: Macdonald, 1981.

Landau, Elaine.*The Warsaw Ghetto Uprising.* New York: Macmillan, 1992.

Pettit, Jayne. *A Time to Fight Back: True Stories of Wartime Resistance.* Boston: Houghton, Mifflin, 1996.

Stadtler, Ben. *The Holocaust: A History of Courage and Resistance.* West Orange, NJ: Behrman House, 1974.

Stein, R. Conrad. *Resistance Movements.* Chicago: Children's Press, 1982.

Vinke, Hermann. *The Short Life of Sophie Scholl.* New York: Harper & Row, 1984.

Vogel, Ilse-Margaret. *Bad Times, Good Friends.* New York: Harcourt Brace Javanovich, 1992.

Weinstein, Irving. *That Denmark Might Live; The Saga of Danish Resistance in World War II.* Philadelphia: Macrae Smith, 1967.

Zeinert, Karen. *The Warsaw Ghetto Uprising* Brookfield, CT.: Millbrook Press, 1993.

Secret Weapons, Spies, Sabotage:

Andryszewski, Tricia. *The Amazing Life of Moe Berg: Catcher, Scholar, Spy.* Brookfield, CT: Millbrook Press, 1996.

Daily, Robert. *The Code Talkers.* New York: Franklin Watts, 1995.

Goldstone, Robert C. *Sinister Touches; The Secret War Against Hitler.* New York: Dial Press, 1992.

Jones, Catherine. *Navajo Code Talkers; Native American Heroes.* Greensboro: Tudor Publications, 1997.

Halter, Jon C. *Top Secret Projects of World War II.* New York: J. Messner, 1978.

Lawson, Don. *The Secret World War II.* New York: Franklin Watts, 1978.

Marrin, Albert. *The Secret Armies.* New York: Atheneum, 1985.

Index

A

Aachen, Germany *2:* 302 (ill.)
Abwehr (German military
    counter-intelligence) *2:* 350
Abbey, at Monte Cassino *2:*237,
    238 (ill.), 239 (ill.)
Action in the North Atlantic
    2: 384–385
Advisory Council for Italy *2:* 220
Africa (*see* North Africa)
African-Americans *1:* 112-119
    and armed services
        1: 114-117, 114 (ill.), 116 (ill.)
    and defense industry jobs *1:* 113
    migration from south of
        1: 108, 118
Afrika Korps *1:* 70-71, *2:* 227
Air force, Allied *1:* 55-60, 57 (ill.),
    2: 253-254, 263-264
Air raids *1:* 182-193
    against Britain *1:* 55-60, 58 (ill.),
        59 (ill.), 185-186, 185 (ill.)
    against Japan *1:* 101, 334-335
    against Germany 188-193
    British civilians killed by *1:* 59

Doolittle raid: *1:* 101
    German civilians wounded by
        2: 394
Airborne troops *2:* 263-264
Aircraft industry (U.S.)
    1: 106-107, 120
AK (*Armia Krajowa*) (*see* Home
    Army [Polish])
Alamein, El *2:* 228
Albania *1:* 72-73
Aleutians *2:* 316-317
Algeria *2:* 228-230
Alliance (French resistance
    network) *2:* 354
Allies *2:* 205-219
Anglo-American Control
    Commission (Italy) *2:* 220
Anschloss 1: 20 (ill.), 21
Anti-Comintern Pact (1936)
    1: 32, 83
Anti-Communism *2:* 371
Anti-Jewish laws *1:* 160
Anti-Jewish propaganda *2:* 375
Anti-Semitism *1:* 2, 157-168
    and Hollywood *2:* 381
    and motion pictures *2:* 375-376

**Italic numerals indicate
volume numbers.**

**Illustrations are marked
by (ill.).**

Anzio *2:* 237-238
Appeasement *1:* 21-22
Arcadia Conference *2:* 208-209
Ardennes Forest *1:* 48-49, 49 (ill.)
    2: 292
Ardennes offensive (*see* Battle of
    the Bulge)
Area bombing *1:* 188-189, 193
Armia Krajowa (AK) (*see* Home
    Army [Polish])
Armistice
    French-German (1940) *1:* 54
    World War I *1:* 4
Army Group Center (German)
    1: 81-82, *2:* 279-280
Army Group North (German) *1:* 81
Arsenal of Democracy *1:* 63, 106
Asia, and the Pacific *2:* 307 (ill.)
Asia for the Asians policy *1:* 31,
    2: 414
Athens *1:* 75-76, 74 (ill.), 136
Atlantic Charter *2:* 208, 414
Atlantic Wall *2:* 254-255,
    255 (ill.), 353
Atlantic, Battle of (*see* Battle
    of the Atlantic)
Atomic bomb *2:* 223, 337-344,
    338 (ill.), 340 (ill.), 363-368
Atrocities *1:* 30, 32, 157-179,
    2: 218-219, 298-299,
Attu *2:* 316
Auschwitz *1:* 178-179, 178 (ill.)
    202, *2:* 297
Australia *1:* 61, 101-102,
    2: 312, 393
Australian troops *2:* 318-319
Austria *1:* 4, 21, 160, 162, *2:* 403
Axis *1:* 69, 72, 75 (ill.), 103,
    2: 205, 224-226
Axis Sally (Mildred Gillars) *2:* 372

B

B-25 bomber *1:* 101
B-29 bomber (superfortress)
    2: 327-328, 334-335
Babi Yar *1:* 171
Baby boom, *2:* 406
Badoglio, Marshal Pietro *2:* 235
Bagration, Operation *2:* 278- 282
Barbarossa, Operation *1:* 77-82,
    79 (ill.)
Bari, Italy *1:* 195

Bataan *1:* 96-97, *2:* 327
Bataan Death March *1:* 97
Battle of Britain *1:* 55-60, 58 (ill.),
    59 (ill.), 182 (ill.), 185-186,
    2: 201 (ill.), 360
Battle of Midway *1:* 102-103
Battle of the Atlantic *1:* 66-69,
    68 (ill.), *2:* 227
Battle of the Bulge *2:* 292 (ill.),
    292-294
    and African-American troops
    1: 115
    and intelligence *2:* 346
Battle of the Coral Sea *1:* 100
    (ill.), 101-102
BBC (*see* British Broadcasting
    Corporation)
Beethoven's Fifth Symphony
    2: 371
Belarus (*see* White Russia)
Belgium *1:* 47-48, 49 (ill.), 138,
    183, *2:* 270, 355, 396
Belorussia (*see* White Russia)
Belzec concentration camp *1:* 173
Bengal, famine in (1943) *2:* 412
Bergman, Ingrid *2:* 382, 382 (ill.)
Berlin *1:* 191, *2:* 395 (ill.), 397 (ill.)
Berlin, Battle of *2:* 301-304
Bethe, Hans *2:* 366
Bielsko *1:* 164
Blücher (German battleship) *1:* 47
Black Code (American attaché
    code) *2:* 357
Black market *1:* 110, 112, 136
Black shirts (Italy) *1:* 12
Blackout *1:* 187, 200
Bletchley Park (Ultra
    headquarters) *2:* 358
Blitz (*see* Battle of Britain)
Blitzkrieg *1:* 40-41
Bogart, Humphrey *2:* 382, 382 (ill.)
Bohemia *1:* 23
Bombardment air, D-Day *2:* 264
Bombardment, naval, D-Day
    2: 264
Bomber Command (Royal Air
    Force) *1:* 188-189, 193
"Bomber" Harris (*see* Harris,
    Sir Arthur)
Bond drives *1:* 108
Bonin Islands *2:* 326 (ill.)
Book burnings *2:* 373
Bosnia *1:* 154-155

Bougainville *2:* 318, 357
Bourke-White, Margaret *2:* 387
Boycott, anti-Jewish *1:* 159
Braun, Eva *2:* 303
Britain (*see* Great Britain)
British Army
    and Battle of Falaise
      (Normandy) *2:* 269
    evacuation from Dunkirk
      1: 51-53
    in Greece *1:* 76
    in invasion of Normandy 260,
      265
    in North Africa 69-72
    women in *1:* 197-198
British Broadcasting Corporation
    (BBC) *1:* 138, *2:* 370
British Expeditionary Force (BEF)
    1: 48, 50-53
Broad front strategy *2:* 292
Brotherhood of Sleeping Car
    Porters *1:* 112
Broz, Josip (*see* Tito)
Brussels, liberation of *2:* 270
Bulgaria *1:* 73-74, *2:* 225-226,
    298-299
Bulge (*see* Battle of the Bulge)
Burma *1:* 84-85, 99, *2:* 305
Burma Road *1:* 84-85, *2:*306 (ill.)
Buzz-bomb *see* V-1

C

Caen, France *2:* 260, 268
Cairo, Egypt *2:* 357
Cavalry (Polish) *1:* 40-41, 41 (ill.)
Canada *1:* 61
    joint defense planning with
      U.S. *1:* 65
    losses in the war *2:* 393
Canadian Army
    and Battle of Falaise
      (Normandy) *2:* 269
    and D-Day *2:* 260
    and Dieppe raid *2:* 257
Canaris, Admiral Wilhelm
    2: 350, 354
Capra, Frank *2:* 379
Casablanca, Morocco *2:* 228, 230
Casablanca Conference
    2: 214 (ill.), 215-216
Casablanca 2: 382 (ill.), 382-383
Casualties *2:* 391-393

Cassino *2:* 236-238, 238 (ill.),
    239 (ill.)
Caucasus *2:* 242, 246
Censorship *1:* 138, *2:* 376
Central Pacific Area (Nimitz)
    2: 312 (ill.)
Ceylon, Japanese naval raid on
    (1942) *2:* 311
Chain reaction, nuclear
    2: 364-265
Chamberlain, Neville *1:* 22, 48
Chelmno *1:* 173
Chetniks *1:* 153-154
Chiang Kai-Shek *1:* 33,
    2: 222 (ill.)
Children *1:* 121, 124-125,
    199-204, 201 (ill.), 203 (ill.),
    2: 304 (ill.), 338 (ill.)
China
    and Korea *1:* 28
    Civil war in *1:* 33
    Communist Party of *1:* 33
    establishment of Republic *1:* 33
    Japanese atrocities in *1:* 30
    Japanese troops in *2:* 305
    Japanese invasion of *1:* 27-29,
      32-34
    losses in the war *2:* 411
Choltitz, Dietrich von *2:* 273, 275
Chuikov, Vasili *2:* 244
Churchill, Winston *1:* 48, 53,
    2: 207- 211, 214 (ill.),
    221 (ill.), 230, 252, 336 (ill.)
Codes and code-breaking *1:* 66,
    2: 356-359
Cold War *2:* 397
Collaboration *1:* 148, 149 (ill.)
Collective security *1:* 6
Cologne, air raid *1:* 189, 190 (ill.)
Colonies *2:* 208, 413
Combined Chiefs of Staff *2:* 209
Commandos *2:* 257, 266
Common Market *2:* 396
Communism *1:* 151-152, *2:* 206,
    219, 283
Communist Party *1:* 7, 16, 17, 33,
    2: 272, 411
Concentration camps *1:* 16,
    172-176
Confessions of a Nazi Spy 2: 379
Convoys, ship *1:* 66
Copenhagen *1:* 46
Coral Sea, Battle of *1:* 100 (ill.),
    101-102

Corregidor *1:* 96-97, 97 (ill.),
   2: 327
Correspondents, war *2:* 285-286
Cotentin peninsula *2:* 259, 268
Counter-intelligence and
   intelligence *2:* 345-359
Crete *1:* 76
Crimean Peninsula *2:* 242
Croatia *1:* 74, 153-156
Crystal Night *1:* 160
Curfew *1:* 137, 141
Curzon Line *2:* 216
Czechoslovakia *1:* 21-23, 23 (ill.)
   resistance in *1:* 141, 143-145

D

D-Day (invasion of Normandy)
   2: 251- 267, 253 (ill.), 260
   (ill.), 278, 347
Dachau concentration camp *1:* 16
   (ill.), *2:* 301
Daladier, Edouard *1:* 22
Danzig *1:* 23, 35, 36 (ill.)
Darlan, Admiral Jean François
   2: 230-231, 231 (ill.)
Davies, Joseph E. *2:* 384
Davis, Benjamin O. *1:* 117
De Gaulle, Charles *1:* 146,
   2: 213-215, 214 (ill.),
   230, 272
Death camps *1:* 172-173
Death march
   Bataan *1:* 97
   from Auschwitz *2:* 297
   from Dachau *2:* 301
Defense Stamps *1:* 108
Denazification *2:* 399
Denmark *1:* 46
   and U.S. defense of Greenland
     1: 66
   anti-German strikes in *1:* 143
   non-violent resistance in *1:* 142
   underground newspapers
     1: 138
Deportations *1:* 172-173
Depression (economic) *1:* 8-10,
   9 (ill.)
Desert Fox (*see* Rommel, Erwin)
Desert War *1:* 69-72
Destination Tokyo *2:* 385
Destroyers for bases agreement
   (1940) *1:* 64-65

Detroit, migration to *1:* 108, 118
Detroit riot (June 1943) *1:* 118
DeWitt, John L. *1:* 127
Die Grosse Liebe (The Great Love)
   2: 378
Dieppe *2:* 256-257
Discrimination
   against African Americans
     1: 114-118
   against Japanese Americans
     1: 125-129
   against Jews *1:* 157-179
   in U.S. armed services
     1: 114-117
Dönitz, Admiral Karl *2:* 304
Donovan, William J. "Wild Bill"
   2: 354
Doolittle, James *1:* 101
Double-Cross System *2:* 349
Double-V campaign *1:* 113
Dover *2:* 259
Drôle de guerre *1:* 44
Draft, military *1:* 106
   of women (Britain) *1:* 197
Dresden, air raid *1:* 191-193,
   192 (ill.)
Dulles, Allen *2:* 206 (ill.), 354,
   354 (ill.)
Dunkirk *1:* 51-53, 49 (ill.), 51
   (ill.), 52 (ill.)
Dutch East Indies *1:* 85, 99-100

E

East Africa, Italian campaign in
   1: 69
East Asia *1:* 28 (ill.), 84 (ill.)
East Prussia *1:* 35, *2:* 296-297,
   402-403
Eastern front *1:* 77-82, *2:* 238-249,
   243 (ill.), 278-281, 281 (ill.)
Economic policy
   in occupation of western
     Europe *1:* 135
   in occupied Poland *1:* 133
Economy, U.S. *1:* 105-108
Edelweiss Pirates *1:* 204
Egypt *1:* 69, 72, *2:* 227
Eiffel Tower *2:* 273
Eighth Army (British) *2:* 227
82nd Airborne Division (U.S.)
   2: 263

Einsatzgruppen *1:* 134, 162, 170
Einstein, Albert *2:* 366
Eisenhower, Dwight D.
    2: 263 (ill.)
    and broadfront strategy *2:* 292
    and Montgomery-Patton dispute *2:* 292
    and opposition to use of
        atomic bomb *2:* 341
    and surrender of Germany
        2: 304
    decides to launch D-Day *2:* 262
    message on D-Day *2:* 262
El Alamein *2:* 227-228
Emperor of Japan (Hirohito)
    1: 25, *2:* 335-337, 339-340
Emperor-system (Japan) *2:* 337
Enabling Act *1:* 17
England (*see* Britain)
English Channel *1:* 50, *2:* 253
    (ill.), 254
Enigma *2:* 358
Enterprise, USS *1:* 103
Estonia *1:* 38, 151, 403
Ethiopia *1:* 13, 69
Evacuations, from London
    1: 200-203, 203 (ill.)
Executive Order 8802 (Fair
    Employment Practices)
    1: 113
Extermination camps *1:* 173

F

Fair Employment Practices
    Commission (FEPC) *1:* 113
Fall of France *1:* 53-55
Fascism *1:* 10-13
Fashion *1:* 111, 200
FEPC (Fair Employment Practices
    Commission) *1:* 113
Fermi, Enrico *2:* 366
Fighting France (*see* Free French
    movement)
The Fighting Lady 2: 379
The Fighting Seabees 2: 385
Film (*see* motion pictures)
Film industry, American *2:* 378
    (*see also* Hollywood)
Final solution *1:* 172
Finland *2:* 226, 279
Firestorm *1:* 190, 192

1st Marine Division (U.S.) *2:* 316
First United States Army Group
    (FUSAG) *2:* 348
Flag raising at Iwo Jima
    2: 329 (ill.)
Forced labor *1:* 138-139, 165-166
Fortitude, Operation *2:* 347-349
442nd Infantry Regiment (Nisei)
    1: 129
Fourcade, Marie-Madeleine
    2: 354-355
4th Infantry Division (U.S.)
    2: 265, 274
France
    and Czechoslovakian crisis *1:* 21
    defeat of (1940) *1:* 53-55
    destruction in *2:* 394
    German invasion of (1940)
        1: 49-53, 49 (ill.)
    German economic policy in
        1: 135
    losses in the war *2:* 392
    rationing in *1:* 136
    resistance *1:* 145-147
    underground newspapers *1:* 138
    under occupation 135-149
Franco, Francisco *1:* 13, 21 *2:* 224
Frank, Hans *1:* 133
Free French movement *2:* 146,
    213, 230
French Indochina *1:* 84, 88
French navy
    scuttling of fleet at Toulon
        2: 232
French North Africa *2:* 251
French resistance 140 (ill.),
    146, 150 (ill.), *2:* 213, 230,
    354-355
Frisch, Otto *2:* 365
FUSAG (*see* First United States
    Army Group)

G

Göring, Hermann *2:* 386
Gandhi, Mohandas *2:* 416
Garson, Greer *2:* 381
Gas chambers *1:* 177, 179
Gasoline, rationing of *1:* 110
Gaulle, Charles de
    (*see* de Gaulle, Charles)
Gdansk (*see* Danzig)

General Government (Poland)
   1: 133
General Winter *1:* 82
Generals, German
   and Hitler *2:* 240-242, 290
Generals' Plot (*see* Plot to
   kill Hitler)
German air force (*see* Luftwaffe)
German army
   and attack on Poland *1:* 38-43,
      42 (ill.)
   children in *2:* 304 (ill.)
   in Africa *1:* 70-72, *2:* 227-228,
      231-233
   in Greece *1:* 73-76, 74 (ill.)
   in Italy *2:* 233, 236-238
   in Russia *1:* 77-81, 78 (ill.),
      80 (ill.), *2:* 238-240, 241-249,
      246 (ill.)
   losses in Soviet Union *2:* 239
Germany
   after World War I *1:* 4-22
   air raids in *1:*189-192
   Allies in *2:*295-304, 302 (ill.)
   border changes (1945)
      1: 5 (ill.), 36 (ill.),
      2: 402 (ill.), 403
   children in *1:* 203-204
   civilians wounded in air raids
      in *2:* 394
   destruction in *2:* 395
   division of *2:* 396, 398 (ill.)
   home front *1:*122-124
   industrial production in *1:* 193
   joins with Austria *1:* 21
   losses in the war *2:* 393
   Morgenthau Plan *2:* 396
   relations with other Axis
      powers *2:* 224-226
   treaty with Japan
      (Anti-Comintern Pact)
      (1936) *1:* 32
   treaty with the Soviet Union
      (Nazi-Soviet Pact) *1:* 37-38, 76
Germany first (U.S. war strategy):
   1: 103-104, 307-308, 311
Gestapo *1:* 160
   and counter-intelligence *2:*
      349, 356
   and Edelweiss Pirates *1:* 204
   and plot to kill Hitler *2:* 290
   and spy hunting *2:* 355
Ghetto, Warsaw uprising (1943)
   2: 286

Ghettos (Poland) *1:* 165-167,
   167 (ill.)
GI Bill (Servicemen's
   Readjustment Act of 1944)
   2: 405-406
Gilbert islands *1:* 95, *2:* 319
Gillars, Mildred (Axis Sally)
   2: 372, 373 (ill.)
Giraud, Henri *2:* 214-215,
   214 (ill.)
Gliders *2:* 254
Goebbels, Josef *2:* 373-374, 383
Gold Beach (D-Day) *2:* 260,
   260 (ill.), 264-265
"Gothic Line" (Italy)
   2: 233 (ill.), 238
Government Code and Cipher
   School (Bletchley Park)
   2: 358
Government-in- exile
   Polish *2:* 218-219, 282
   Netherlands *1:* 85
Graf Spee *1:* 45
"Grand Alliance" *2:* 207
Great Britain *1:* 61-70, 253 (ill.)
   and Czechoslovakian crisis
      1: 21-22
   and second front *2:* 210
   and the Blitz *1:* 58-60
   Battle of Britain *1:* 55-60,
      185-186
   evacuations from London
      1: 199-202
   home front *1:* 122, 124
   in armed services 197-198
   losses in the war *2:* 393
   oil embargo against Japan *1:* 88
   relations with other Allied
      countries *2:* 206-213
   relations with United States
      2: 207-210
Great Depression *1:* 8-9
Great Marianas Turkey Shoot
   2: 320
Greater East Asia Coprosperity
   Sphere *1:* 100
Greece
   and Italian army *2:* 225
   execution of hostages in by
      Germans *1:* 142
   German invasion of *1:* 73-75
   Italian invasion of *1:* 72-73
   losses in the war *2:* 392

under occupation *1:* 136
withdrawal of German troops
from *2:* 299
Greenland *1:* 66
Grossen-Wannsee Conference
(*see* Wannsee Conference)
Groves, Leslie *2:* 367 (ill.)
Grynszpan, Hershel *1:* 160
Guadalcanal *2:* 314 (ill.), 314-316
and Navajo code-talkers *2:* 358
Guadalcanal Diary 2: 385
Guam *1:* 95, *2:* 320
Guernica (Spain), bombing of
1: 21
Guerrilla warfare
in Ethiopia *1:* 69
in occupied Europe *1:*144-147,
149-152, 155-156
"Gustav Line" (Italy)
2: 233 (ill.), 236

H

Halsey, Admiral William *2:* 313
Hamburg *1:* 190-191, 191 (ill.)
Hanford, Washington *2:* 366
Harlem riot (August 1943) *1:* 118
Harris, Sir Arthur
1: 189, 189 (ill.)
Hawaii *1:* 89
Health and disease
in occupied Europe *1:* 137
Hedgerows (Normandy) *2:* 268,
269 (ill.)
Heisenberg, Werner *2:* 364
Hepburn, Katherine *2:* 378
Heydrich, Reinhard *1:* 141,
164-165, 165 (ill.), 172
Himmler, Heinrich *1:* 134, 172
Hindenburg, Paul von *1:* 13-14,
18
Hirohito (Emperor of Japan)
1: 25, *2:* 335-337, 339-340
Hiroshima *2:* 224, 337-338,
338 (ill.), 340
Hitchcock, Alfred *2:* 379
Hitler Youth *1:* 204, *2:* 304 (ill.)
Hitler Youth Division (Waffen SS)
1: 204
Hitler, Adolf *1:* 19 (ill.), 20 (ill.),
54, 54 (ill.), 73, 76, 133, 157,
2: 210, 240 (ill.), 245, 273,
349, 256, 273, 356

death of *2:* 303
plot to kill *2:* 287-290
relations with generals
2: 240-241
rise to power *1:* 10-18
Hitler-Stalin Pact
(*see* Nazi-Soviet Pact)
HMS *Prince of Wales 1:* 98
HMS *Repulse 1:* 98
Hollywood *2:* 378-379, 383
Holocaust *1:* 157-179, 158 (ill.),
163 (ill.) 167 (ill.), 169 (ill.),
175 (ill.), 178 (ill.)
and children *1:* 202
Home Army (Polish) *1:* 35,
2: 282-284
and Warsaw uprising (1944)
2: 282-286
Home front *1:* 105-129
Hong Kong *1:* 95
Honolulu *1:* 89
Honshu *2:* 332
Hornet *1:* 103
Hostages *1:* 140-142
France *1:* 142
Greece *1:* 142
Hungarian army *1:* 78
Hungary *2:* 225
and communism *2:* 220
and Yugoslavia *1:* 74
army in Soviet Union *2:* 244
attack by Romania on *2:* 298
deaths in *2:* 393
German economic policy in
1: 135
Hunger winter (Netherlands)
1: 136
Hyper-inflation *1:* 8

I

Iceland *1:* 66
Ie Shima *2:* 388
Ikoku, Iva Toguri (TokyoRose)
2: 373
The Immortal Sergeant 2: 385
Imperialism *1:* 27
Incendiary bombs *1:* 188
India *1:* 61, 62 (ill.), 99
and Atlantic Charter *2:* 208
Bengal famine (1943) *2:* 412
independence movement in
2: 415 (ill.), 416
losses in the war *2:* 393

Indochina *1:* 84, *2:* 416
Indonesia *1:* 85. *2:* 415
   (*see also* Dutch East Indies)
Industry
   American *1:*106-108, 109 (ill.),
     111-112
   and Battle of the Atlantic *1:* 66
   women in *1:* 119-124, 119 (ill.),
     120 (ill.)
Inflation *1:* 8
Intelligence *2:*345-359
International Military Tribunal
   (*see* Nuremberg trials)
Internment, Japanese-Americans
   1: 127
Iraq *1:* 69
Irish-Americans *1:* 113
Ironbottom Sound (Guadalcanal)
   2: 315
Island hopping strategy
   2: 307-310, 318
Isolationism *1:* 6, 62-63
Issei *1:* 125
It's A Wonderful Life 2: 379
Italian army
   in Albania *1:*72-73
   in Greece *1:* 73
   in invasion of Soviet Union
     1: 78
   in East Africa *1:* 69
   losses in Russia and Africa
     2: 234
Italian Socialist Republic *2:* 235
Italian-Americans *1:* 127
Italy *1:* 12
   Allied invasion of *2:* 233 (ill.),
     233-238, 234 (ill.), 251
   Allied military government in
     2: 220
   and aid to Ustashi *1:* 154
   and Albania *1:* 72-73
   and Desert War *1:* 69
   and Greece *1:* 72
   and Soviet Union *2:* 220
   and Yugoslavia *1:* 74
   anti-war sentiment in *1:* 72
   army in Soviet union *2:* 244
   declaration of war against
     Germany (1943) *2:* 236
   disarming of troops by
     Germany *2:* 236
   losses in the war *2:* 393
   relations with Germany
     2: 224-225, 235

   rise of Fascism *1:* 12
   strikes in *1:* 144
Iwo Jima *1:* 195, *2:* 309 (ill.),
   326 (ill.), 327 (ill.), 327-328,
   329 (ill.)

J

Japan *2:* 333 (ill.)
   and Germany *2:* 224
   and Soviet Union *1:* 37, 87,
     2: 220
   before World War II *1:* 24-27
   losses in the war *2:* 410
   modernization of *1:* 25-26,
     27 (ill.)
   negotiations with U.S. (1941)
     1: 88
   occupation of French
     Indochina *1:* 85
   oil embargo against *1:* 88
   seizure of Manchuria (1931)
     1: 29
   Soviet Union declares war on
     2: 222
   surrender of *2:* 339-340, 343
     (ill.), 344
   tensions with United States
     1: 32
   territories *1:* 84 (ill.)
   treaty with Nazi Germany
     (Anti-Comintern Pact) (1936)
     1: 32
   use of poison gas by *1:* 195
   war crimes trials *2:* 410
   war strategy *1:* 93
   war with China (1937-1945)
     1: 32-34
Japanese army
   atrocities in China by *1:* 30, 32
   conflicts w/Japanese Navy
     2: 311
Japanese-Americans *1:* 125-129
Japanese-Soviet Neutrality Treaty
   (1941) *1:* 87
Jasenovac concentration camp
   1: 154
Java *1:* 99
Java Sea, Battle of *1:* 99
Jets, German *2:* 362-363
Jewish Council (Judenrat)
   1: 165-166

Jewish star *1:* 166, 172
Jews
and building of atomic bomb
2: 366
and German occupation
policies *1:* 132, 162-163,
163 (ill.)
and German propaganda *2:* 371
and Hollywood *2:* 381
and Holocaust *1:* 157-179, 158
(ill.), 175 (ill.), 178 (ill.)
Eastern European *1:* 77
Nazi racial theories concerning
1: 77
removal of from teaching jobs
in Netherlands *1:* 143
Jews, Finnish *2:* 279
Jews, Polish *2:* 392
Jews, Russian *1:* 168-170, 169 (ill.)
Joyce, William (Lord Haw Haw)
2: 372
Jud Süss 2: 375
Judenrat (Jewish Council)
1: 165-166
July Plot *2:* 287-290
Juno Beach *2:* 260, 260 (ill.),
264-265

K

Kaiser (German Emperor),
abdication of *1:* 4
Kamikaze *2:* 325, 329, 331-332
Kasserine Pass *2:* 232
Katyn Massacre *2:* 218-219
Kenya *1:* 69
Khan, Noor Inayat *2:* 355
Kharkov *2:* 242, 247
Kiev *1:* 171
battle of *1:* 78
liberation of *2:* 248
Kindertransporte 1: 202
King, Admiral Erneŝt
and Germany first strategy
2: 310
Kirkpatrick, Helen *2:* 387
Klisura *1:* 142
Kolberg 2: 376
Kolombangara *2:* 318
Kolomyja *1:* 174
Korea *1:* 27-28, 31
Kovno *1:* 170
Kremlin *1:* 81

Kristallnacht (see Crystal Night)
Kulmhof (Chelmno)
concentration camp*1:* 173
Kuomintang (Chinese Nationalist
Party) *1:* 33, *2:* 411
Kursk *2:* 247-249
Kursk salient *2:* 247-248
Kwajalein *2:* 320
Kyushu, planned invasion of
2: 332

L

Labor camps *1:* 166
The Lady Vanishes 2: 379
Lake, Veronica *1:* 121
Lang, Fritz *2:* 383
Latin America, U.S. influence in
2: 208
Latvia *1:* 38, 76, 151, *2:* 403
Laval, Pierre *1:* 148
League of German Girls *1:* 204
League of Nations *1:* 6, *2:* 408
Leahy, William D. *2:* 341
Leander, Zarah *2:* 378
Lebensraum *1:* 76, 132
Leclerc, Phillip *2:* 274
Leipzig *1:* 161
Lend-Lease Act *1:* 65, 87, 106,
2: 207, 213
Lenin, Vladimir Ilich *1:* 81
Leningrad
losses in the war *2:* 392
siege of *1:* 81, *2:* 377
Leningrad
Symphony(Shostakovitch)
2: 377
Levittown, NY *2:* 407 (ill.)
Lewis, John L. *1:* 112
Lexington, USS, sinking of *1:* 101
Leyte *2:* 324-326
Leyte Gulf *2:* 324-325
The Liberation of Rome 2: 379
Liberty ships *1:* 66, 67 (ill.)
Libya *1:* 69, 70, *2:* 227
Liddell Hart, B. H. *1:* 188, *2:* 216
Lidice *1:* 141
Lindbergh, Charles *1:* 63
Lithuania *1:* 38, 76, 170, *2:* 280
collaboration with Germans
in *1:* 151
incorporated in Soviet Union
2: 403

Litvak, Anatole *2:* 379
Litvak, Lily *1:* 197
Lodz ghetto *1:* 166-168
London
    and V-1 *2:* 361
    attacks on in Battle of Britain
        1: 57-60, 182 (ill.), 186
    evacuations from 199-202,
        203 (ill.)
London Poles *2:* 218, 282-286
    and Warsaw uprising(1944)
        2: 284-286
    anti-communism of *2:* 283
Lord Haw Haw (William Joyce)
    2: 372
Los Alamos, New Mexico
    2: 367
Los Angeles
    migration to *1:* 108
    riots in (June 1943) *1:* 118
Louis, Joe *1:* 117
Louvre Museum *2:* 273
Lübeck *1:* 188
Lublin *1:* 166, 173-174
    liberation of *2:* 280
Lublin Committee *2:* 219, 283
    and Warsaw uprising (1944)
        2: 283
Luftwaffe *1:* 42, 182, *2:* 253
    and Battle of Britain *1:* 185
    and Battle of Stalingrad
        2: 245
    and strafing of refugees
        1: 53, 183
    at Dunkirk *1:* 52
    bombing of Rotterdam *1:* 48
    bombing of Warsaw *1:* 42
    first attack on London by
        1: 185
    in Battle of Britain *1:* 56
    in Battle of France *1:* 53
    in Crete *1:* 76
    in German invasion of
        Soviet Union *1:* 77
    in Norway *1:* 47
    in Soviet Union *2:* 240
    in Yugoslavia *1:* 74
    night bombing of Britain
        1: 186
Luxembourg *2:* 292, 396
Luzon *1:* 96, *2:* 326
Lvov *1:* 173, *2:* 280

M

MacArthur, Douglas *1:*98
    and Army-Navy rivalry *2:* 312
    and Japanese surrender cere-
        mony *2:* 344
    and Chester Nimitz *2:* 313
    and occupation of Japan *2:* 410
    in the Philippines 95-98, *2:* 324
Magic (American interception of
    Japanese codes) *2:* 357
Maginot Line *1:* 48-50, 49 (ill.)
Malaya *1:* 97
Malaysia *1:* 97
Malmédy massacre *2:* 293,
    294 (ill.), 295 (ill.)
The Man Who Never Was *2:* 346
Manchukuo *1:* 30-31
Manchuria *1:* 28-29, *2:* 221-222,
    333, 342, 339, 411
Manhattan District of the Army
    Corps of Engineers *2:* 366
Manhattan Project *2:* 223,
    365-368
Manila *1:* 96, *2:* 326
Manzanar *1:* 129
Mao Zedong *2:* 413 (ill.)
Maquis *1:* 140 (ill.)
March on Washington
    Movement. *1:* 112
Mariana Islands *2:* 320, 323,
    326 (ill.)
Marine Corps Monument to Iwo
    Jima *2:* 328
Marine Corps (U.S.)
    and African-Americans
        1: 114-115, 117
    and Nimitz *2:* 311
    at Guadalcanal *2:* 313-316,
        314 (ill.)
    at Iwo Jima *2:* 309 (ill.),
        327-328
    at Okinawa *2:* 328-332,
        330 (ill.), 331 (ill.)
    at Tarawa *2:* 319
Marseille *2:* 271
Marshall, George C. *2:* 209-211
    and African-Americans *1:* 114
    as Roosevelt's top military
        advisor *2:* 209
Marshall Islands *2:* 319-320
Master race *1:* 157
Mauldin, Bill *2:* 389, 389 (ill.)
Medical experiments *1:* 179

Meiji Restoration *1:* 26
Memorial Day Massacre *1:* 105
Meredith, Burgess *2:* 390
Meuse River *1:* 49
Mexican-Americans *1:* 118
Midway Island *1:* 100
Midway, Battle of *1:* 102-103,
     2: 357
Migration *1:* 108
Mihailovic, Draza *1:* 153, 154, 156
Milice (France) *1:* 148
Militarism, Japanese *1:* 30-31, 83
     2: 410
Military strategy
   common U.S.-British *2:* 207
   in Pacific war *1:* 103
Miller, Dorie *1:* 118
Mines *2:* 255, 265, 334
Minsk, liberation of *2:* 280
Mission to Moscow *2:* 384
Mobilization *1:* 39
Monte Cassino (*see* Cassino)
Montenegro *1:* 154-155
Montevideo *1:* 45
Montgomery, Bernard L. *2:* 228
   dispute with Patton *2:* 291
   in Italy *2:* 235
   in Sicily *2:* 233
   named ground commander for
      D-Day *2:* 252
   troops of cross Rhine *2:* 299
The Moon is Down *2:* 383
Moravia *1:* 23
Morocco *2:* 228-230
Mortain counter-offensive *2:* 359
Moscow, Battle of *1:* 81
Motion pictures
   American *2:* 378-385
   German *2:* 374
   in occupied Europe *1:* 137
Mountbatten, Lord Louis
     2: 415 (ill.)
Mrs. Miniver *2:* 380, 382
Mt. Suribachi (Iwo Jima) *2:* 328
Mulberries (artificial harbors)
     2: 258-259, 259 (illus.)
Münchhausen *2:* 378
Munich Conference *1:* 21
Murmansk *2:* 213
Muslims (Bosnian), persecution
     by Ustashi of *1:* 154
Mussolini, Benito
   and Albania and Greece *1:* 72
   and Desert War *1:* 69

and Germany *2:* 224
and Italian Social Republic
     2: 235
at Munich Conference *1:* 21
declares war on France and
      Britain *1:* 53
declining popularity of *1:* 72
execution of *2:* 235
fall of *2:* 235
jealousy of Hitler *1:* 72
loss of empire *2:* 234
rescue of by Germans *2:* 235
rise of *1:* 12
Mustang (American fighter plane)
     1: 194
Myanmar *1:* 99

N

*Nacht und Nebe*l (Night and Fog)
     1: 142
Nagasaki *2:* 224, 338, 340 (ill.)
Nanking, Rape of *1:* 32
Nantes *1:* 142
Naples, liberation of *2:* 236
Narvik *1:* 46, 46 (ill.)
Nationalist Party—China
     (Kuomintang) *1:* 33, *2:* 411
Nationalist Party (Germany)
     1: 17-18
Native Americans *2:* 358
Navajo code-talkers *2:* 358,
     359 (ill.)
Navy, British
   blockade of Germany in World
      War I *1:* 4
   in Battle of the Atlantic *1:* 66
Navy, Canadian
   in Battle of the Atlantic *1:* 66
Navy, U.S.
   and protection of convoys to
      Britain (1940-41) *1:* 65
   and rivalry with army *2:* 310
Nazi-Soviet Pact *1:* 37-38 (ill.),
     43, 76, *2:* 215,
   and Polish-Soviet relations
     2: 283
Nazis *1:* 10-18
Nehru, Jawaharlal
     2: 415 (ill.), 416
Netherlands *2:* 396
   and Dutch East Indies
      (Indonesia) *1:* 85

deaths in *2:* 392
evasion of forced labor in *1:* 139
food rationing and starvation
  in *1:* 136
German reprisals in *1:* 141
invasion of *1:* 47
non-violent resistance in *1:* 142
starvation in (1944-45) *2:* 394
student protests in *1:* 143
underground newspapers *1:* 138
Networks, intelligence
  in occupied Europe *2:* 352-353
New Britain *2:* 317, 319
New Georgia *2:* 317
New Guinea *1:* 101, *2:* 317 (ill.),
  318, 321, 323
New Ireland *2:* 319
New Order *2:* 371
Newfoundland
  meeting of Roosevelt and
    Churchill (August 1941)
    2: 207
Newspapers, underground *1:* 138
Newsreels *2:* 376
Nice *2:* 271
Nigeria *1:* 69
Night and Fog (*Nacht und Nebel*)
  1: 142
Night bombing by RAF *1:* 187
Night witches *1:* 197
Nimitz, Chester *2:* 311, 313, 316
92nd Infantry Division *1:* 115
93rd Infantry Divisions *1:* 115
99th Fighter Squadron *1:* 117
Nisei *1:* 125
No-strike pledge *1:* 108, 112
Noah's Ark (intelligence network)
  2: 354
Normandy *2:* 253 (ill.), 260 (ill.)
  262, 269 (ill.)
  and Allied bombing campaign
    1: 189
  and Ultra *2:* 359
  Polish troops in *1:* 43
  intelligence *2:* 347
  (*see also* D-Day)
Normandy, Battle of (June-Aug
  1944) *2:* 268-271, 270 (ill.),
  271 (ill.)
  (*see also* D-Day)
Normandy Invasion (*see* D-Day)
North Africa *1:* 69-72, 71 (ill.),
  2: 227-233, 229 (ill.)

Allied invasion of *2:* 211, 212
  (ill.), 228-230
  Italian invasion of 69-70
North Pacific Area *2:*312 (ill.), 313
Norway *1:* 46 (ill.)
  German invasion of *1:* 45-47
  German reprisals in *1:* 141
  in American motion pictures
    2: 383
Notre Dame Cathedral (Paris)
  2: 387
Nuremberg laws *1:* 159
Nuremberg rallies *2:* 374
Nuremberg trials *2:* 399-401,
  400 (ill.)
Nurses, U.S. Army *1:* 198, 198 (ill.)
Nutrition
  during occupation *1:* 136

O

Oahu *1:* 89
Oak Ridge, Tennessee *2:* 366
Occupation *1:* 131-156
Office of Price Administration
  and Civilian Supply (OPA)
  1: 110
Office of Production Manage-
  ment (OPM) *1:* 106
Office of Strategic Services (OSS)
  1: 155, *2:* 354
Office of War Information (OWI)
  2: 382
Officers, German
  and relations with Hitler *2:* 287
Oil fields *1:* 69, 73
Okinawa *2:* 306, 326 (ill.), 328,
  330 (ill.), 332
Olympic Games (Berlin 1936)
  2: 374
Omaha Beach *2:* 260, 260 (ill.),
  266-267, 267 (ill.)
Onderduikers (divers) *1:* 140
101st Airborne Division (US)
  2: 263
OPA (*see* Office of Price Adminis-
  tration and Civilian Supply)
Operation Anvil *2:* 271-272,
  272 (ill.)
Operation Barbarossa *1:* 77
Operation Overlord (*see* D-Day)
Operation Torch *2:* 211,
  212 (ill.), 228

Oppenheimer, J. Robert
  2: 367 (ill.), 367-368
Oran *2:* 228, 230
Orphans *1:* 202-203
Oslo *1:* 47, 46 (ill.)
Oslo Report (British intelligence)
  2: 350
OSS (*see* Office of Strategic
  Services)
Overlord, Operation (*see* D-Day)
OWI (*see* Office of War
  Information)
Oxford, England *2:* 358

P

Pétain, Marshal Henri Phillippe
  1: 54
  and end of French democracy
    1: 145-146
P-51 Mustang (American fighter
  plane) *1:* 194
Pacific Command division
  2: 312 (ill.)
Pacific ocean, islands *1:* 94 (ill.),
  2: 307 (ill.)
Pacific war
  American strategy for *2:* 306
  size of Japanese forces in *2:* 310
  size of U.S. forces in *2:* 309,
    2: 310
Panzer (tank) divisions (German)
  1: 39, 77
Papua, New Guinea *2:* 318, 319
Parachute troops
  at D-Day *2:* 260
  and capture of Crete *1:* 76
Paratroopers (illus) *2:* 263
Paris
  and plot to kill Hitler *2:* 289
  food rationing in *1:* 136
  liberation of *2:* 271-274
  surrender to Germans of *1:* 53
Partisans
  and Operation Bagration
    (White Russia) *2:* 279
  in Slovakis *1:* 145
  in the Soviet Union *1:* 149-152,
    196-197, 196 (ill.)
  in Yugoslavia *1:* 155
  liberation of Belgrade by *2:* 299
  women *1:* 197
Pas de Calais *2:* 259, 271

Patton, George S. *2:* 270-271
  and African-American troops
    1: 115
  and FUSAG *2:* 348
  and Normandy *2:* 269
  and Bill Mauldin *2:* 390
  dispute with Montgomery
    2: 291
  in North Africa *2:* 233
  in Sicily *2:* 233
  reaction to Buchenwald *2:* 301
  troops of cross Rhine *2:* 298
Paul, Prince (Yugoslav Regent)
  1: 73
Pearl Harbor *1:* 89-92, 92 (ill.)
  and intelligence *2:* 345
  and President Roosevelt *1:* 90
  Japanese attack on *1:* 89-91,
    91 (ill.)
Peenemünde *2:* 363
Peierls, Rudolf *2:* 365
Peking *1:* 32
People's Republic of China *1:* 33
Percival, Sir Arthur *2:* 344
Perry, Matthew *1:* 25
Petroleum
  in Caucasus *2:* 242
Philippine Sea, Battle of the *2:* 320
Philippines *1:* 86, *2:* 324 (ill.)
  American policy towards *2:* 323
  American reconquest of *2:* 323
  guerrillas in *2:* 324
  Japanese invasion and conquest
    of *1:* 95
Phony War *1:* 43
Pianists (radio operators) *2:* 356
Picasso, Pablo *1:* 21
Planes *1:* 106
  production of by U.S., Japan,
    Germany *2:* 308
Plot to kill Hitler *2:* 287, 289
Poison gas *1:* 194-195
Poland
  and border changes *2:* 217,
    217 (ill.), 403
  and Soviet-Western differences
    2: 215
  attitude towards Soviet Union
    (1939) *1:* 36
  border with Soviet Union *2:* 217
  disease in *2:* 394
  expulsion of German popula-
    tion from *2:* 402
  German invasion of *1:* 23-24,
    38-43, 42 (ill.)

German demands on *1:* 23, 35
German economic policy in
    1: 133
German occupation policies
    1: 133
Jewish population of *1:* 162
losses in the war *2:* 392
orphans in *1:* 202-203
territorial gains from Germany
    1: 5
Polish army *1:* 39-43
Polish Committee of National
    Liberation (*see* Lublin
    Committee)
Polish Corridor *1:* 6, 35, 36 (ill.)
Polish troops
    and capture of Cassino *2:* 237
Polish-Soviet relations *2:* 218, 282
Port Arthur *1:* 29
Port Moresby *2:* 318
Potsdam Conference *2:* 336 (ill.)
Potsdam Declaration *2:* 335-337
Poznan *1:* 134
Prague *1:* 143
Prelude to War 2: 379
Prisoners-of-war
    American *1:* 97, 124
    French *1:* 139
    Soviet *1:* 132
    German *1:* 202
Production, industrial 106-108
Propaganda *2:* 370-371, 373
Protests, against German
    occupation *1:* 142-143
Proximity fuse *2:* 360
Psychological warfare *2:* 372
Pulitzer Prize *2:* 387, 388
Purple Code *2:* 356, 357
The Purple Heart 2: 385
Putten *1:* 141
Pyle, Ernie *2:* 387-388,
    388 (ill.), 390

R

Rabaul *2:* 317, 319
Racial theories, Nazi *1:* 77, 132
Racism
    against African Americans in
        the military 114-117
    against Japanese Americans
        1: 125-129, 128 (ill.) *2:* 383

against the Japanese *1:* 96,
    125-126, 126 (ill.)
in Japan *1:* 31
Radar
    and Battle of Britain *1:* 56,
        2: 360
    and invasion of Normandy
        2: 349
    development of *2:* 360
    German *2:* 360
    in Battle of the Atlantic *1:* 68
Radio *2:* 372-374
Radio transmitters
    and intelligence work
        2: 352, 355
RAF (*see* Royal Air Force)
Railroads
    government seizure of *1:* 112
    destruction of Soviet *2:* 394
Rains, Claude *2:* 382 (ill.)
Randolph, A. Philip *1:* 112, 113
Rangers, U.S.
    and D-Day *2:* 266
Rape of Nanking *1:* 32
Rationing *1:* 109-111, 110 (ill.),
    136, 200
Ray, Satyajit *2:* 412
Rearmament
    German *1:* 19
    British and French *1:* 22
Recruitment films *2:* 378
Red Army *1:* 77-82, *2:* 240-249
    and actions against civilians
        (East Prussia) *2:* 296
    and Warsaw uprising (1944)
        2: 285
    and winter 1945 offensive
        2: 296
    massacres in East Prussia (1945)
        2: 393
    Operation Bagration *2:* 278-282
    origin of name *2:* 356
    takes Warsaw *2:* 295-296
Red Ball Express. *2:* 291
Red Orchestra (intelligence
    network) *2:* 355-356
Refugees *1:* 159
    and atomic bomb *2:* 366
    and intelligence work *2:* 353
    in Battle of France *1:* 53
    in Dresden *1:* 192
    in East Prussia *2:* 296
Reich Citizenship Law (*see*
    Nuremberg laws)

Reichskristallnacht,
   (*see* Crystal Night)
Reichstag fire *1:* 15, 15 (ill.)
Reims *2:* 304
Relocation, of Japanese-Ameri-
   cans *1:* 127-128, 128 (ill.)
Remagen *2:* 298
Renault *1:* 137
Reparations (repayments) *1:* 7
Replacement Army (Ersatzheer)
   2: 288
Reprisal *1:* 140-141, 145
Republic of China *1:* 33
Reserve Police (German) *1:* 174
Resistance
   and forced labor *1:* 139
   and intelligence work *2:* 352
   and internal divisions *1:* 144
   in occupied Europe *1:* 140 (ill.)
      142-156, 150 (ill.)
   Poland *1:* 135
   punishment for *1:* 142
Resistance movements
   and intelligence work *2:* 352
   and Normandy invasion *2:* 353
   armed *1:* 144
   and North Africa *2:* 230
   attitude towards Giraud *2:* 214
   in France *1:* 140 (ill.), 146,
      148, 150 (ill.), *2:* 213,
      268, 353
   in the Soviet Union *1:* 150-152,
      151 (ill.)
   in motion pictures *2:* 382, 383
Retaliation *1:* 140
Rhine River *2:* 291, 298, 300 (ill.),
   301 (ill.)
Rhineland *1:* 5, 19, 204, *2:* 241
Ribbentrop-Molotov Pact (*see*
   Nazi-Soviet Pact)
Riefenstahl, Leni *2:* 374, 375 (ill.)
Riots
   Los Angeles (zoot suit riots)
      1: 118
   Detroit (June 1943) *1:* 118
   Harlem (August 1943) *1:* 118
   racial, in military *1:* 117
Roma (Gypsies) *1:* 154
Romania *2:* 225, 298
   army in Soviet Union *2:* 244
   German economic policy in
      1: 135
   losses in the war *2:* 393

Rome, liberation of *2:* 238
Rommel, Erwin *1:* 70-71, 70 (ill.),
   2: 228, 231, 232
   and breaking of American
      attache code *2:* 357
   and plot to kill Hitler *2:* 290
   in Normandy *2:* 261
   suicide of *2:* 290
Roosevelt, Eleanor *2:* 378
Roosevelt, Franklin D. *1:* 63, 90,
   93 (ill.), 103-104, 113, 127,
   2: 207-210, 214-216,
   214 (ill.), 221 (ill.), 303,
   341, 365-366, 408, 414
Rose of Stalingrad *1:* 197
Rosenthal, Joe (photographer)
   2: 328
Rosie the Riveter *1:* 119-121,
   109 (ill.)
Rostock *1:* 188
Rotterdam *1:* 48, 182
Royal Air Force (RAF) *1:* 55-59,
   57 (ill.), 183-193, 184 (ill.),
   187 (ill.)
   and D-Day *2:* 264
   and night bombing of
      Germany *1:* 187
   and strategic bombing *1:* 183
   at Dunkirk *1:* 52
   in Battle of Britain *1:* 55-56
   in motion pictures *2:* 380
Rubber, synthetic *1:* 107
Ruhr *1:* 189, *2:* 299
Rumania *2:* 225
Rumanian army *1:* 78
Rundstedt Offensive (*see* Battle
   of the Bulge)
Russia (*see* Soviet Union)
Russo-Finnish War *2:* 279
Russo-Japanese War (1905) *1:* 29
Ryukyus Islands *2:* 326 (ill.), 328

S

Sabotage
   by French resistance
      1: 147 (ill.), *2:* 268
   by young Germans *1:* 203-204
   in occupied Europe *1:* 142-143
Sahara 2: 385
Saipan *2:* 320, 326 (ill.), 328
Salerno *2:* 236
Samurai *1:* 30

San Diego, migration to *1:* 108
Sardinia *2:* 347
Schultz, Sigrid *2:* 385
Science *2:* 359-368
Scientists
    and atomic bomb *2:* 364-365
    German *2:* 399
    Jewish *2:* 366
    refugees *2:* 366
Scorched earth *1:* 80
SD (*Sicherheitsdienst*) *1:* 168
Seattle *1:* 121
2nd Cavalry Division *1:* 115
Second front *2:* 210-212, 252, 277
Secret agents *2:* 245-359
    in Yugoslavia *1:* 74
Secret police
    German *1:* 31, 134, 163, *2:* 349
    Japanese *2:* 352
    Russian *1:* 151, *2:* 219
Secret societies (Japanese) *1:* 30-31
Segregation, and U.S. military
    1: 113-117, 114 (ill.)
Seine *2:* 271
Selective Service Act (draft)
    1: 114
Serbia *1:* 74, 154
Serbs *1:* 154-154
Sergeant York 2: 380, 380 (ill.)
Service de Travaille Obligatoire
    (compulsory labor service)
    France *1:* 139
Sevastopol *2:* 242
761st Tank Battalion *1:* 115
Seventh Army (U.S.) *2:* 299
Seventh Symphony
    (Shostakovich) *2:* 377
Shanghai *1:* 32
Sherman tanks *2:* 228
Ships for Victory *1:* 121
Ships, merchant (Japanese) *2:* 334
Ships, production of *1:* 106
Shostakovitch, Dmitri *2:* 377
Sicily *2:* 233, 234, 251
    Allied invasion of *2:* 211, 346
Siegfried Line *2:* 291
Signal Corps, U.S. Army *2:* 379
Sikorski, Wladyslaw *2:* 218 (ill.),
    283 (ill.)
Singapore *1:* 99
Sino-Japanese War (1895-95)
    1: 28, 32
Sit-down strikes *1:* 105

Sixth Army (German) *2:* 244-246
Skorzeny, Otto *2:* 235
Slave Labor *1:* 123, 124, 165-166
Slovak National Rising. *1:* 145
Slovakia *1:* 23, 41, 144,
    2: 226, 403
Slovenians *1:* 154
Sobibór death camp *1:* 174
Social Democrats (Germany)
    1: 7, 14, 17
SOE (*see* Special Operation
    Executive)
Sofia *2:* 299
Solomon Islands *2:* 314, 317,
    317 (ill.)
Somalia *1:* 69
Somaliland *1:* 69
Somme River *1:* 50
Song of Russia 2: 384
Sorge, Richard *2:* 350-351,
    351 (ill.)
South Africa *1:* 61
South Pacific Area Command
    (Halsey) *2:* 312 (ill.), 313
South-Eastern Europe
    2: 297 (ill.), 298
South-West Pacific Command
    2: 312 (ill.), 313
Soviet Army *1:* 43, *2:* 268
    women in *1:* 196-197, 197 (ill.)
Soviet Union
    American Lend-Lease aid to
        1: 65
    entry into war against Japan
        2: 222
    border battles with Japan *1:* 37
    border dispute with Poland
        2: 216
    German invasion of *1:* 77-82,
        79 (ill.)
    in American motion pictures
        2: 384
    Katyn massacre *2:* 218
    losses during the war *2:* 392
    military production by *2:* 248
    negotiation with Britain and
        France (1939) *1:* 36
    partisans in *1:* 149-152,
        151 (ill.), 196-197, 196 (ill.)
    physical destruction in *2:* 394
    pressure on Allies for second
        front *2:* 252
    relations with other Allied

powers *2:*206-207, 212, 215-222
relations with Japan *1:* 29, 87, *2:* 220-222
spying on atomic bomb project *2:* 223
war with Japan *2:* 332-333, 339
war with Germany *1:* 77-82, *2:* 278-282, 281 (ill.), 295-297, 301-304
Soviet-Japanese Neutrality Treaty (1941) *1:* 87, *2:*220
Soviet-Polish relations *2:* 282
Spanish Civil War *1:* 13, 21, *2:* 224
Special Operations Executive (British) *2:* 353
Special Operations Executive (SOE)–British *2:* 353-355
and Belgium, Netherlands *2:* 355
and French resistance *2:* 354
and recruitment of refugees *2:* 353
and Yugoslavia *1:* 155
Spies *2:* 349-356
(*see also* Intelligence)
Sri Lanka (*see* Ceylon)
SS *1:* 148, 160, 164-165, 166, 176, 179
St. Petersburg (*see* Leningrad)
St.-Lô *2:* 269
Stalcup, Ann *1:* 202
Stalin, Joseph *1:* 37, 151, *2:* 213, 217, 220, 221 (ill.), 223, 245, 285, 336 (ill.), 351, 384
Stalingrad, Battle of *2:* 244-246, 246 (ill.)
women in *1:* 197
Staple Inn, London *1:* 182 (ill.)
Star and Stripes (U.S. Army newspaper) *2:* 389
Starvation *1:*136, *2:* 394
Stauffenberg, Count Claus von *2:* 288-289
Steinbeck, John *2:* 383
Stimson, Henry *1:* 114
STO (*see* Service de Travaille Obligatoire)
Stormtroopers *1:* 10, 11 (ill.), 158, 160
The Story of G.I. Joe 2: 390
Strategic air offensive *1:*189, 193

Strategic bombing *1:* 183-193
American bombing of Germany *1:* 194
American bombing of Japan *2:* 334
Strikes *1:* 105, 112, 142-143
Submarines *1:* 45
and intelligence work *2:* 355
U.S. campaign against Japan *2:* 333-334
in Battle of the Atlantic *1:* 66-69, 68 (ill.)
Suburbs, growth of in U.S. *2:* 406-407, 407 (ill.)
Subways (London) as bomb shelters *1:* 185 (ill.), 200
Sudan *1:* 69
Sudetenland *1:* 21, *2:* 402, 404
Suez Canal *1:* 69
Suicide
of Japanese soldiers on Attu *2:* 316
kamakazi pilots 325, 329, 331-332
Supreme Court (U.S.)
and Japanese-Americans *1:* 129
Surrender, German *2:* 304
Sweden *1:* 45-47, 46 (ill.)
Switzerland
and intelligence work *2:* 354
radio broadcasting *1:* 138
Sword Beach (D-Day) *2:* 260, 260 (ill.), 264-265
Synagogues *1:* 160, 164
Szilard, Leo *2:* 366

T

Taiwan *1:* 28, *2:* 411
Tanks, production of *1:* 106
Tarawa *2:* 319
Teenagers *1:* 121
Teheran Conference (November 1943) *2:* 217
Televaag *1:* 141
Terkel, Studs *1:* 108
Thames River,bombing of docks on *1:* 57, 186
Third Army (U.S.)
crosses the Rhine *2:* 298
in Normandy *2:* 269
Thirty Seconds Over Tokyo 2: 385

Tinian *2:* 320
Tiso, Father Josef *1:* 145
Tito, Josip Broz *1:* 155-156
Tojo, Hideki *1:* 88, 88 (ill.)
Tokyo
    American bombing of (March
        1945) *2:* 335
    bombing of by Doolittle *1:* 101
Tokyo (Edo) Bay *1:* 25
Tokyo Express (Guadalcanal)
    2: 315
Tokyo Rose (Iva Toguri Ikoku)
    2: 373
Tolstoy, Leo *2:* 377
Tomara, Sonia *2:* 387
Torch, Operation *2:* 228
Total war *1:* 181-204
Toulon, French fleet at *2:* 232
Transports to death camps *1:* 174,
    174 (ill.)
Treaty of Versailles *1:* 4, 19
Treblinka death camp *1:* 174
Tregaskis, Richard *2:* 385
Tripartite Pact *1:* 86 (ill.), 87,
    2: 225-226
Triumph of the Will 2: 374
Truman, Harry S. *2:* 223, 336
    (ill.), 341
Tube Alloys(British atomic bomb
    project) *2:* 365
Tunisia *2:* 229, 231
Turkey *1:* 4
Tuskegee Airmen *1:* 117
20th Century-Fox *2:* 380, 381

U

U-boats (*see* Submarines)
Ukraine *1:* 76, 171
    collaboration with Germans in
        1: 151
    communist repression in *1:* 151
    fighting in during invasion of
        Soviet Union *1:* 78
    Soviet recapture of *2:* 248
Ultra *2:* 358
    and Battle of Normandy *2:* 359
Unconditional surrender
    2: 216, 335
Underground, Polish *2:* 282
    (*see also* resistance)
Unemployment (Germany) *1:* 10

Union of Soviet Socialist
    Republics (*see* Soveit Union)
Unions *1:* 105, 112
    and no-strike pledge *1:* 108
United Nations *2:* 409 (ill.),
    409-410
United States
    aid to Britain (1940-41) *1:* 63
    aid to China *1:* 84
    aid to Soviet Union *2:* 240,
        248, 404
    and relations with Britain
        2: 207
    anti-Japanese racism in *1:* 96
    anti-Nazi feelings in *1:* 63
    conflicts with Soviets and use
        of atomic bomb *2:* 342
    economic conditions, 1945
        2: 403, 405
    enters World War I *1:* 4
    home front *1:* 105-129
    isolationism in *1:* 62
    joint defense planning with
        Canada *1:* 65
    negotiations with Japan
        (1941) *1:* 88
    oil embargo on Japan *1:* 88
    peacetime draft introduced
        1: 65
    pressure on Soviets to enter
        war against Japan *2:* 221
    pro-Allied feelings in *1:* 61
    reaction to Nazi anti-Semitism
        in *1:* 63
    rejects of Treaty of Versailles
        1: 6
    relations with Japan *1:* 86
    sends warships to Japan (1853)
        1: 25
    tensions with Japan *1:* 31
United States Steel Corporation
    1: 107
Unoccupied zone (France)
    2: 232
Uprising, Warsaw (1944) *2:* 283
USS *Arizona 1:* 90, 92, 118
    memorial to *1:* 92 (ill.)
USS *Bunker Hill 2:* 331 (ill.)
USS *California 1:* 90, *2:* 325
USS *Hornet 1:* 101
USS *Lexington 1:* 101, 102 (ill.)
USS *Liscome Bay 1:* 118
USS *Missouri 2:* 344

USS *Oklahoma 1:* 90
USS *Shaw 1:* 91 (ill.)
USS *West Virginia 1:* 90, *2:* 325
USS *Yorktown 1:* 101
USSR (*see* Soviet Union)
Ustashi *1:* 154, 156
Utah Beach *2:* 260,
    260 (ill.), 265

V

V for victory *1:* 48, *2:* 371
V-1 (flying bomb) *2:* 353, 360
V-2 (rocket) *2:* 361, 361 (ill), 362
Vella Lavella *2:* 318
Veterans *2:* 406
Vichy France *1:* 146, 148
    and French Indochina *1:* 85,
        2: 229
    and North Africa *2:* 229
    occupation of *2:* 232
Victor Emmanuel III, King of Italy
    2: 235
Victory gardens *1:* 111
Victory in the West 2: 376
Vienna *2:* 211
Viet Minh *2:* 416
Vietnam
    independence movement in
        2: 416
    railroad to China from *1:* 84
Vilna *1:* 134, *2:* 280
Vistula *2:* 280
Vistula River *2:* 295
Vogelkop (New Guinea) *2:* 321
Volga *2:* 244
Volksdeutche (ethnic Germans)
    1: 133
Vom Rath, Ernst *1:* 160
Von Choltitz (*see* Choltitz,
    Dietrich von)

W

WAAC (Women's Auxiliary
    Army Corps) *1:* 198
WAC (Women's Army Corps)
    1: 198
Waffen-SS 1: 162, *2:* 293
Wagner, Richard *2:* 377

Wainwright, Gen. Jonathan
    2: 344
Wake Island *1:* 95
Wake Island 2: 385
Wannsee Conference *1:* 171
War bonds *1:* 107-108
War correspondents *2:* 385-387,
    386 (ill.), 388 (ill.)
War crimes *2:* 400
War crimes trials (Tokyo) *2:* 410
    (*see also* Nuremberg trials)
War Guilt Clause (Treaty of
    Versailles) *1:* 6
War ships *1:* 27 (ill.)
Warlords (China) *1:* 33
Warner brothers *2:* 381
Warner, Jack *2:* 384
Warsaw *1:* 166, *2:* 280
    bombing of *1:* 182
    capture of (1939) *1:* 42
    casualties during uprising
        (1944) *2:* 286
    Red Army enters *2:* 296
    treatment during German
        occupation of *2:* 282
    uprising in (1944) *2:* 285-286
Warsaw ghetto *1:* 167
Warsaw ghetto uprising (1943)
    2: 286
Warsaw uprising (1944) *2:* 219,
    285-286
Wasilewska, Wanda *2:* 284 (ill.)
WASPs (Women's Airforce Service
    Pilots) *1:* 199
WAVES (Women's Naval Service)
    1: 116
Weinberg, Gerhard L. *2:* 412
Wellman, William *2:* 390
West Germany *2:* 396
West wall (or Westwall) *2:* 291
Westermann *1:* 174
Western Allies
    and Soviet Union *2:* 206
Western front *2:* 251-275, 278,
    291-300
White Russia (Belarus) *1:* 76,
    2: 279
    German casualties in battle of
        (1944) *2:* 280
    liberation of (Operation
        Bagration) *2:* 278, 280
    Soviet claims to *2:* 282
    Soviet recapture of *2:* 248

Why We Fight 2: 379
Willie and Joe (Bill Mauldin
    cartoon characters) *2:* 389
Wilson, Woodrow *1:* 6
Winter Line (*see* Gustav Line)
Winter position (*see* Gustav Line)
Winter War (1939-40) *2:* 279
*With the Marines at Tarawa
    2:* 379
Wloclawek *1:* 164
Wolf-packs *1:* 66
Women *1:* 196
    and war work *1:* 108, *2:* 369
    as war correspondents
        2: 385-386, 386 (ill.)
    in armed forces *1:* 196-199,
        197 (ill.), 199 (ill.), 200 (ill.)
    in Britain *1:* 122, 197
    in Germany *1:* 122
    in industry *1:* 119-120
    in Japan *1:* 31, 124
    in the Soviet Union *1:* 122, 196
Women in Defense 2: 378
Women's Voluntary Service
    (WAS) (Britain) *1:* 197
World War I *1:* 3-8, 54,
    2: 252, 391
Wroclaw *2:* 296

Y

Yalta conference *2:* 221 (ill.)
Yamamoto, Admiral Isoroku
    2: 357
Yamato (Japanese battleship)
    2: 329
A Yank in the RAF 2: 380, 381
York, Alvin *2:* 380
Yorktown *1:* 103
Yugoslavia *2:*298- 299
    deaths in *2:* 392
    division of by Axis *1:* 74
    German invasion of *1:* 73
    Italian troops in *2:* 236
    resistance in *1:* 152-156,
        153 (ill.)

Z

Zanuck, Darryl F. *2:* 380-381
Zealand *1:* 61
Zhukov, Marshal Georgi K.
    and battle of Moscow *1:* 82
    and winter offensive (1945)
        2: 296
    at Leningrad *1:* 81
Zoot suit riots *1:* 118